Jubilee Bible Monograph

Jubilee Bible Monograph

American Bible Society
101 North Independence Mall East FL8, Philadelphia, PA 19106
www.americanbible.org

Page design concept by The Williams
Group, Inc.
New York

Item: 124736

Acknowledgments

THE JUBILEE BIBLE PROJECT was championed by the Reverend Charles H. Smith, a former employee of the American Bible Society who saw the need to bridge the teachings of the Bible with the realities of African-American day-to-day living. In his capacity as Assistant Director for Heritage Markets, Reverend Smith traveled extensively throughout the United States for several years gathering research data, interviewing church and denominational leaders, speaking to clergy, laypersons, and youth, attending conferences and seminars, reading the latest books, and listening intently to people to determine the type of supplementary material that would make the Jubilee Bible relevant to the African-American community and beyond. From such exhaustive research comes the Jubilee Bible. The American Bible Society gratefully acknowledges Reverend Smith's determination, indefatigable spirit, and deep commitment to the Bible cause.

The Society gratefully acknowledges the contributions of Dr. Virgil A. Wood, pastor emeritus, educator, and American Bible Society consultant, whose concept of biblical jubilee was instrumental in laying the foundation for this project.

The Society also acknowledges the Rev. Dr. Thomas L. Hoyt, Jr. Presiding Bishop, Seventh Episcopal District, Christian Methodist Episcopal Church, and Dr. Dennis C. Dickerson, Professor of History at Vanderbilt University in Nashville, Tennessee, historiographer, ordained minister, and Chairman of the Board of Trustees at the American Bible Society, for their roles as senior advisors for the Jubilee Bible.

The Society owes much gratitude to the Rev. Diane M. Ritzie, Ph.D candidate in Old Testament at Graduate Theological Foundation in Mishawaka, Indiana, and former consultant to the American Bible Society for serving as project manager for the Jubilee Bible; and to Barbara Bernstengel and Dorette Saunders of the American Bible Society's Nida Institute for Biblical Scholarship for serving as project editors.

Acknowledgments

Contributors

William H. Collins. Jr. has served as the Minister of Music at the Mount Hermon Baptist Church in the Bronx, New York, for over 35 years. He directs his own music studio in Harlem. He earned a Bachelor of Music degree from the Candell Conservatory of Music in Oakland, California, and his Master of Music degree from Manhattan School of Music in New York City. Professor Collins is listed in Distinguished Musicians in the United States. He has served in music ministry for more than 50 years.

Robert L. Cvornyek is Professor of History and Labor Studies at Rhode Island College in Providence and chair of the History Department. He is a former historical researcher at the American Bible Society and is the author of The Bible in Slavery and Freedom: The American Bible Society and the Afro-American Community, 1816-1960 (1990) and Baseball in Newark (2003).

Elliott Cuff is the pastor of Lincoln Heights Missionary Baptist Church in Wood-lawn, Ohio. He is a graduate of Harvard University, Cambridge, Massachusetts, and New York Theological Seminary, where he earned a Master of Divinity degree, and the United Theological Seminary in Dayton, Ohio where he earned the Doctor of Ministry degree. His preaching motto is, "Be Radical, Be Relevant, but most of all, Be Right!"

Michael I. N. Dash is Professor of Ministry and Context at the Interdenominational Theological Center in Atlanta, Georgia. He served as co-director of the ITC Faith Factor Project 2000 Study of Black Churches, which had as its focus African-American congregational life. He received his Seminary Diploma from Union Theological Seminary in Kingston, Jamaica, a Diploma of Theology from the University of London, a Master of Sacred Theology from Christian Theological Seminary, Indianapolis, Indiana, and his Doctorate of Ministry from the School of Theology at Boston University. He has co-authored Hidden Wholeness: An African American Spirituality for Individuals and Communities; The Shape of Zion: Leadership and Life in Black Churches," and The Mark of Zion: Congregational Life in Black Churches.

Dennis C. Dickerson is James M. Lawson, Jr. Professor of History at Vanderbilt University in Nashville, Tennessee. He served as Chairman of the Board of

Trustees at the American Bible Society. Dr. Dickerson is an ordained minister in the African Methodist Episcopal Church and has served his denomination as a General Officer since 1988. He is the Historiographer and Editor of the A.M.E. Church Review. He received his Bachelor's degree from Lincoln University in Pennsylvania, and earned a Master of Arts and Ph.D. from Washington University, as well as a Master of Divinity from Vanderbilt. Dr. Dickerson has also written extensively on African-American Religious History with his works appearing in many scholarly journals and anthologies. He is the author of several books, including Militant Mediator: Whitney M. Young, Jr. (1998), A Liberated Past: Explorations in A.M.E. Church History (2003), and his soon-to-be released title, African American Preachers and Politics: The Careys of Chicago.

Cain Hope Felder is Professor of New Testament Language and Literature at the Howard University School of Divinity in Washington. D.C., and serves as chair of the Ph.D. program. He has been on Howard's faculty since 1981, having come to Washington from Princeton Theological Seminary. He is an ordained elder in the Methodist Church, and served as pastor of Grace United Methodist Church in New York City. Dr. Felder earned a Ph.D. and a Master of Philosophy in Biblical Languages and Literature from Columbia University, a Diploma of Theology from Oxford University in England, and a Master of Divinity from Union Theological Seminary in New York and a Bachelor of Arts in Philosophy, Greek and Latin from Howard University. A prolific writer, he is the editor of The Journal of Religious Thought and has authored and edited several works including Troubling Biblical Waters: Race, Class, and Family (1989); Stony the Road We Trod: African American Biblical Interpretation (1991); The Original African Heritage Study Bible (1993) and True to Our Native Land (2007).

Frank L. Gipson received his Ph.D. in Hebrew Bible and Ancient Near Eastern Studies in 2003 from the Graduate School, Drew University, Madison, New Jersey. His dissertation entitled "Lineage Structure and Local Authority in Ancient Israel," describes local leadership via social structure and organization visible within the text of the Hebrew Bible.

Thomas L. Hoyt, Jr. is the 48th Bishop of the Christian Methodist Episcopal Church. Upon his election to the Episcopacy in 1994, he was assigned to the Fourth Episcopal District (Mississippi and Louisiana), and at the 2006 General Conference, to the Seventh Episcopal District (Inclusive of 10 eastern states in the United States and the District of Columbia). He received his Bachelor's degree from Lane College, Jackson, TN; the Master of Divinity degree from the Interdenominational Theological Center, the Master of Sacred Theology degree from Union Theological Seminary in the City of New York; and the Ph.D. from Duke University. Bishop Hoyt also received honorary degrees from Trinity College, Hartford, CT; Rust College, Holly Springs, MS; Lane College, Jackson, TN; and The Interdenominational Theological Center, Atlanta, GA. He served on the Faith and Order Commissions of the World Council of Churches and the National Council of Churches of Christ in the USA. He has written more than forty articles for professional journals and publications, and has served as lecturer for the Lyman Beecher Series at Yale Divinity School. He was Professor of New Testament Studies for 25 years at the Interdenominational Theological Center, Howard University School of Religion and Hartford Seminary.

Murray L. Newman was educated at Phillips University in Enid, Oklahoma, where he received his Bachelor's and Master of Arts degrees. He attended Union Theological Seminary in the City of New York where he received his B.D. and . He also attended the University of Basel in Switzerland and the University of Heidelberg in Germany. He is an ordained priest of the Episcopal Church who served as Professor of Old Testament at Virginia Theological Seminary, Alexandria from 1955-1996; and Visiting Lecturer at Howard Divinity School, Howard University. Dr. Murray is the author of People of the Covenant, The Continuing Quest for the Historical Covenant, Rahab and the Conquest, and other articles and book reviews.

Prince Vuyani Ntintili received a Master in Theology from Dallas Theological Seminary, a Master of Philosophy from Drew University, a Doctor of Theology from Christian Leadership University in Florida, and a Ph.D. in Ethics from Drew University. He is the founder and president of Christian Leadership Equipping and networking (CLEAN) ministries in South Africa.

Gene Rice is Professor of Old Testament Language and Literature at the Howard University School of Divinity in Washington, D.C. He received his Bachelor's degree from Berea College, Berea, Kentucky, his Master of Divinity from Union Theological Seminary in the City of New York, and his Ph.D. from Columbia University. He is the author of 1 Kings: Nations Under God and more than twenty articles in various scholarly journals, among which is Africans and the Origin of the Worship of Yahweh which was published in The Journal of Religious Thought 50 (1993-94).

Diane M. Ritzie served as a consultant to the American Bible Society and as a New York State Chaplain for the Department of Corrections. She received her Bachelor's degree from Lehman College of the City University of New York, a Master of Science degree from Columbia University, a Master of Divinity degree from Seminary of the East, a Master of Philosophy from Drew University, and is currently a Ph.D. candidate in Old Testament at Graduate Theological Foundation in Mishawaka, Indiana. She was the first African American to teach Old Testament at Nyack College.

Jerome Clayton Ross is Associate Professor, Department of Religious Studies, at Randolph-Macon College in Ashland, Virginia. He is also the pastor of Providence Park Baptist Church in Richmond, Virginia. Dr. Ross received his Bachelor's degree from Randolph-Macon College, his Master of Divinity from Virginia Union, and his Ph.D. in Old Testament from the University of Pittsburgh. His dissertation is entitled The Composition of the Holiness Code (Leviticus 17-26), his review of Stony the Road We Trod was published in A Journal of Bible and Theology (April 1993), and his book, The History of Ancient Israel and Judah: A Compilation was published in 2003.

Mitzi Jane Smith holds a Ph.D. in New Testament from Harvard Divinity School. She received her Bachelor's degree in Theology from Columbia Union College, Takoma Park, Maryland, a Master of Arts in Black Studies from Ohio State University, and a Master of Divinity from Howard University School of Divinity. She is the author of A Tale of Two Sisters: Am I My Sister's Keeper? which was published in The Journal of Religious Thought: Volume 52:253:1 (June 1996).

Maxine M. Walker (d. 2007) was the first African-American chaplain for the entire hospital system of Greenville, South Carolina. She was also the Minister of Pastoral Care and Counseling at Cedar Grove Baptist Church in Simpsonville, South

Carolina. Chaplain Walker received her Bachelor's degree from the University of Central Florida in Orlando, and her master of Divinity degree from the Interdenominational Theological Center. One of her sermons was featured in the third edition of Those Preachin' Women. She was also the author of My Round Rainbow, a children's story/activity book.

Virgil A. Wood is an ordained Baptist minister who became actively involved in the Civil Rights Movement. He served with Dr. Martin Luther King, Jr. as a member of his National Executive Board of the Southern Christian Leadership Conference for the last ten years of Dr. King's life and coordinated the state of Virginia in the historic March on Washington in 1963. Dr. Wood received his Master of Divinity from Andover Newton Theological School in Newton, Massachusetts, and his Doctorate in Education from Harvard University. He served as Dean and Director, the African American Institute, and Associate Professor at Virginia Seminary and College in Lynchburg, and a visiting lecturer, Research and Teaching Fellow at Harvard University. Dr. Wood is the author of several books including Introduction to Black Church Economic Studies. He retired in 2005 as pastor of Pond Street Baptist Church in Providence, Rhode Island after a twenty-five year tenure.

Edwina Maria Wright (d. 2007) received her Bachelor's degree from Douglass College, Rutgers University, her Master of Arts degree from Eastern Baptist Seminary, Master of Divinity from McCormick Theological Seminary, and her Ph.D. in Comparative Semitic Philology from Harvard University. She served as Assistant Professor of Old Testament at Union Theological Seminary in the City of New York. Prior to accepting the post at Union, Dr. Wright lectured at Rutgers University and was a teaching fellow at Harvard University.

Acknowledgments

Reviewers

Shaykh Abd'Allah Latif Ali, Chairman, *Imams Council of New York City, New York, New York*

Amir Al-Islam, Professor African American History, Islam and World Civilization, *Medgar Evers College, Brooklyn, New York*

Dr. Randall C. Bailey, Andrew W. Mellon Professor of Hebrew Bible, *Interdenominational Theological Center, Atlanta, Georgia*

The Rev. Simon Barnes, Executive Vice President for Development, Marketing and Research, *the American Bible Society, New York, New York*

The Rev. Frederick J. Bryant, Jr., Pastor, *Trinity Lutheran Church, Jersey City, New Jersey*

The Rev. Dr. David G. Burke, former Dean, Nida Institute for Biblical Scholarship, *American Bible Society, New York, New York*

Bishop Clarence Carr (Retired), *African Methodist Episcopal Zion Church, Western District, St. Louis, Missouri*

Bishop Ronald M. Cunningham, Chairman, College of Bishops, *Christian Methodist Episcopal Church, Memphis, Tennessee*

Dr. Michael I.N. Dash, Professor, Ministry and Context, *Interdenominational Theological Center, Atlanta, Georgia*

Dr. Cain Hope Felder, Professor of New Testament Language and Literature *Howard University, School of Divinity; Chairman, Biblical Institute for Social Change, Washington, D.C.*

The Rev. Dr. Edward L. Foggs, *Sherman Street Church of God, Anderson, Indiana; former General Secretary, Leadership Council of the Church of God, Anderson, Indiana*

The Rev. Dr. Robert M. Franklin, President, Morehouse College, *Atlanta, Georgia*

The Rev. Dr. Will Herzfeld (d. 2002), Director for Global Community and Overseas Operations, Division for Global Mission, *Evangelical Lutheran Church in America, Chicago, Illinois*

The Rev. Dr. Darcel M. Holloway, Pastor, singer, songwriter and author of several books including "Woman of the Cross" (1998) and "Come Out De Wilderness" (2006).

Dr. Dwight N. Hopkins, Professor of Theology, *The Divinity School, University of Chicago, Chicago, Illinois*

The Rev. Dr. Arnold W. Howard, Pastor, Enon Baptist Church, Baltimore, Maryland

Dr. David Matthews, past Vice President, *National Baptist Convention USA, Indianola, Mississippi*

Bishop Felton Edwin May (Retired), Dean, *Kendall Science and Health Mission Center, Philander Smith College, Little Rock, Arkansas*

The Rev. Dr. Dale A. Meyer, President, Concordia Seminary, St. Louis, Missouri

Mrs. Bobbie Patterson, former Associate Executive Director, *Southern Baptist Convention, Women's Missionary Union, Birmingham, Alabama*

The Rev. Dr. Staccato Powell, Pastor, *Grace AME Zion Church, Raleigh, North Carolina;* former Executive Director, National Ministries Unit, *National Council of Churches of Christ, USA, New York, New York*

Dr. Gene C. Rice, Professor of Old Testament Language and Literature, *Howard University, School of Divinity, Washington, D.C.*

Dr. Jerome C. Ross, Assistant Professor of Old Testament, *The Samuel Dewitt Proctor School of Theology, Virginia Union University, Richmond, Virginia*

The Rev. Dr. John R. Scott, Jr., former Pastor, *Gethsemane Baptist Church, Baltimore, Maryland*

Dr. Linda E. Thomas, Professor of Theology and Anthropology, Lutheran School of Theology at Chicago, Chicago, Illinois

The Rev. Dr. Ralph G. Thompson, Field Representative for the Ellen G. White Estate, former Secretary, *General Conference of Seventh-Day Adventists, Silver Spring, Maryland*

The Rev. Dr. Eugene G. Turner (Retired), former Associate Stated Clerk for Governing Bodies, Ecumenical Agencies, *Presbyterian Church (USA), Louisville, Kentucky*

The Rev. Dr. Angelique Walker-Smith, Executive Director, The Church Federation of Greater Indianapolis, Indianapolis, Indiana

The Scripture references cited in the articles in Section Two are drawn from a variety of translations. These translations are referenced as follows:

CEV	*Contemporary English Version*
KJV	*King James Version*
NKJV	*New King James Version*
NIV	*New International Version*
NRSV	*New Revised Standard Version*
RSV	*Revised Standard Version*

The African American Jubilee Edition

Preface

THE AFRICAN AMERICAN JUBILEE EDITION of the Bible heralds a call to engage anew the Holy Scriptures, through the lens of the African American experience, and to be renewed by the intentional moving of the Holy Spirit in the lives of a Covenant people.

The Jubilee Bible, with its supplementary material, presents a way for African Americans to see how they are inextricably connected to the ancient world of the Bible; it allows them to fully understand the inter-relatedness of the biblical stories and their own rich heritage by critically examining the elements of place, people, culture, and story. This culturally-relevant edition of the Bible invites readers to reconnect with the historic struggles of their ancestors whose lives were fashioned by Jubilee Laws; and it reminds them that despite dispersion, social dislocation, and disenfranchisement, God's enabling Spirit has been present all the time.

The supplementary material is designed to encourage readers, especially those of this contemporary generation, to read and, in some instances, re-read the Bible in light of their own cultural and social locations. As readers bring their own experiences to the biblical text and interact with the various stories, remarkable similarities will emerge between the issues they face today and those of the ancient world. Issues of race, gender, oppression, exploitation, prejudice, and xenophobia are all addressed in the Bible. God, who is God of all wisdom and all knowledge, reconciled those issues in Christ and has provided, through the Scriptures, guidance for our life in a faith community.

The Jubilee Bible challenges today's African Americans to move beyond religious rhetoric to more communal relationships. It encourages them to look within the sacred pages and unanimously define themselves as God defines them, "wonderfully made." It invites them to affirm God as the center of their being and urges them to move toward Jubilee by accepting God's plan of redemption, reconciliation and release.

As members of the body of Christ, we need to know one another's story. We embrace this opportunity to share the African American story as part of the restoration and healing that is needed to bring all of us into a Jubilee community. It is a story that bears repeating; it is the sacred history of a people and their engagement with the God of liberation.

Contents

The African American Jubilee Edition

Acknowledgments *v*

Preface *xiii*

Jubilee Biblical Mandates *xviii*

- *Leviticus 25.8-12*
- *Isaiah 61.1-4*
- *Luke 4.16-21*

Questions for Reflection *xix*

Section One

The Biblical Jubilee 1
by Virgil A. Wood

The African American Experience 9
From Experience to Biblical Image

Diaspora 18
From Africa to the United States
From Africa to the West Indies and South America
Since 1619: A Faith Journey
Faith-based Freedom

African Culture 24
Kinship
Religion
Worship
Music

The Black Church 26
Leadership and Politics
Preaching in the Black Church
The Black Church and Education
The Black Church and the Black Family

Creating a Jubilee World 32
Practice Jubilee!
Celebrate Jubilee!

Selected Chronology 37
Struggles and Victories (1619-2009)

Section Two

Understanding the Bible and the World of Biblical Antiquity

One — Interpretation of Scripture 47
by Murray L. Newman

Two — Jubilee in Leviticus 17-26 59
by Jerome Clayton Ross

Three — The Message of Salvation 75
by Thomas L. Hoyt, Jr.

Four — The Relationship between Hebrew and African Languages 89
by Edwina M. Wright

Five — The Presence and Role of Africans in the Bible 97
by Prince Vuyani Ntintili

Six — The Presence of Blacks in Biblical Antiquity 109
by Cain Hope Felder

Seven The Alleged Curse on Ham 127
by Gene Rice

Eight Slavery in the Ancient Near East and, Particularly, in Israel 145
by Frank L. Gipson

Nine Roman Slavery in Antiquity 157
by Mitzi Jane Smith

The Black Church

Ten A History of the Black Church 187
by Dennis C. Dickerson

Eleven A Hidden History: African American Contributions to the Bible Cause 203
by Robert L. Cvornyek

Twelve Black Preaching in the Church 213
by Elliott Cuff

Thirteen Music in the Black Church 229
by William H. Collins, Jr.

Interpreting the Bible for African Americans Today

Fourteen The Bible in African American Spirituality 245
by Michael I. N. Dash

Fifteen Homegoing 259
by Diane M. Ritzie

Sixteen The Blessing: Restoring Hope for African American Youth 273
by Maxine M. Walker

Bible Study Helps *(In the Back of the Bible)*

Chronology of the Bible 3

Maps 6

Bible Study Notes 19

Chart of the Bible 20

What's in the Bible 21

How to Read the Bible 26

Read through the Bible in a Year 28

Some Readings for Special Days 33

Famous Passages of the Bible 34

Finding Help in the Bible 38

What the Bible Says about God's Forgiveness 41

Jubilee Biblical Mandates

Leviticus 25.8-12

Contemporary English Version

The LORD *said to his people:*

"Once every forty-nine years on the tenth day of the seventh month, which is also the Great Day of Forgiveness, trumpets are to be blown everywhere in the land. This fiftieth year is sacred—it is a time of freedom and of celebration when everyone will receive back their original property, and slaves will return home to their families. This is a year of complete celebration, so don't plant any seed or harvest what your fields or vineyards produce. In this time of sacred celebration you may eat only what grows on its own."

Leviticus 25.8-12

King James Version

And thou shalt number seven sabbaths of years unto thee, seven times seven years; and the space of the seven sabbaths of years shall be unto thee forty and nine years. Then shalt thou cause the trumpet of the jubilee to sound on the tenth day of the seventh month, in the day of atonement shall ye make the trumpet sound throughout all your land. And ye shall hallow the fiftieth year, and proclaim liberty throughout all the land unto all the inhabitants thereof: it shall be a jubilee unto you; and ye shall return every man unto his possession, and ye shall return every man unto his family. A jubilee shall that fiftieth year be unto you: ye shall not sow, neither reap that which groweth of itself in it, nor gather the grapes in it of thy vine undressed. For it is the jubilee; it shall be holy unto you; ye shall eat the increase thereof out of the field.

Isaiah 61.1-4

Contemporary English Version

The Spirit of the LORD God has taken control of me!
The LORD has chosen and sent me
  to tell the oppressed the good news,
to heal the brokenhearted,
  and to announce freedom for prisoners and captives.
This is the year when the LORD God
  will show kindness to us and punish our enemies.

The LORD has sent me to comfort those who mourn,
  especially in Jerusalem.
He sent me to give them flowers in place of their sorrow,
  olive oil in place of tears,
  and joyous praise in place of broken hearts.
They will be called "Trees of Justice,"
  planted by the LORD to honor his name.
Then they will rebuild cities that have been in ruins
  for many generations.

Isaiah 61.1-4

King James Version

The Spirit of the Lord GOD is upon me; because the LORD hath anointed me to preach good tidings unto the meek; he hath sent me to bind up the brokenhearted, to proclaim liberty to the captives, and the opening of the prison to them that are bound; to proclaim the acceptable year of the LORD, and the day of vengeance of our God; to comfort all that mourn; to appoint unto them that mourn in Zion, to give unto them beauty for ashes, the oil of joy for mourning, the garment of praise for the spirit of heaviness; that they might be called Trees of righteousness, The planting of the LORD, that he might be glorified. And they shall build the old wastes, they shall raise up the former desolations, and they shall repair the waste cities, the desolations of many generations.

Luke 4.16-21

Contemporary English Version

Jesus went back to Nazareth, where he had been brought up, and as usual he went to the meeting place on the Sabbath. When he stood up to read from the Scriptures, he was given the book of Isaiah the prophet. He opened it and read,

"The Lord's Spirit has come to me,
because he has chosen me
to tell the good news to the poor.
The Lord has sent me to announce freedom for prisoners,
to give sight to the blind, to free everyone who suffers,
and to say, 'This is the year the Lord has chosen.'"

Jesus closed the book, then handed it back to the man in charge and sat down. Everyone in the meeting place looked straight at Jesus.

Then Jesus said to them, "What you have just heard me read has come true today."

Luke 4.16-21

King James Version

And he came to Nazareth, where he had been brought up: and, as his custom was, he went into the synagogue on the sabbath day, and stood up for to read. And there was delivered unto him the book of the prophet Isaiah. And when he had opened the book, he found the place where it was written,

The Spirit of the Lord is upon me,
because he hath anointed me to preach the gospel to the poor;
he hath sent me to heal the broken-hearted,
to preach deliverance to the captives,
and recovering of sight to the blind,
to set at liberty them that are bruised,
to preach the acceptable year of the Lord.

And he closed the book, and he gave it again to the minister, and sat down. And the eyes of all them that were in the synagogue were fastened on him. And he began to say unto them, This day is this Scripture fulfilled in your ears.

Questions for Reflection

(see also Deuteronomy 15.1-18)

1. How would you summarize the main aims of the "Jubilee Year?" Do you know of any attempts today to translate some of these aims into practical initiatives or policies?

2. So far as we know historically, the provisions of the Jubilee Year were never put into practice. Why do you think this was so? What would be the difficulties of carrying out this vision?

3. The Jubilee tradition speaks of giving "rest" to the land (Leviticus 25.11). What does it mean to "give rest" to the land? Can we relate this today to an ecological system in danger of collapse?

4. What themes from Jesus' proclamation in Luke 4.16-21 can you relate to the Jubilee tradition?

Source: *"Turn to God: Rejoice in Hope,"* prepared for the Eighth World Council of Churches Assembly, held in Harare, Zimbabwe, December, 1998

EQUAL
RIGH

Section One

The Biblical Jubilee

Virgil A. Wood

"And ye shall hallow the fiftieth year, and proclaim liberty throughout all the land unto all the inhabitants thereof: it shall be a *jubilee* unto you; and ye shall return every man unto his possession, and ye shall return every man unto his family." (Leviticus 25.10, *KJV*)

◂ "400 Years of Our People." Art Resource, New York, NY © 2010 Michael Escoffery/ Artists Rights Society (ARS), New York, NY

The story of Jubilee is well established in both the Old and New Testaments, although the record of its practice is barely known. For African Americans, it was their slave ancestors' love for the Bible which drew them to embrace certain biblical beliefs which kept the spirit of Jubilee alive. The collective activity of enslaved blacks immediately after the emancipation in 1865 shows that those newly freed blacks created, within the first 50 years after slavery, the institutional framework for black churches, black colleges, the black press, and black businesses. The foundation has been so solidly laid that these institutions have been able to survive to the present time. (See Section Two: "A Hidden History: African American Contributions to the Bible Cause," by Robert L. Cvornyek.)

In modern society, the word Jubilee strikes an unfamiliar sound with little known historical connections. Most Americans would be surprised to learn that the Jubilee Scripture, Leviticus 25.10, is inscribed on the Liberty Bell, and that the British and American legal systems of bankruptcy laws come out of the Jubilee tradition.

The Jubilee tenets are practiced in some parts of the world to this day. The Gabbra, a nomadic people in the Northeast of Kenya, "live in one of the driest areas of East Africa. In 1981, they celebrated their year of Jubilee, ending another cycle of fifty years in their existence. In the year of Jubilee crooked affairs are straightened out, injustice is righted, debts are settled, cattle (the only property) are reallotted and sins are forgiven. This is not a myth; it is not a story; it is not an ideal that they believe should be fulfilled. It really happened in 1981 after a year of preparation."[1]

Provisions of Jubilee

The Jubilee provisions are cited in Leviticus 25, Isaiah 61, and Luke 4. The original text in Leviticus 25.10 (KJV) reads, "And ye shall hallow the fiftieth year, and proclaim liberty throughout all the land unto all the inhabitants thereof: it shall be a ***jubilee*** unto you; and ye shall return every man unto his possession, and ye shall return every man unto his family." The text focuses on provisions relative to land use, redemption of lost land, pricing and selling considerations in relation to Jubilee guidelines, and later gives the injunction "ye shall not therefore oppress one another" (v.17).

In the Leviticus account, we discover that God was preparing the various tribes who yearned to become the nation of God's original promise to Abraham, to move from a nomadic existence to a people of settlement (25.2). There were core beliefs which had to be observed if the People of Promise were to become the Nation of Promise with their own Land of Promise. However, the provisions of Jubilee were to be kept within the Hebrew nation.

"Liberty Bell." Courtesy of National Archives, Washington, DC

We also note that the Jubilee is the fiftieth year, the year after the succession of seven sabbatical years*, in which all the land which had been taken from its owners, for whatever reason, was to be returned. The land was to lie fallow, and slaves were to be set free.[2]

Jubilee is a biblical concept and we begin a retrospective examination of Jubilee with the Leviticus passage which speaks to justice, freedom, restoration, and reparation. Much of this concept is mirrored by our Lord, as recorded in Luke 4.16-30. There, Jesus reads the well-known Scripture which begins, "the Spirit of the Lord is upon me, because he hath anointed me to preach the gospel to the poor." (v.18, *KJV*). After Jesus was finished reading, he sat down and said to the people, "Today this Scripture is fulfilled in your hearing" (v. 21, *NIV*). In essence, at the end of this his inaugural sermon, Jesus endorses Jubilee.

There were six provisions set forth in Jesus' message: (1) to preach the gospel to the poor; (2) to heal the broken-hearted; (3) to proclaim liberty to the captives; (4) to restore sight to the blind; (5) to set at liberty those that are oppressed; and (6) to proclaim the acceptable year of the Lord.

Luke's account of Jubilee differs slightly from the passage in Isaiah 61 in that Luke adds, "recovery of sight to the blind," and

* Sabbatical year is defined as every seventh year during which time debts are forgiven, debtors/slaves are released and the land would remain uncultivated. See Deuteronomy 15.1-18.

Luke's liberation of the oppressed is rendered as "the opening of the prison to them that are bound," in the Isaiah text. When Jesus announced his central mission, he illustrated how the Jubilee would work by extending the traditional boundaries of family beyond the nation of Israel. Jesus now included foreigners and all the nations of the earth in the provisions of God's Jubilee. He went far beyond the concept of physical liberation to offer spiritual liberation—salvation through God's grace. (For further study, see Section Two: "The Message of Salvation," Thomas L. Hoyt, Jr.)

Jubilee Now

What, then, are the implications for Jubilee today? As the Church moves toward a better understanding of the biblical Jubilee, some elements will be apparent. First, the Jubilee is always associated with the activity and presence of God's Spirit as explicitly stated in the Isaiah 61 and Luke 4 accounts; in the Leviticus account, the Lord speaks directly to Moses. The Church will yield abundant fruitfulness of Jubilee wisdom as it considers the biblical Jubilee through its consistent surrender to God's Holy Spirit.

Second, we will find the provisions of Jubilee as enduring objectives and outcomes in the life, ministry, and work of Jesus, especially following Jesus' announcement of Jubilee and its fulfillment in himself, in the Nazareth hometown synagogue. Thirdly, after the resurrection, the new band of Jesus' followers, first the twelve, then the 120, then the 3,000, committed themselves to these core beliefs by the day of Pentecost, just fifty days following Easter. In a sense, we find the first significant manifestation of the Jubilee in the life of the new community, as recorded in the following passage from the Acts of the Apostles.

"This Jesus God has raised up, of which we are all witnesses... And they continued steadfastly in the apostles' doctrine and fellowship, in the breaking of bread, and in prayers. Then fear came upon every soul, and many wonders and signs were done through the apostles. Now all who believed were together, and had all things in common, and sold their possessions and goods, and divided them among all, as anyone had need." Acts 2.32, 42-45 *(NKJV)*

Maria Harris, an author and professor of Religious Education, offers significant insight into the first century church by discussing the broad curriculum which they embraced, and which we, the current Church, would benefit from adopting.

Harris states:
"The first time these forms are named for us is in the book of Acts. There we find in one place the most detailed description of the first Christian community doing what will in time become the classical activities of ecclesial ministry: ***kerygma,*** proclaiming the word of

"Three Women of America," 1990. Art © Elizabeth Catlett/Licensed by VAGA, New York, NY

Jesus' resurrection; ***didache***, the activity of teaching; ***leiturgia***, coming together to pray and to represent Jesus in the breaking of bread; ***koinonia***, or community; and ***diakonia***, caring for those in need."[3] If we are to engage in biblical Jubilee, those five elements need to be present in the life of the church and the community.

Finally, attaining Jubilee may be a painfully slow journey. However, as the Church makes its way on such a Jubilee pilgrimage, it will move every wall of religious separation and undertake this journey, beseeching and welcoming brothers and sisters of all faith communities to join in. The Church will share the message of salvation as it seeks the kingdom in the midst of a world filled with chaos and pain. As we journey together, we will make discovery after joyful discovery, many of which are beyond our imagination.

▸ Detail, "400 Years of Our People," Michael Escoffery/Art Resource, New York. © 2010 Michael Escoffery/ Artists Rights Society (ARS), New York, NY

To understand our history as African Americans, as the people of America, we must understand our continuing need, if less than constant commitment, "to define and refine our common understanding of the very idea and fact of liberty."[4] It is this commitment to liberty that the Jubilee Bible invites and requires all of us to proclaim.

As a Church, as a nation, as a people, the whole polity, the whole family, the whole of humanity, we will remember to the profit of ourselves and our common future, that Jubilee is a universal mandate for a civil world and a civil society. No Jubilee, no justice. No justice, no Jubilee. No Jubilee, no civility. Despite neglect, disdain, and irreverence, earth shall have a Jubilee. Jubilee will not be denied. And, with our whole-hearted participation, it will be a Jubilee of justice, peace, security, and the kingdom of character. But there will also be judgment. Is not judgment already upon America and the world? Witness the conflicts and hatreds we once thought obsolete; the rash of violence now rampant and destructive, on a scale unmatched at home and abroad.

As we explore its practices we will discover that Jubilee *is* the guarantor of the Good Society, with its provisions for self-adjudication of every kind of injustice and hostility that builds up in individuals, families, and societies. Skeptics say that Jubilee cannot work. But, it can also be said that whether or not Jubilee can work, we will not know, until we have put its principles into practice.

As a People of Promise, *coming* into a Land of Promise, *having* in our hand the Book of Promise, we can do no better than study God's Word and pray earnestly that God who gives us the courage to keep faith in his promises, will show us the way to a bright, new Jubilee future.

Sources Cited

1. Joseph Donders, *Non-Bourgeois Theology, An African Experience of Jesus,* (Maryknoll, NY: Orbis Books, 1985), 75-79.

2. *Smith's Comprehensive Dictionary of the Bible,* Samuel Barnum, 1893.

3. Maria Harris, *Fashion Me A People,* (Louisville, KY: Westminster John Knox Press, 1989), 16, 17.

4. James McGregor Burns and Stewart Burns, *A People's Charter: The Pursuit of Rights in America,* (New York: Alfred A. Knopf), 1991.

The African American Experience

From Experience to Biblical Image

◂ "I'm Harriet Tubman. I Helped Hundreds to Freedom," 1975. Art © Elizabeth Catlett/Licensed by VAGA, New York, NY

African Americans have known slavery. They have known it as brutally as the suffering Israelites in Pharaoh's Egypt. To speak of the African American experience is to speak of the experience of slavery. This horrific experience dates back to 1619 when Africans arrived in Jamestown, Virginia, and were thereafter forced into slavery. Their European captors were "Bible Christians" and, as noted by New Testament scholar, Vincent L. Wimbush, the Africans were quick to notice the influence the Bible had on the "self-image, culture, and orientation" of these slave owners. Slaves heard their captors refer to the Bible as "Holy Scripture" or "Holy Book," and they soon began to associate the Bible with power.[1] According to Wimbush, African slaves sought to engage "the Book" and thus demonstrated their "ability to adapt themselves to different understandings of reality."[2] Inasmuch as slaves were forbidden to read, they were denied access to "the Book;" hence, the biblical narratives they heard were filtered through the lens of their experience in bondage. The Bible came to represent a body of literature that contained stories of enslavement and liberation.

The events recorded in the book of Exodus concerning the escape of Israelites from bondage in Egypt would have resonated with the Afri slaves. They would have identified with the struggles of the Hebrews come to know God as one who heard their cries and who would deli them from bondage. Clarice Martin, a New Testament scholar, points that this particular biblical narrative (most notably, Exodus 14) "has tioned as a vivid and explicit symbol that confirms that God is a God liberates, who secures justice for the people of God."[3]

Another New Testament scholar, Brian K. Blount, observes that, for th slaves, the critical starting point in any engagement with the Bible was historical circumstance. According to Blount, "the interpretative move from experience to biblical image, not the other way around... They b with the horrors of their experience and then interpret those horrors through their understandings of biblical images. Their key intent is not much to understand the Bible as it is to understand their historical circ stance."[4] The Exodus event, as noted above, is an example of this move ment from experience to biblical image. As slaves became increasingly familiar with the Bible, they interpreted their experiences as parallel to sufferings of the Israelites while they were in bondage in Egypt. Inasm as the slaves were illiterate, they had, as Blount points out, "but one int pretative lens through which they instinctively analyzed the Bible: thei own historical experience," which led them into an interpersonal engag ment with the biblical text and fostered their own spiritual formation.[5]

This interpersonal engagement, or interpretation of the Scriptures, wa often done through song. Images drawn from the Bible were wedded music, and the songs represented a voice against institutionalized slav The words from the following spirituals demonstrate interpretations Scripture in light of the experience of African Americans as slaves and illustrate a "process of the transformation of the Book Religion of the dominant peoples into the religion reflective of the socio-political and economic status of African slaves:"[6]

Go down, Moses
'Way down in Egypt land,
Tell ole Pharaoh,
Let my people go.

* * *

Dey crucified my Lord,
An' He never said a mumblin' word.
Dey crucified my Lord,
An' He never said a mumblin' word,
Not a word – not a word – not a word.

Katie Cannon in her book, "Womanism and the Soul of the Black Community," notes that the slaves, as spiritual singers, "were not bothered by the chronological distance between the biblical era and their present." They operated on "a sense of sacred time" and experienced "an immediate intimacy with biblical persons as faith relatives." People and events from the past world of the Bible came alive in the midst of their present circumstances.[7] And stories such as the Israelites' freedom from Egyptian bondage (Exodus 14) and Daniel being protected while in a lions' den (Daniel 6) represented stories of deliverance and hope.

▸ Detail of Ethiopian religious painting representing the Crucifixion of Christ. © Robert Huberman/Superstock

African Americans thus "saw themselves as *hermeneutically* free"[8]—that is, they were free to engage, interpret, and refashion Scripture in light of their experience. And since their engagement with the biblical texts was primarily based on oral transmissions, "a strict literalism did not characterize their engagement of the Bible."[9] As noted by Renita Weems, an Old Testament scholar, the illiteracy of the slaves liberated them from any "allegiance to any official text, translation, or interpretation; hence once they heard biblical passages read and interpreted to them, they in turn were free to remember and repeat in accordance with their own interests and tastes."[10] Thus, the slave experience became the interpretative lens or *hermeneutic* for engaging the biblical texts, and listening and remembering were the key *hermeneutical* tools.

Wimbush further points out that, during the eighteenth century revival movements in the North and the South, "Africans began to convert to Christianity in significant numbers," and they took "note of the diversity of views that reading the Bible could inspire" and "learned that they, too, could read 'the Book' freely" – reading certain parts and ignoring others.[11] Nowhere is this more vividly evidenced than in the account of Howard Thurman's story of his grandmother's listening habits and how in the early 1900s she would not let her grandson read from any of the Pauline letters (with the exception of 1 Corinthians 13) inasmuch as, when she was a slave, she often heard her master's white minister preach from the text: "Servants, be obedient to them that are your masters according to the flesh, with fear and trembling, in singleness of your heart, as unto Christ" (Ephesians 6.5, *KJV*). Because the minister had interpreted this passage to mean that the existence of slavery was God's will, the grandmother vowed that if ever she learned to read and became free she "would not read that part of the Bible."[12]

The ways in which African Americans have appropriated Scripture interpretation in light of their experiences illustrates what Wimbush has termed "a culture-specific reading of the Bible" which has shifted "the focus of interpretation away from objective text toward 'world' or culture" and has laid the foundation for continued African American and other culturalist readings of the Bible.[13]

The Word of God in African American Culture

The Jubilee Edition of the Bible is designed to help readers connect their histories, cultural images, moral visions, and perspectives to the ancient Scriptures in such a way that the Word of God becomes authentic, relevant, and intimate. Readers are thus invited to examine and study the Bible through the lens of African American historic and culturally relevant understandings of the Scriptures.

The textual theme for this Jubilee Edition of the Bible is grounded in Scripture: Leviticus 25.8-12; Isaiah 61.1-4; and Luke 4.16-21. (For a further examination of these textual themes, see the following articles in Section Two: "Jubilee in Leviticus 17-26," by Jerome C. Ross, and "The Message of Salvation," by Thomas L. Hoyt, Jr.) The Jubilee theme is rich in historic interpretation and offers a message of hope for all humankind to live as the family of God, as evidenced by the vision recorded in the Letter to the Ephesians 2.19b, CEV: "You are citizens with everyone else who belongs to the family of God."

In studying the Scriptures and exploring their connections to one's social reality, the reader is encouraged to examine the biblical text from four perspectives: **Place, People, Culture, and Story.**

1. Where does the event take **place**? Study the ancient lands and geography.

2. Who were the **people**? From where did they migrate and at what period in history?

3. What was the **culture**; e.g., habits, traits, language, occupations, survival skills, faith systems, judicial systems, and power relationships?

4. What was their "**story**?" The Bible is lived history—human stories, both oral and written—of pilgrimages, faith journeys, struggles, triumphs, temptations, testings, stories of achievements and failures, of relationships, coping strategies, and spiritual encounters, to name a few.

New Testament scholar Brad Ronnell Braxton has drawn upon Jesus' parable of the Good Samaritan (Luke 10.25-37) as an example for examining a biblical text within the context of today's social reality. He points out the following:

> Historically, the ill will between blacks and whites in America has always been a useful point of connection, because social tension is at the heart of this text. African American preachers have drawn strong parallels between Samaritans and their own

community. Both groups were considered racially inferior by the ruling culture. Both groups were objects of bitter feelings.

In spite of his social status, the Samaritan in the text acted in a commendable manner. Many African American preachers have lifted up the Samaritan as an example for behavior. This example applies not only to some far-off time and setting. It applies now—to the real world of racism, second-class citizenship, police brutality, and economic exploitation.

For African Americans this parable has been a weapon in the warfare for human rights and equality. It has served as a clarion call to act in an ethically responsible way, even if the wounded victim on the road is not part of one's social group. Even more, if the person is the oppressor.

In the face of oppression, African Americans have found great solace in Jesus' story. Here was a man from society's margins who stopped on a dangerous road. He helped a traveler who appeared to be the other, but in reality was the brother.[14]

Read the parable of the Good Samaritan. Examine the story in light of the four perspectives outlined above. How does your interpretation of the story compare with Braxton's? What were your interpretative lenses? What insights did you gain? What connections do you see between this parable and the six provisions of the Jubilee set forth by Jesus in Luke 4?

By reading the stories and events in the Bible, discover ways in which they connect to your experiences. For a guide to interpreting the Scriptures, see the article in Section Two: "Interpretation of Scripture," by Murray L. Newman. And, for a more in-depth examination of the presence of Africans in the Bible, see also in Section Two: "The Presence and Role of Africans in the Bible," by Prince V. Ntintili, and "The Presence of Blacks in Biblical Antiquity," by Cain Hope Felder.

An exciting Jubilee journey awaits you! Discover the transforming power of God's Word and the insights God has in store for you as you engage the world of the Bible through the lens of your own unique experience.

Let the wonderful kindness and understanding that come from our Lord and Savior Jesus Christ help you to keep on growing. Praise Jesus now and forever! Amen! (2 Peter 3.18, *CEV*)

Africa

A discussion on the Jubilee concept would not be complete without the inclusion of Africa, the place where the history of African Americans began.

Africa was the seat of civilization, a continent of vast empires. Among its peoples were great prophets, teachers and leaders who had distinguished themselves through their visionary acuity, knowledge, and prowess. These mighty empires maintained their prominence by aggressively trading with faraway cities and expanding their territory through conquest of other lands. Thus, through commerce and wars, the people of Africa began a migratory pattern that took them away from their original regions. Such migration eventually spawned powerful kingdoms especially in West Africa. Ghana, Mali, Songhay, and the Mossi States are among the most notable.

Ghana dates back to the seventh century B.C. Long before A.D. 1000, it was a major, well-organized empire, which had intricate systems of democracy. Its riches came from an abundance of gold, a lively slave trade, and a tax system not unlike our own. Mining, farming, and artistry made the region thrive, but later internal strife, invasions from rival neighboring states, and severe climatic changes caused Ghana to fall in the thirteenth century.

▸ Egypt, near Luxor, Valley of the Kings. Interior frescoes of King Ramesses VI's tomb. © Wolfgang Kaehler/ Superstock

▸ Close-up of the Map of Africa, Joan Bleau, 1630. © Steve Vidler/ Superstock

MOZAMBIQVE
CANARIA
NATOLIA
Cyprus
Candia
MEDITERRANEUM
AFRICÆ
nova descriptio.
Auct: Guiljelmo Blaeuw.
ASIAE
PARS
ARABIA
OCEANI
ORIEN:
TALIS
PARS
SINUS
BARBARICUS
NUBIA REGN.
Barca desertum
Zocotora
Dangali
Mozambique
Zefala
MADAGASCAR, que et
S. LAURENTII INSula dicitur
Ægypti

With the collapse of Ghana came Mali, a more powerful state whose famous capital, Timbuktu, and equally famous city, Djenne, were highly regarded as Islamic centers of culture and education as well as trade and commerce. Mali's most famous emperor, Mansa Musa (who ruled 1312-1337), is remembered for making a pilgrimage to Mecca through Cairo dressed in full regalia, with a large entourage of slaves, elephants and camels who were ornately groomed, and several trunks filled with gold. Musa gave lavish presents of gold as he traveled, and it is believed that he caused the price of Egypt's gold to fall because of his actions. Although Musa was skilled in military tactics, he is also credited for boosting commerce and "proselytizing Islam more than any one of his predecessors."[15]

Despite Mali's military and commercial successes, it was eventually eclipsed by the Songhay empire. Like Mali, the Songhay empire profited greatly from shrewd trading. Its people, who were primarily traders, also flourished as farmers, fishermen, shepherds, and craftsmen. Their military skills kept them safe from attack but widespread rebellion, coupled with an invasion of Timbuktu by the Moroccans in 1591, caused the empire to collapse.

The Mossi States (later known as Upper Volta, and today as Burkino Faso) succeeded Songhay. It became the most powerful and most industrial state in the region. It survived as an African state for over 500 years and was the last of the great black West African states. When it was subjugated by the French in 1896, it opened the way to European dominance in West Africa, which was by then a major source for the Atlantic slave trade.

Diaspora

The word ***diaspora*** is defined as the scattering of people with a common origin, background, and belief. It has been used traditionally to describe the experience of the Jews who were dispersed from Judah in the sixth century and exiled in Babylonia (587- 483 B.C.). Diaspora is now also used to define the forcible dispersal of peoples of African descent beyond the boundaries of the continent of Africa. Unlike the Jews in captivity, the millions of uprooted and enslaved Africans were heterogeneous peoples from a wide range of tribal groups and cultures who spoke different languages. (See Section Two:

"The Relationship Between Hebrew and African Languages," by Edwina M. Wright.)

Slavery, the practice of owning another person as property, was not a new idea. The forcible dispersal of Africans can be traced as far back as classical antiquity when small numbers of Africans were sold into slavery in the Mediterranean region. Others were shipped to western India, southern Iraq, and as far away as China. The African slave trade, however, was not based on race and did not carry the stigma of inferiority. In fact, many of the enslaved were educated and skilled people. (For further study, see Section Two: "Slavery in the Ancient Near East and, Particularly, in Israel," by Frank Gipson, and "Roman Slavery in Antiquity," by Mitzi Jane Smith.)

The colonization of the New World by the Europeans during the 1500s and 1600s only served to expand the booming slave trade. In the mid-sixteenth to nineteenth centuries, the Portuguese, Spaniards, Dutch, English, and French were the main perpetrators. It is estimated that during these three centuries slave ships scattered some ten to twelve million Africans across the New World (North and South America, the West Indies and Mexico). Millions more died in Africa during, or after, their capture, or as a result of the horrific conditions on the ships transporting them to North America.

It is significant to examine the African culture and trace the diaspora from Africa to the Western Hemisphere because it provides a fuller understanding as to the importance and necessity of Jubilee. It also provides a historical link and cultural identity to the people we call African Americans.

From Africa to the United States

Most of the Africans who were enslaved in the United States came from the western part of Africa. Many came from the area near the seacoast, from the Senegal River in the north to the area which is now known as Angola. Others came from Zaire, Nigeria, Ghana, Senegambia, the Ivory Coast, Liberia, and Sudan. Still others were brought from East Africa from Mozambique and Madagascar. Among these ethnic groups were the Wolof, Mandingo, Bambara, and Yoruba, all of whom had a significant Muslim population, as well as the Akan, Kru, Fon, Ibo, and various Kongo people.

▶ African-Americans picking cotton on plantation beside the Mississippi, ca. 1883. © Image Asset Management Ltd./Superstock.

Paddle Steamer River Agriculture textile Landscape, USA. Plantation house left, workers' cabins to its right. Jetty for loading cotton bales, center.

African slaves first arrived in the British North American colonies in 1619 in Virginia. Slavery spread to Maryland, the Carolinas, and later Georgia where Africans cultivated tobacco, rice, and indigo. South Carolina depended upon black labor to such an extent that by 1720 more Africans inhabited the colony than Europeans. This demographic reality caused one observer in 1737 to note that South Carolina "looks more like a Negro country than like a country settled by white people."[16] Although large scale agriculture required major importations of African slaves, farm and urban necessities in northern colonies also put Africans into bondage in New England and in the Middle Atlantic. The rhetoric of liberty during the Revolutionary War period, however, compelled the authors of the Declaration of Independence to proclaim slavery as incompatible with democratic ideas. As a result, slaves were increasingly manumitted in the North and in some parts of the Upper South, particularly in Virginia and Maryland. Nonetheless, the Constitution which established the United States in 1789 recognized black slaves as three-fifths of a person and permitted the slave trade to continue until 1808. The invention of the cotton gin in 1793 revived slavery in the South and inaugurated its spread elsewhere in the region and beyond.

From the beginning, African slaves worked without pay in grueling conditions. Freedom of movement, family disruption, ties to tribes, language, religion, and culture all yielded to the necessities of American slavery. A congressional gag rule forbade the discussion of slavery in the U.S. Capitol while fugitive slave provisions in the Constitution and in a congressional enactment seemed to fix the servile status of blacks into an indefinite future. No state in the Union had been immune from the practice of involuntary servitude. It took a Civil War from 1861 through 1865 to free slaves from permanent bondage in the United States. (See Section Two: *"The Alleged Curse on Ham,"* by Gene Rice.)

From Africa to the West Indies and South America

One scholar has estimated that 9,566,100 Africans survived the "Middle Passage" and were enslaved in the Western Hemisphere.

Estimated Slave Imports into the Americas by Importing Region (1451-1870)

British North America	339,000
Spanish America	1,552,100
British Caribbean	1,665,000
French Caribbean	1,600,200
Dutch Caribbean	500,000
Brazil	28,000
Old World	175,000
Total	**9,566,100**[17]

▸ "Gathering Fruit," by Emile. Private Collection/ Beth Hinckley/ Superstock

Africans went in the largest numbers into the Caribbean while Brazil was the primary single destination for this tragic traffic in human beings. Slaves were shipped first to South America or the West Indies where they would be trained or "seasoned" for work in the United States. By 1700, the major Caribbean islands, including Jamaica and Barbados, enslaved thousands of slaves.[18] Sugar plantations flourished and many absentee masters had their slaves worked to death.

In South America, the Spanish and Portuguese colonists who practiced slavery met little opposition from the Roman Catholic Church. Slaves were considered a labor system, a part of the monarch's property and the Church sought to maintain some semblance of human rights for the enslaved. Marriage among slaves, for example, was recognized. Such "humane" treatment did not prevent uprising by some slaves. But, in Brazil especially, there was considerable intermingling between slaves and masters until a significant mulatto population emerged. After emancipation, this group occupied a higher status than blacks in Brazilian society.[19]

Since 1619: A Faith Journey

The articles in Section Two of the Jubilee Bible examine the ugly beginnings of slavery in American society and weave a story of torturous exile to one that continuously unfolds in triumphant exodus under the guidance of Almighty God.

Dr. Samuel D. Proctor in *The Substance of Things Hoped For: The Faith Epic of African Americans* describes a pilgrimage of "a handful of slaves (20) who disembarked in Jamestown to 32 million African American citizens, from 244 years of physical bondage of slavery to positions of trust and responsibility in the highest levels of government, religion, education, business, industry, sports, arts/entertainment, medicine, and jurisprudence." Proctor sees this journey as one that is unparalleled; an epic of a unique people of faith who persevered, endured, and maintained their spirituality despite the harshness of their lives.

Faith-based Freedom

The African Americans' view of the sacred and divine is inextricably linked to their African heritage, their inherent values of freedom, justice, and racial equality, and their early experiences in the U.S. Although many blacks voluntarily embraced Christianity, some whites used selected biblical teachings of obedience and suffering to keep the slaves submissive. Despite this, blacks adopted the salvation story as their own and were quick to accept the freedom it offered. Consequently, their music, dance, prayer and secret gatherings reflected the theme of freedom. (See Section Two: "The Bible in African American Spirituality," by Michael I. N. Dash.) They strongly identified with the suffering of Jesus and held the hope that one day Jesus' message of Jubilee—his proclamation of freedom from oppression—would eventually be realized. This faith lies at the heart of the African American experience.

"Faith became their bridge," says Proctor. "Their depth of faith required the special preparation for living on tirelessly, living on unfulfilled hopes and desires, which have not been paralleled. This faith brought them through sheer pain and brutality of the lash, the chains, the whip, and the burden; this faith sustained them in the anguish of the separation from their parents, children and spouses... More particularly, this faith enabled them to envision that a day of freedom would come, and they could begin that long trek toward an education, and respectability, independence, security, leisure, and personal privacy, which was the most cruel denial of all."[20]

What African Americans needed was not just freedom from servitude, but the freedom to make their own choices, to attain their full potential, and to knock on the doors of justice and be let in.

African Culture

Kinship

Most of the indigenous peoples of Africa live in clusters or units commonly called tribes. In modern times, the word "tribe" is viewed as derogatory and it is often replaced by the term "people." Each people is seen to have their own language, occupy a specific geographical region, share a common culture, and hold similar religious beliefs.

The African family includes the extended family, "a more or less close-knit group of relatives comprising several pairs of grandparents or possibly great-grandparents and all their living descendants except those who had married out of the group into another comparable group."[21] Family also includes those who were yet to be born.

As an individual, each person is a valued member of the group. The individual exists because of the community and people of present and past generations. This interdependence creates a strong bond within the community.

Religion

Most scholars agree that, while African American Christianity developed orthodox adherence either to Catholicism or Protestantism, preserved remnants drew from the African religious heritage. Some slaves in spiritual ecstasy engaged in ring shouts. Others decorated the graves of departed family members with items that would be useful to the deceased in the afterlife. Blacks integrated these and other practices with their Christian beliefs and developed the cultural richness that characterizes African American Christianity.

Worship

"Africans in their act of worship live close to the land. Prayers to God relate directly to rain, fertility, and the welfare of humans, cattle and fields. Since animals and plants constitute food for humans, it is not surprising that Africans have many religious ceremonies associated with them. Their act of worship is aided by sacrifices, offerings, prayers, and invocations. God is the one who makes the sun rise and set, the rain fall, the mountains quake, and the rivers overflow. He heals the sick, helps the barren, and aids those in distress."[22]

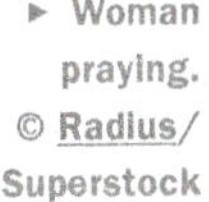

▸ Woman praying. © Radius/ Superstock

Music

Music played an integral role in the life of the African people. Oral history and traditions were recited and sung by traveling troubadours who would often perform in a public place. Laws, customs, national and family history, and even news were often handed down in this way by these professional ***griots*** or storytellers. Such singing invited rhythmic action. Singers would snap their fingers while onlookers would pat their feet, clap their hands, and move their bodies rhythmically to the beat. In most cases, dancing accompanied the singing. Africans are known to dance for all occasions: in happy or sad times, and simply to pass the time. These cultural practices are clearly a large part of the heritage of the African American people and have been incorporated into their religious experience. (See Section Two: "Music in the Black Church," by William H. Collins, Jr.)

The Black Church

"O, freedom over me.
And before I'd be a slave
I'll be buried in my grave
An' go home to my Lord
An' be free."

Negro Spiritual

▸ Mourning family of one of the four African-American girls killed in the 16th Street Baptist Church bombing on September 15, 1963. © Everett Collection/ Superstock

▸ Church Choir
© Exactostock/
Superstock

If Jubilee is to be established, it must first start with the church. The church has been the bedrock of faith, a balm of healing for the hurting and weary, and a strong voice on behalf of the oppressed. The black church is not a single institution, but it can be identified as a distinctive community whose faith is rooted and grounded in an interpretation viewed through the lens of a people victimized by almost three centuries of slavery. The black church has sought to acquire justice and rights which have been enjoyed, primarily, by the dominant culture of this country.

At its inception, the black church has been the most important and dominant institutional reality in African American communities. The black church carries burdens, and performs roles and functions beyond the boundaries of spiritual nurturing, in politics, economics, education, music, and culture. It has been involved in missions that embrace domestic activities such as family, education, urban ministries, and the institutional church, to name a few.

Leadership and Politics

The black church is not just a building for the "gathering of the saints." It is a community whose influence is reflected in politics, civil rights, militancy, outreach programs and economic independence contributions. The fundamental values of survival and liberation are deeply embedded in the primary biblical doctrine of the "belief systems" of the black faith community, and involvement is motivated by convictions.

Historically, the black church was primarily the natural training ground for the development of leadership skills. This was seen especially in the areas of politics and community development. This accounts for many of the famous historical figures who were involved in slave revolts, abolitionism, electoral politics and civil rights protests. These figures have been either clergy, or closely identified with black churches, and history reflects their accomplishments in the black community. Clergy leadership of the black church tends to be strong and decisive, though it is increasingly being shared with mission-driven laypersons who are being led into multiple ministries and are becoming more vocal in decision-making. Likewise, African American leaders from predominately white churches played significant roles. For example, Dr. Elder G. Hawkins, and many others like him, was a staunch supporter of the Civil Rights Movement. Dr. Gayraud S. Wilmore, a theologian and author, did much to advance black theology.

Preaching in the Black Church

The black preacher is integral to the nurture of the spiritual life of the black church. The preacher is often pastor, community leader, prophet, civil rights advocate, and the chief administrator of the black community's most independent enterprise, the black church. The preacher played a significant part in the social and religious development of "Negro" life. First, preaching was an outlet for leadership ability. It was the one position of leadership permitted Negroes, and the office carried prestige. The black preacher was able to communicate religion in a useful and intimate form to those enslaved. As one of the people suffering with them, the minister made religion not only a discipline but also a living ground of hope. This preacher was the first shepherd to the people of diverse languages and customs who were brought from diverse parts of Africa and thrown into slavery. Though the black church gave them their first sense of unity and solidarity, it was the "ole time" preacher who for generations was the mainspring of hope and inspiration for blacks in America. (For further study, see Section Two: "Black Preaching in the Church," by Elliott Cuff.)

The following excerpt of a sermon/poem by James Weldon Johnson pays tribute to all African American preachers who inspire their congregations with the excitement, the dramatic cadences, and the illuminating Word of God.

▸ Aspects of Negro Life: The Negro in an African Setting, by Aaron Douglas, 1934. Oil on Canvas. © Arts and Artifacts Division, Schomburg Center for Research in Black Culture, The New York Public Library. Used by permission.

Go Down Death–A Funeral Sermon

Weep not, weep not,
She is not dead;
She's resting in the bosom of Jesus.
Heart-broken husband–weep no more;
Grief-stricken son–weep no more;
Left-lonesome daughter–weep no more
She's only just gone home.

Day before yesterday morning,
God was looking down from his great, high heaven,
Looking down on all his children,
And his eye fell on Sister Caroline,
Tossing on her bed of pain,
And God's big heart was touched with pity,
With the everlasting pity.

And God sat back on his throne,
And he commandeth that tall, bright angel standing at his right hand:
Call me Death!
And that tall, bright angel cried in a voice
That broke like a clap of thunder:
Call Death–Call Death!
And the echo sounded down the streets of heaven
Till it reached away back to that shadowy place.
Where death waits with his pale, white horses.

And death didn't say a word,
But he loosed the reins on his pale, white horse,
And he clamped the spurs on his bloodless sides,
And out and down he rode,
Through heaven's pearly gates,
Past suns and moons and stars;
On Death rode,
And the foam from his horse was like a comet in the sky;

While we were watching round her bed,
She turned her eyes and looked away,
She saw what we couldn't see;
She saw Old Death. She saw Old Death
Coming like a fallen star.
But death didn't frighten Sister Caroline;
He looked to her like a welcome friend.
And she whispered to us: I'm going home,
And she smiled and closed her eyes.

Weep not–weep not,
She is not dead;
She is resting in the bosom of Jesus.[23]

(See Section Two: "Homegoing," by Diane M. Ritzie.)

The Black Church and Education

Since the institution of slavery, the question of black education has been an important issue in the United States. Early slaveholders believed that if slaves received an education, it might inspire them to revolt, ultimately resulting in the destruction of the institution of slavery. If this had happened, the celebration of slavery's end would have been Jubilee! Rather than cause for celebration, the

Reconstruction period proved to be an unplanned system that had no significant benefit for the slave, resulting in individuals who had not been prepared, socially or economically, to succeed in America.

No other area of black life received a higher priority from black churches than education. Despite the fact that teaching a slave to read and write was illegal during slavery, one of the most persistent desires of the slaves was to be educated. Blacks knew instinctively that literacy would provide untold opportunities and it would give them access to reading the Bible for themselves.

▸ "Booker T. Washington: The Apostle of Learning." Detail of print, "Afro-American Monument." Chromolithograph ca. 1897. © Everett Collection/ Superstock

Proverbs 4:7, "In all thy getting, get wisdom."

The Black Church and the Black Family

The church is the one institution in the community where its congregants can find a focal place to express their God-given gifts, receive recognition, develop raw talents, and cultivate inner strength for self-determination and worth. The church enables the family to find ways to give positive meaning to potentially stressful life events. The black church plays an indispensable role as "the extended family" where the roles of "brother, sister, aunt, and uncle" take on new meanings. Social outings, rituals, baptisms, graduation, celebrations, funerals, and other church-focused activities have provided cultural systems for church-centered lives. Church-sponsored meals have provided the elderly with fellowship and nourishment. The growth of whole life centers in urban settings attempts to recapture the holistic role of the church as the primary spiritual center for the entire life of the individual, thus, taking steps toward creating Jubilee. (For further study, see Section Two: "A History of the Black Church," by Dennis C. Dickerson.)

Creating a Jubilee World

Practice Jubilee!

Throughout the Scriptures, the Jubilee refrain resounds with themes of forgiveness, liberty, and justice. To forgive and be forgiven; to be free to return to one's traditions and to remember bondage and freedom from bondage; to strive for justice in the biblical sense, both economically and socially, with regard to equitable distribution of the earth's resources and concern for the family—these tenets are at the heart of true Jubilee that culminates in gratitude to God, the source of "every perfect gift" (James 1.17).

In her book *"Proclaim Jubilee!"* Religious Education Professor Maria Harris states that she has "found no people more involved with living the Jubilee than African Americans" inasmuch as they "preserve in their own experience a history of the slavery and suffering and longing for liberation that the Jubilee sought to address."[24] From the Jubilee Emancipation of 1865, through the post-Civil War Reconstruction period, up to the Civil Rights' movements in the twentieth century, the Jubilee pilgrimage for African Americans has continued with the quest for forgiveness, liberty, and justice.

To apply the Jubilee model and understand its significance in daily life "requires that people dwell in God's creative presence" and "experience God's forgiveness; hope in God's promises; and practice God's justice." Such "religious wholeness characterizes Jubilee."[25]

To practice jubilee requires the people of God to engage in the struggle to "see that justice is done" (Micah 6.8b, *CEV*)—locally, nationally, and globally. In communities where people are oppressed, their cries echo the words of the prophet Habakkuk:

> Our LORD, how long must I beg for your help
> before you listen?
> How long before you save us
> from all this violence?
> Why do you make me watch
> such terrible injustice?
> Why do you allow violence,
> lawlessness, crime, and cruelty
> to spread everywhere?
> Laws cannot be enforced;
> justice is always the loser;
> criminals crowd out honest people
> and twist the laws around.
> *(Habakkuk 1.2-4, CEV)*

To strive for justice now is what the prophets Micah, Amos, Isaiah and others are calling us to do if we are to understand the significance and relevance of jubilee today.[26] To practice Jubilee is to worship the LORD as the prophet Isaiah declares:

> Remove the chains of prisoners
> who are chained unjustly.
> Free those who are abused!
> Share your food with everyone
> who is hungry;
> share your home
> with the poor and homeless.
> Give clothes to those in need;
> don't turn away your relatives.
> *(Isaiah 58.6b, 7, CEV)*

Implicit in the struggle is the call for economic justice—equal access to capital and expanding economic opportunities for those excluded from the economic mainstream. Church and community leaders, along with directors of financial institutions, are being challenged to foster the creation of equitable local financial policies so that communities are strengthened for the benefit of all people.[27] Such a challenge is grounded in Scripture and teaches the value of everyone becoming a wise steward of financial resources (see Matthew 25.14-30).

As you study the Holy Scriptures, reflect on ways in which you can participate in the struggle and practice Jubilee. Some suggested Scripture passages for you to examine are:[28]

Exodus 21.1-11 (giving freedom to slaves)
Exodus 22.25-27 (lending money to the poor without interest)
Exodus 23.10-13 (the sabbath year and providing for the poor)
Leviticus 25 (laws for observing the sabbath year)
Deuteronomy 15.1-18 (sharing with the poor and setting slaves free)
Nehemiah 5 (removing the burden of debt)
Isaiah 5.8-10 (condemnation of greed)
Isaiah 58 (true worship by striving for justice)
Isaiah 59 (social injustice condemned)
Amos 5 (justice demanded by the LORD)
Luke 3.11 (sharing with those in need)
Luke 7.18-23 (good news proclaimed to the poor)
Luke 10.25-37 (offering compassion to your neighbor)

How do these passages speak to you today? What are you called to do?

Celebrate Jubilee!

The ending of the twentieth century marks the beginning of a new millennium, and author Maria Harris calls humankind to celebrate Jubilee as a way of responding "to the challenges with which the twentieth century leaves us and the twenty-first century confronts us."[29] Her call is one of celebration and an acknowledgement "that the world continues to be charged with the grandeur of God," and that "proclaiming Jubilee is an act of faith, an act of hope, and an act of conviction that grace, goodness, and holiness exist, even though none of them has triumphed fully."[30]

To celebrate Jubilee is

- to proclaim Jubilee and announce a new social order is at hand
- to acknowledge one's sins and seek forgiveness from others
- to listen quietly and wait upon the Lord both privately and in community
- to give thanks to God and respond with songs of gratitude
- to make a commitment to strive for justice and freedom for all people.[31]

The Holy Scriptures invite you to celebrate Jubilee. Examine the following passages in light of the five points noted above:

Isaiah 61 (good news is proclaimed)
Isaiah 65.17-25 (a vision of the Lord's new creation)
Matthew 5-7 (Jesus outlines a vision for living in community)
Luke 4.16-19 (Jesus preaches good news to the poor)

How will ***you*** celebrate Jubilee?

"For it is a jubilee; it shall be holy to you." (Leviticus 25.12a, *NRSV*)

Empowered by the Holy Spirit, humanity can celebrate that the kingdom of God is truly at hand (Mark 1.15).

- Jubilee ushers in the new social order as ordained by God.
- Jubilee is a universal mandate for a civil society and a civil world.
- Jubilee can bring connectedness among all peoples.
- Jubilee empowers the Black Church, even in the midst of chaos and pain, to lead all Christians to a beloved Jubilee community as envisioned by Jesus and as recorded in the 4th chapter of the Gospel according to Luke.

Join hands with your neighbor and celebrate God's kingdom in your midst. Celebrate the fullness of life that is intended for all God's children (John 10.10). (See Section Two: "The Blessing: Restoring Hope for African American Youth," by Maxine Walker.)

Proclaim Jubilee!

Practice Jubilee!

Celebrate Jubilee!

FREE
ALL SLAVES

Selected Chronology (1619-2009)

Struggles and Victories

1619 The first Africans are brought to British North American colonies when a Dutch ship lands 20 black laborers in Jamestown, Virginia.

1638 Native Americans are transported from Salem, Massachusetts to the West Indies and exchanged for African laborers, opening the New England slave trade.

1641 Massachusetts becomes the first colony to legalize slavery.

1761 Jupiter Hammon, a New York slave, publishes his poem "An Evening Thought: Salvation by Christ, with Penitential Cries." He is probably the first published slave poet.

1770 Runaway slave Crispus Attucks is the first of five killed in the Boston Massacre. Attucks is recognized as the leader of the action that eventually led to the American Revolution.

1776 United States Declaration of Independence

1787 Establishment of the Free African Society

1808 Ban on slave trade put into effect. In accordance with provisions of the Constitution, Congress outlaws the African slave trade. The slave trade continues illegally, with greatly reduced numbers of Africans being smuggled into the United States thereafter.

1820 Start of "Back to Africa" movement: 20,000 blacks will eventually leave the United States for Liberia.

1827 ***Freedom's Journal***, the first black newspaper in America, is published in March in New York City.

◂ "Juneteenth," (Emancipation Proclamation), Michael Escoffery/Art Resource, New York, NY. Private ollection. ©2010 Michael Escoffery/Artist Rights Society (ARS), New York, NY

1829 In September, David Walker, a free black man from North Carolina living in Boston, publishes his militant anti-slavery tract ***An Appeal to the Colored People of the World.*** Its publication gives rise to panic in the South and there are efforts to restrict its circulation.

1857 In March, the Supreme Court of the United States renders the Dred Scott decision, declaring that black people are not and cannot be citizens of the United States. Dred Scott remains a slave even though he has lived for a long period outside the jurisdiction of slavery. It also ruled that Congress has no right to bar slavery from western states.

1863 Lincoln's Emancipation Proclamation. On January 1, President Lincoln issues the Proclamation freeing slaves in areas then in rebellion against the United States. The Proclamation does not free slaves in areas under the control of the United States.

1865 Juneteenth is the oldest known celebration signaling the ending of slavery. On June 19th, Union soldiers at Galveston, Texas, brought the news that the war had ended and that all slaves were to be freed. This was more than two years after the Emancipation Proclamation.

1875 The Civil Rights Act concerns itself primarily with the prohibition of racial discrimination in places of public accommodation. In 1883, however, the Supreme Court rules the law unconstitutional. This decision virtually removes the federal government from the civil rights arena, particularly in regard to enforcement of the 14th Amendment.

1875 James Augustine Healy is named as the first African American bishop in the Roman Catholic Church.

1885 Rev. Samuel David Ferguson is consecrated as the first African American Protestant Episcopal Bishop in the United States.

1889 Black Lutherans in North Carolina organizes the Alpha Evangelical Lutheran Synod of Freedmen in America, the first and only separate black Lutheran ecclesiastical organization in United States history.

1905 W. E. B. DuBois, William Monroe Trotter and other blacks establish the Niagara Movement in Fort Erie, NY, forerunner of the integrated NAACP.

1909 Establishment of the National Association for the Advancement of Colored People in New York City on the 100th Anniversary of Lincoln's birth.

1910 Establishment of the National Urban League with support from Booker T. Washington and affluent whites.

1914 Marcus Garvey founds the Universal Negro Improvement Association to promote racial pride and emigration to Africa.

1935 Mary McLeod Bethune establishes the National Council of Negro Women.

1947 John Hope Franklin publishes his comprehensive black history, *From Slavery to Freedom.*

1950 Ralph Bunche is awarded the Nobel Peace Prize for successful mediation between the Arabs and Israelis in Palestine.

1954 In the case of *Brown vs. Board of Education* of Topeka, the Supreme Court rules that segregation in public education is unconstitutional, declaring that separate is "inherently unequal."

1954 Dr. James Joshua Thomas becomes the first African American pastor of the Reformed Dutch Church.

1955 Rosa Parks refuses to surrender her seat in the front of a bus to a white man. She is jailed. This sparks the Montgomery Bus Boycott.

1957 Congress passes the first important civil rights legislation since 1857, protecting the right to vote.

1963 Medgar Evers, a prominent Civil Rights activist, is assassinated.

1964 Congress passes, and President Lyndon B. Johnson signs, the Civil Rights bill banning discrimination in education, employment, and public accommodations.

1966 Constance Baker Motley, former NYC Borough President and NAACP lawyer, is appointed the first black female federal judge.

1967 President Lyndon Johnson appoints Thurgood Marshall first black Justice to the U. S. Supreme Court.

1968 Reverend Dr. Martin Luther King, Jr. is assassinated in Memphis, Tennessee.

1969 Shirley Chisholm is elected as the first African American Congresswoman in the United States. She makes a bid for the presidency in 1972.

▶ Detail, "Juneteenth," (Emancipation Proclamation) Michael Escoffery/Art Resource, New York, NY. Private Collection. © 2010 Michael Escoffery/ Artist Rights Society (ARS), New York, NY

1976 President-elect Jimmy Carter appoints Georgia Representative Andrew Young U. S. Ambassador to the United Nations.

1979 Congress honors the memory of Martin Luther King, Jr. by voting to make him the first African American with his likeness in the Capitol rotunda.

1983 President Ronald Reagan signs a bill into law making the third Monday in January a federal holiday honoring Martin Luther King, Jr.

1984 Reverend Jesse Jackson is the first African American male candidate in a presidential primary.

1988 Barbara Harris is elected the first female Bishop of the Episcopal Church.

1989 Colin Powell is appointed Chairman of the Joint Chiefs of Staff.

1993 Toni Morrison wins the Nobel Prize for Literature for her novel, *Beloved.*

1994 Black and white Pentecostals meet in Memphis, Tennessee and plan a new association, The Pentecostal-Charismatic Churches of North America, to include such largely black denominations as the Church of God in Christ and such largely white denominations as the Assemblies of God.

1997 Reverend Frederick K.C. Price, televangelist and pastor of the 17,500 member FaithDome in Los Angeles, California, starts a nearly two-year series on Race, Religion, and Racism.

1998 Reverend Arnold I. Thomas, the first black pastor of the First Congregational Church of Williamstown, Massachusetts, becomes the Conference Minister of the Vermont Conference of United Church of Christ.

1998 Bishop Wilton D. Gregory of the Diocese of Belleville, Illinois, is elected Vice President of the National Conference of Catholic Bishops.

1999 Reverend Jesse Jackson, accompanied by a delegation of American religious leaders, travels to Belgrade, Yugoslavia, and secures the release of three U. S. servicemen being held as prisoners in the Serbian-Albanian conflict.

1999 Rosa Parks is honored for her role in the civil rights movement with the Congressional Gold Medal. The Medal is the highest civilian award given by Congress.

1999 The American Bible Society publishes "The African American Jubilee Bible" in the *Contemporary English* and *King James Versions.*

1999 *Africana,* a comprehensive encyclopedia of the African and African-American experience, is edited by Harvard scholars Kwame Anthony Appiah and Henry Louis Gates, Jr.

2000 The National Council of Churches USA, an agency for ecumenical cooperation among Christians in the U.S., celebrates its 50th anniversary. Several historic black churches are members of the NCC USA.

2001 General Colin Powell is appointed Secretary of State by President George W. Bush.

2001 Condoleeza Rice is appointed National Security Advisor.

2001 Brown University names Ruth J. Simmons president of the University. She is the first African American to hold that post.

2001 Carolyn Payton, first black and first woman to head the Peace Corps (1977), dies.

2002 Halle Berry becomes the first African American to win the Academy Award for Best Actress.

2003 African-American astronaut Michael P. Anderson dies in the Columbia space shuttle disaster.

2004 Phylicia Rashad is the first African American to win a Tony Award for Best Actress in a play.

2005 Condoleeza Rice is appointed Secretary of State by President George W. Bush.

2005 Deadly Hurricane Katrina paralyzes the states of Louisiana, Alabama, Mississippi and parts of Florida. Many poor blacks are among the hardest hit.

2006 Civil rights stalwarts Coretta Scott King and Rosa Parks, die.

2006 Singer Lou Rawls, who hosted a telethon for more than 25 years to benefit the United Negro College Fund, dies.

2007 Tony Dungy, Indianapolis Colts, becomes first African-American NFL head coach to win the Super Bowl.

2008 U.S. presidential candidate, Barack Obama, is nominated by the Democratic Party.

2008 CNN airs "Black in America," a documentary on the struggles and successes of blacks 40 years after Martin Luther King, Jr.'s death.

2009 Barack Obama becomes the first African-American President of the United States, and his wife, Michelle, becomes the first African-American First Lady.

2009 Eric Holder becomes the first African-American U.S. Attorney General.

2009 Musician Duke Ellington is honored on a U.S. coin, the District of Columbia quarter.

2009 Ursula Burns is named CEO of Xerox Corporation, the first female African-American head of a Fortune 500 company.

2009 The National Association for the Advancement of Colored People celebrates its 100th anniversary.

2009 U.S. President Barack Obama wins the Nobel Peace Prize.

Section Two

"Then shalt thou cause the trumpet of the jubilee to sound on the tenth day of the seventh month, in the day of atonement shall ye make the trumpet sound throughout all your land."

(Leviticus 25.9, *KJV*)

The preceding material gave an overview of the Jubilee system and some historical background on African American heritage. The sixteen articles that follow in Section Two extend an invitation to examine issues today in light of the Jubilee mandate and the Holy Scriptures. The articles are designed to help you explore your own connection between the world of the Bible and the social issues you face on a day-to-day basis.

If Jubilee must begin with the Church, how are Scriptures interpreted? What part does music play? What is spirituality? How does one view death? What legacy do we leave our youth? How does God's salvation impact our lives?

◂ Shofar. North Africa or Middle East, 19th century. Ram's Horn engraved. The Jewish Museum, New York/Art Resource, New York, NY

Most of the articles are replete with Scripture references. The topics, in conjunction with biblical citations, could well serve as the foundation for some lively discussions and Bible study. Readers are encouraged to examine the issues set forth and journey with God's people to "Proclaim Jubilee" and spread God's Word of liberation, justice, and reconciliation.

"Proclaim the year of the Lord's favor." (Luke 4.19, *NRSV*)

OSEE
OR · OMNIV

One

Interpretation of Scripture

Murray L. Newman

The Bible may be viewed as the Word of God in the words of the people of God. Its focus and center is that stream of history which emerged with Abraham and Sarah, and flowed through the subsequent centuries to reach a climax in Jesus of Nazareth— his life, death, and resurrection. The thoughtful interpreter approaches the Bible with humility, always open to Christian insights of the centuries. In addition, the interpreter is sensitive to the literary composition of both the Old and New Testaments, their historical value, and above all their theological message. Jesus Christ, the incarnate Word, is the measure of all other words in the Bible.

◂ The Prophet Hosea, from the Prophets' window in the Augsburg Catherdral, C. 1130. © Universal Images Group/ Superstock.

Interpretation of Scripture involves a knowledge of its contents, origin, nature, and authority, as well as principles and guidelines for understanding and applying its meaning for contemporary hearers and readers.

I. The Protestant Bible

For Protestant Christians, the Bible consists of 66 books, 39 in the Old Testament (almost all originally in Hebrew) and 27 in the New Testament (all originally in Greek). Although the canons of the Roman Catholic and Orthodox churches contain additional books, clearly the 66 books are fundamental for all Christians and they are the ones assumed to comprise the Bible for purposes of this article.

The Scriptures of the Old and New Testaments represent a collection of writings authored by many different people in different historical periods from at least the 13th century B.C. to the first century A.D. Those of the Old Testament (or Old Covenant) come from the people of ancient Israel who stood in a covenant relation with God. Those of the New Testament (or New Covenant) were written by early Christians who recognized Jesus of Nazareth as the Jewish Messiah and were entrusted with the task of extending God's covenant to all the world.

II. The Word of God in the Words of the People of God

A basic assumption in this article is that the Bible is the Word of God in the words of the people of God.

A. The Word of God

Although not encompassing its totality, from a Christian perspective the central thrust of the Bible may be viewed as that stream of history witnessed to in the Book of Genesis that began with the call of Abraham. The account of Abraham's call is preceded by the narrative of creation and the disobedience of the first couple, which resulted in human estrangement from God and the breakthrough of evil in the world. This disobedience affected nature itself, as well as all human beings, who were not only estranged from God, but from one another. Abraham's destiny under God was to become the father of a people with a land, from whom would come a blessing for all the families of the earth, thus counteracting human estrangement from God and neighbor (Genesis 12.1-3). This stream flowed from Abraham, Sarah, and the other ancestors, to Moses and Miriam, with the liberating events of the exodus and the covenant between the ancient Hebrews and God, with his commandments. It moved into the Promised Land under Joshua, then to the kingship of David, bringing order and security to God's people. There followed the Prophets with their messages of both judgment and salvation. From this same stream also emerged the Psalmists and Writers of Wisdom. It then flowed to the Exile and beyond, to reach a climax with God's perfect revelation in Jesus of Nazareth, whose life, death, and resurrection are recounted in the four Gospels and other writings of the New Testament Church. Both the Old and New Testaments unequivocally affirm that God was uniquely involved in this stream of biblical history to manifest his presence, power and purpose in the world, and to achieve human salvation. For this reason the biblical writings, which witness to these events of God's self-revelation, can be called the Word of God.

In this special history, God is revealed as the Creator, holy, righteous, commanding, and loving. He is concerned with saving people from all earthly bondage, as witnessed particularly by the Exodus event and the prophets of the Old Testament, as well as from the deeper bondages of sin and death, proclaimed with power by the New Testament.

B. In the Words of the People of God

Although the people of God who were responsible for the emergence, formulation, and transmission of the biblical writings were inspired by the Holy Spirit, their words, although also inspired, are human and fallible. These writings always point beyond themselves to the God who is the Creator and Lord of nature, acts in human history, and will bring all things to their consummation with the Second Coming of Christ.

The life of the Christian Church represents a continuation of the biblical history. The Bible, which the people of the covenants produced, is therefore indispensable for worship, discipline, theologizing, and the very existence of the Christian Church. Under the guidance of the Holy Spirit the members of the Church, individually and collectively, have the responsibility of interpreting the Scriptures. However, every interpretation is ultimately subject to reinterpretation in the light of new reading and hearing of its words in new historical situations.

III. Principles of Interpretation

A. The Principle of Humility

The first principle of biblical interpretation is *humility.* For the individual Christian, as well as the larger Christian community with its various leaders and scholars, humility is the point of departure. The Christian does not stand in authority above the Bible; rather, the Bible stands in authority over the Christian. All human beings, including all Christians, are sinful and fallible, and none can ever claim to have the final, infallible interpretation of any biblical passage.

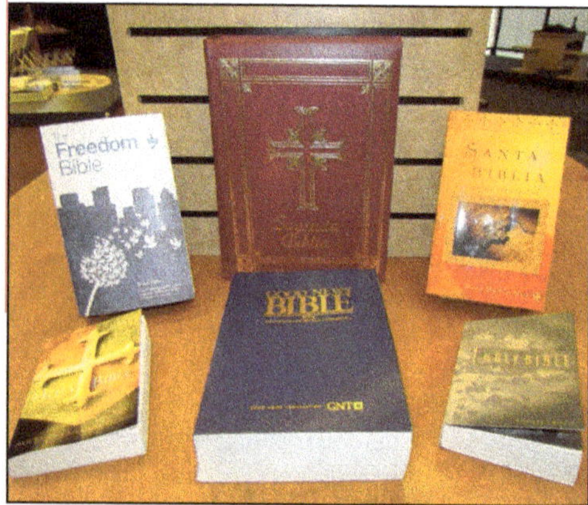

▸ Bible resources, American Bible Society. Used by Permission

B. The Principle of Reason

At the same time, Christians do in fact have the responsibility of interpreting the Bible to the best of their intellectual ability. Christians are not called to stand passive before the Bible. Every human being has been granted the gift of *reason.* Reason is a human faculty that comes from being created in God's image. With the gift of reason, the believer will use his or her mind as responsibly as humanly possible in biblical interpretation.

C. The Principle of Tradition

A third principle of interpretation is the use of the *tradition* of the people of God. No one interprets Scripture in a vacuum. Both the Christian individual and the Christian community stand as members of the ongoing life of the covenant people and their tradition. Tradition includes the collective reflection of the Church on the biblical revelation through the centuries. This would encompass Christian thinkers and theologians from New Testament times to the present, as well as hymns, sermons, prayers, liturgies, Creeds, biblical commentaries, and whatever else has helped people of the past to understand the nature and will of God as revealed in Holy Scripture.

D. The Literary Principle

Whatever else the Bible may be, it is certainly a *literary* document. Its 66 books comprise the collection of a rich variety of literature. The thoughtful believer recognizes it as such, and uses principles employed for the study of any great work of literature.

Just as in reading a newspaper it is essential to distinguish among news articles, editorials, obituaries, cartoons, and other literary forms in order to understand each one and the role it plays in contemporary life, it is equally important to distinguish the many different literary forms in the Bible. There are too many different types to mention them all. Thus only a few are noted here.

Some are unique, such as the four Gospels in the New Testament. They tell of the life and ministry of Jesus, and in that sense are biographies. But they are more than biographies; they are proclamations of God's saving work through his only Son. They are Gospels, that is, proclamations of the Good News concerning the life, death, and resurrection of Jesus of Nazareth, the Messiah.

Within the Gospels there are the smaller units, termed pericopes, such as parables, sermons, teachings, miracle stories, the birth accounts, and especially the passion narratives. Each has its own meaning, but must also be considered in the larger context of the entire Gospel.

One should mention the apocalyptic passages in the Gospels, as well as the entire book of Revelation. These apocalyptic writings do not speak of the past, but of what God will do in the future with the Second Coming of Christ and the consummation of all things. The apocalyptic writings contain a great deal of highly symbolic language, which frequently is difficult to understand. The thoughtful person of faith will be slow to interpret the symbols too literally.

The Book of Acts appears as a history of the early Church, stressing particularly the activities of Peter and Paul. The letters, or epistles, of Paul and other early Christians provide yet another New Testament form.

In the Old Testament one is aware of an even greater variety of literary types. A great deal of the Old Testament comes in the form of historical narrative: Genesis– 2 Kings, as well as 1 and 2 Chronicles, Ezra and Nehemiah. Within these larger narratives are numerous smaller units, such as theological myths, sagas, parables, genealogies, liturgies, laws, sermons, and a number of others.

In addition to the writings that tell of past historical events, there are those that speak of the future. The oracles of Israel's Prophets spoke of the future, usually of the near future. Their primary concern was with God's righteousness and his desire for justice in Israel's life. Some, however, were inspired to look further into the future and anticipate a perfect messianic savior and leader of God's people.

On the other hand, the Book of Daniel, like the Book of Revelation, is an apocalyptic work which looks into the more distant future. Again, as in the apocalyptic writings of the New Testament, the thoughtful interpreter will avoid trying to press all the details of such writings, but will recognize that their final and most important message is the ultimate triumph of God in human history.

One should also mention the Psalms (a collection of Israel's hymns), traditionally ascribed to King David, and also the Wisdom literature (Proverbs, Job, Ecclesiastes), in which the writers of Wisdom reflect on order in nature and human life.

The discerning Christian is always sensitive to the literary character of each passage, and avoids interpreting it in the same way. The reader is also aware that each individual passage must finally be considered in the larger context of the book in which it appears, as well as the entire Old Testament in the case of Old Testament passages; the entire New Testament with New Testament passages; and finally the entire Bible; with its rich variety of literary forms.

E. The Historical Principle

Another principle of biblical interpretation has to do with *history*. By historical principle we mean that the biblical traditions are rooted in the actual events of human life. Scripture witnesses to real happenings in space and time involving the ancient Hebrews, Jesus of Nazareth, and the earliest Christians.

For the Christian, the historical point of departure in this regard is the Incarnation of Jesus Christ. *God was in Christ.* God acted uniquely in the life, death, and resurrection of Jesus of Nazareth, a real historical person. Jesus was born during the reign of Herod the Great, preached, taught, and healed in Galilee while Tiberius was the Roman Emperor, and was crucified and raised again while Pontius Pilate was Governor of Judea. In addition, the apostles who accompanied Jesus in his ministry and experienced his resurrection were actual historical people, as were Peter, Paul and the other Christians whose activity is recorded in the New Testament.

The same can be said of the historical people of ancient Israel, from Abraham and Sarah and the other ancestors, to Moses and Miriam, Joshua, David and the other kings, Amos and the other Prophets, the Psalmists and Wisdom writers. Further, the great events to which the Old Testament bears witness actually happened— the Exodus, the Covenant at Sinai, the entrance into the land of Canaan, the emergence of the kingship, the kingdoms of Judah and Israel, the Assyrian threat, the Babylonian exile and return, actually happened.

In this connection, the use of maps of the Holy Land, Jerusalem, the Ancient Near East, as a whole, as well as Greece and Italy, can be invaluable in understanding the geographical settings of the various biblical events.

To be sure, none of the books of the Old Testament or the New Testament were intended to be scientific, secular histories. They were composed as proclamations of God's involvement in the lives of the people of ancient Israel and new Israel. So the wise interpreter does not expect inerrant scientific accuracy in all respects. At the same time, the great biblical events can be accepted as basically historical, and certainly the traditions of the Bible were inspired by God in such a way that his nature and purposes for human life and its salvation are revealed.

F. The Theological Principle

The word *theology* comes from Greek and means the "word of God." Is the Bible really the Word of God in the words of the people of God? Is God living and active and the Bible his living and active Word? Is it the most important means of God's self-revelation to people? If the interpreter approaches the Bible with the openness of faith in the living and active God, it can indeed be a revelation of the nature and will of God, of his power and presence and purposes, of his Word for people today.

1. The Incarnate Word

God inspired many words from many different voices through the centuries of biblical history. The result was the unparalleled theological richness contained in the Holy Scriptures. These words have continued to speak to the faithful through the centuries following that special history to this very day. Since the Bible is so rich in theological content, it is self-evident that different words from God can come through its pages to different people in different circumstances. At the center of this richness, it must be emphasized, stands Jesus Christ in his incarnation, life, atoning death, and resurrection. The Word Incarnate is the measure of all other words in the Bible.

2. The Entire Bible as Authoritative

Although the Christian's knowledge of God's nature and will comes most fully through the witness of the New Testament to Christ, it must be recognized that all 66 biblical books are authoritative for the Church— Old Testament as well as New Testament.

No Christian should undervalue the divine significance of the Old Testament. It was the Bible of Jesus and the earliest Christians, and their primary knowledge of God's nature and will came from its pages. One should note that the Old Testament contains a number of truths that are presupposed or not fully developed in the New Testament. Genesis 1, for example, speaks of God's creation of nature and its fundamental goodness. The Exodus event testifies to God's continuing concern to liberate people from all kinds of physical bondage, while the subsequent covenant at Sinai with the Ten Commandments reveals his unchanging moral will, commandments with continuing authority even for today. The prophecies of the prophets, such as the words of Amos, "Let justice roll down like waters, and righteousness like an ever-flowing stream" (5.24 *NRSV*), speak of God's demand for social justice in human society. Of special importance for the Christian believer is the fact that the Old Testament has preserved God's promises concerning the Messiah, the Suffering Servant, the Great High Priest, the Prophet to come, the Mediator of a new covenant, and others, which the New Testament sees as fulfilled in Jesus.

To be sure, if there seems to be a tension between the teachings of the Old Testament and the New Testament, the latter takes precedence for Christians. Through the biblical centuries God was progressively revealing his reality and will, as his people were able to appropriate them, to reach a climax with his perfect Word in Jesus Christ. For example, the destruction of Canaanite men, women, and children during the Conquest under Joshua, which the Hebrews believed to be in accordance with the will of God, may be understandable in certain ways in that time, but it is certainly not a warrant for such actions on the part of present followers of the One who commanded love, not only of neighbor, but of enemy as well.

3. Proof Texts and Theme Texts

In interpreting the entire Bible, one should distinguish between *proof* texts and *theme* texts. A *proof* text is a biblical passage that is taken out of context and is used in an attempt to prove a belief that is contrary to the fundamental thrust of the biblical revelation. An illustration would be the curse on Canaan in Genesis 9.25, originally directed against the immoral Canaanite religion, but which has been misinterpreted to claim the inferiority of black people or even to justify slavery. On the other hand, a *theme* text expresses a fundamental truth of biblical revelation. The statement in Genesis 1.27 affirming that "man" (*adam*, human being) has been created in the image of God reflects a basic theme that becomes ever clearer in the entire Bible. Every human being in God's creation has incomparable value, whose dignity must be respected.

Perhaps, however, the most important theme texts for Christians are John 3.16: "For God so loved the world that he gave his only Son, so that everyone who believes in him may not perish but may have eternal life" (*NRSV*). And: "you shall love the Lord your God with all your heart, and with all your soul, and with all your mind, and with all your strength," ...and "You shall love your neighbor as yourself" (Mark 12.30,31 *NRSV*).

4. Different Words for Different People

The believer always seeks to be open to all of Scripture, while recognizing, of course, that it will speak different words to different people at different times, depending on their situation and needs.

For example, the traditions in the Book of Exodus concerning God's act of liberating the Hebrew people from bondage in Egypt have spoken powerfully to African Americans as well as to other oppressed racial and ethnic groups through the years. Slavery, segregation, prejudice, or any form of racial or ethnic bondage, are repugnant in the eyes of the God of Moses and of the Lord Jesus Christ.

Paul's affirmation in Galatians 3.28 that in Christ there is neither Jew nor Greek, slave nor free, male nor *female* has spoken to contemporary women in their struggle to find their rightful place under God in the Church and larger society.

The biblical words from God come not only to groups but also to individuals. To one believer, as with Moses in the Old Testament, or to Paul in the New Testament, is addressed a call to a special vocation; to another, a word of judgment for wrongful conduct; to yet another, a word of forgiveness for the same; to a person in deep sorrow, a word of comfort and support; to one facing imminent death: "I am the resurrection and the life. Those who believe in me, even though they die, will live, and everyone who lives and

▸ "The Wise Men Journey to Bethlehem," by James Tissot (1836–1902/ French). Watercolor. Jewish Museum, New York, NY. © Superstock/ Superstock

believes in me will never die" (John 11.25b,26a, *NRSV*). The biblical words do not answer all of life's questions, but they do speak to the deepest human needs.

5. A Few Final Guidelines

Perhaps the most important guidelines for the Christian interpreter are (a) to be continually immersed in reading and listening to the Bible; (b) to think about what each passage meant in biblical times and may mean in contemporary times; (c) to be humble before it as the Word of God; and, above all, (d) to be prayerfully open to the guidance of the Holy Spirit in its interpretation.

IV. A Prayer

Blessed Lord, who caused all Holy Scriptures to be written for our learning: Grant us so to hear them, read, mark, learn, and inwardly digest them, that by the power of your Holy Word, and guidance of your Holy Spirit, we may patiently embrace, ever hold fast, and faithfully proclaim the hope of everlasting life you have given us in our Savior Jesus Christ. In his name we pray. Amen.

curſeth his God, ſhall beare his ſinne.
16 And hee that blaſphemeth the
Name of the LORD, he ſhall ſurely
be put to death, and all the Congregation ſhall certainely ſtone him: Aſwell
the ſtranger, as he that is borne in the
land, when he blaſphemeth the Name
of the LORD, ſhall be put to death.

*Exod. 21. 12. deu. 19. 21.
† Hebr. ſmiteth the life of a man.
† Hebr. life for life.

17 ¶ *And he that †killeth any man,
ſhall ſurely be put to death.
18 And he that killeth a beaſt, ſhall
make it good; †beaſt for beaſt.
19 And if a man cauſe a blemiſh in
his neighbour; as *he hath done, ſo ſhal
it be done to him:

*Exod. 21. 24. deu. 19. 21. matth. 5. 38.

20 Breach for breach, eye for eye,
tooth for tooth: as he hath cauſed a blemiſh in a man, ſo ſhall it be done to him
againe.
21 And hee that killeth a beaſt, hee
ſhall reſtore it: and hee that killeth a
man, he ſhall be put to death.

*Exod. 12. 49.

22 Ye ſhall haue *one maner of law,
aſwell for the ſtranger, as for one of
your owne countrey: for I am the
LORD your God.
23 ¶ And Moſes ſpake to the children
of Iſrael, that they ſhould bring foorth
him that had curſed, out of the Campe,
and ſtone him with ſtones: and the children of Iſrael did as the LORD commanded Moſes.

CHAP. XXV.

1 The Sabbath of the ſeuenth yeere. 8 The Iubile in the fiftieth yeere. 14 Of oppreſſion. 18 A bleſſing of obedience. 23 The redemption of land, 29 Of houſes. 35 Compaſſion of the poore. 39 The vſage of bondmen. 47 The redemption of ſeruants.

AND the LORD ſpake vn-
to Moſes in Mount Si-
nai, ſaying,
2 Speake vnto the chil-
dren of Iſrael, and ſay vn-
to them: When yee come into the land
which I giue you, then ſhall the land
†keepe *a Sabbath vnto the LORD.

† Hebr. reſt.
*Exod. 23. 10.

3 Sixe yeeres thou ſhalt ſow thy
field, and ſixe yeeres thou ſhalt prune
thy Vineyard, and gather in the fruit
thereof.
4 But in the ſeuenth yeere ſhalbe a
Sabbath of reſt vnto the land, a Sabbath for the LORD: thou ſhalt neither ſow thy field, nor prune thy Vineyard.
5 That which groweth of it owne
accord of thy harueſt, thou ſhalt not
reape, neither gather the grapes †of thy
Vine vndreſſed: for it is a yeere of reſt
vnto the land.

† Hebr. of thy ſeparation.

6 And the Sabbath of the land ſhall
be meat for you; for thee, and for thy ſeruant, and for thy mayd, and for thy hired ſeruant, and for the ſtranger that ſo-
iourneth with thee,
7 And for thy cattel, and for the beaſt
that are in thy land, ſhal all the encreaſe
thereof be meat.
8 ¶ And thou ſhalt number ſeuen
Sabbaths of yeeres vnto thee, ſeuen
times ſeuen yeeres, and the ſpace of the
ſeuen Sabbaths of yeeres, ſhall be vnto thee fourtie and nine yeeres.
9 Then ſhalt thou cauſe the trumpet †of the Iubile to ſound, on the tenth
day of the ſeuenth moneth; in the day of
atonement ſhall ye make the trumpet
ſound throughout all your land.

† Hebr. lowde of ſound.

10 And ye ſhall hallow the fiftieth
yeere, and proclaime libertie throughout all the land, vnto al the inhabitants
thereof: It ſhalbe a Iubile vnto you,
and ye ſhall returne euery man vnto
his poſſeſſion, and ye ſhall returne euery man vnto his family.
11 A Iubile ſhall that fiftieth yeere
be vnto you: Ye ſhall not ſow, neither
reape that which groweth of it ſelfe in
it, nor gather the grapes in it of thy Vine
vndreſſed.
12 For it is the Iubile, it ſhall be holy vnto you: ye ſhall eate the encreaſe
thereof out of the field.
13 In the yeere of this Iubile yee
ſhall returne euery man vnto his poſſeſſion.
14 And if thou ſell ought vnto thy
neighbour, or buyeſt ought of thy
neighbours hand, ye ſhall not oppreſſe
one another.
15 According to the number of yeres
after the Iubile, thou ſhalt buy of thy
neighbour, and according vnto the
number of yeeres of the fruits, he ſhall
ſell vnto thee.
16 According to the multitude of
yeeres, thou ſhalt encreaſe the price
thereof, and according to the fewneſſe
of yeeres, thou ſhalt diminiſh the price
of it: for according to the number of the
yeeres of the fruites doeth hee ſell vnto
thee.
17 Yee ſhall not therefore oppreſſe
one another; but thou ſhalt feare thy
God: For I am the LORD your God.
18 ¶ Where-

Two

Jubilee in Leviticus 17-26

Jerome Clayton Ross

The primary text on Jubilee is Leviticus 25, which is contextualized in two respects. First, Leviticus 25 is part of Leviticus 17–26, a three-tiered, five-part manual of discipline that was designed for use by the Aaronite priests. Second, Jubilee is located within the discussion of survival of a post-exilic Judean, and minority, community during the Persian Period. When seen in this respect, Jubilee is a socio-political and economic measure that is intended to secure the survival of the Judean community by means of reconstitution of community, and reclamation of control. Thus, it may best be appropriated as a tool for critique of contemporary discriminatory practices, and for empowerment of equitous communal life.

◂ Page from the King James Version of the Bible, American Bible Society Rare Book Collection, New York, NY

Introduction

As we approach the 21st century, the biblical theme of Jubilee (pronounced *Yôbel*, from the Hebrew) has surfaced. The main text for this theme is Leviticus 25, which is part of the larger law collection called the Holiness Code (or "H"- Leviticus 17–26). Typically, "return" or "restoration" has been regarded as its focus. However, this depends upon the approach that one takes. This discussion of Jubilee takes a different focus, which examines the text from a literary critical approach.

Since our concern is with Jubilee, Leviticus 25 is the focal text for discussion. In the first section, **The Structure of Leviticus 25** is briefly described. In the second section, **The Structure and the Classification of Leviticus 17–26,** its "superstructure," is presented in order to show its levels and interconnections, and to classify it. In this respect, Leviticus 17–26 has a three-tiered, five-part structure, and is best classified as a manual of discipline for use by priests.

The third section, **The Theme of Holiness in Leviticus 17–26: Its Use,** discusses this key theme and shows that it is developed and utilized as a multi-faceted boundary-marker for the community, and as such is employed as a mechanism for survival. In this regard, faith constitutes a way of living that is manifested socially in customs, institutions, practices, and symbols, and conceptually in principles, statements, or theories. Being both theoretical and practical, it is complex, integrating matters pertaining to worship with sociopolitical affairs, all from the perspectives of its drafters. As an expression of biblical faith, Leviticus 17–26 is the indicator of a post-exilic Judean (and thereby minority) community, that was headed by priests, who led a struggle to survive, and secured the existence of their community by means of the "fence" of holiness.

The fourth section, **The Concern with Survival in Leviticus 17–26,** explains the circumstances that necessitated its provisions. Here, it is shown that these laws address the confusion regarding the standards for the community that had ensued due to competing priestly factions within their socially mixed community (which was under Persian supervision) by means of seven principles for survival. The fifth section, **The Message of Leviticus 17–26,** details its basic thrust: its argument is that anyone, regardless of origin or prior affiliations, who lives in the province of Judah, and follows its rulings, is a legitimate worshiper of the LORD, or a Yahwist, and is thereby holy.

In the last section, **Conclusion: The Implications of Jubilee according to Leviticus 17–26,** the key data is summarized, from which implications for living are considered. The premier thesis for understanding Jubilee, according to Leviticus 17–26, is that it is designed to ensure the survival of the Judean community by means of reconstitution of community and reclamation of control on the part of the descendants of the exiled Jews. It is not simply a "return" or "restoration."

The Structure of Leviticus 25

Leviticus 25 is the ninth in a series of ten lessons, of which Leviticus 17–26 is composed. It consists of two parts: 1. an introduction (vv. 1, 2aa); and 2. teachings (vv. 2ab-55), that are followed by an insert (Leviticus 26.1, 2).

The introduction follows the standard, introductory formula (cf. Leviticus 17.1, 2a; 18.1, 2a; 19.1, 2aa) that consists of a quotation formula and a two-fold command ("the LORD told him to say..." [*CEV*]; "And the LORD spake unto Moses in Mount Sinai, saying, Speak unto...and say unto them..." [*KJV*]), and serves the typical function of bracketing, and commissioning, the practical instructions that follow. The teachings are very extensive, including two major sections (vv. 2ab-7, 8-55) that cover regulations pertaining to land sabbaths and Jubilee.

The Structure and the Classification of Leviticus 17-26

Leviticus 25, which contains the discussion of Jubilee, is found in Leviticus 17–26, which has the following structure:

Priestly Regulations
Leviticus 21, 22

Communal Regulations
Leviticus 18–20

Cultic Regulations
Leviticus 23–25

Introduction
Leviticus 17

Conclusion
Leviticus 26

This structure reveals that Leviticus 17–26 is a teaching for priests, having Leviticus 21, 22 as the point of reference for the other chapters, and the land as the pervading focus. First, the instructions in

Leviticus 18–20 have points of contact with Leviticus 21, 22, and Leviticus 18.6-23; 19.3, 4, 20, 22; and 20.9-21 correspond to the regulations on marriage for the priests (Leviticus 21.7-9, 13-15), presenting the rules in the forms of prohibitions, cases that have been deliberated, and punishments.

The morality of the priests is set in the context of communal morality. For example, the purity that is required of the people in marriage is correlated with that of the priests, since it is probable from the general context that wives were sought and taken for these priests. The purity of the priests is, then, partially premised upon the purity of the community.

Second, in Leviticus 25.13-55, the specific cases concerning redemption which build upon the general regulations (vv. 10b-12) for Jubilee have similarities with the passages in Leviticus 18, especially vv. 6-23 and vv. 24-30. The consideration of marital relations betrays an underlying concern: maintenance and protection of land-rights. These were formulated and proposed in order that land may not be lost through exogamous marriages. In this respect, Leviticus 25.13-55 probably served as precautionary measures against the accumulation of land in the hands of a few landowners to the detriment of peasant farmers (called latifundialization). Furthermore, the land is the focus in Leviticus 26, continuing the discussions of Leviticus 25, and thereby relating to the other references to the land (19.23aa; 23.10ab; 25.2ab).

Regardless of whether or not the land-sabbaths and the Jubilee regulations were implemented, the ideals are lifted up, and serve as themes that connect this chapter to the rest of Leviticus 17–26. Several other observations are important: 1. the situation of the Levites (Leviticus 25.32-34); 2. the references to the priests as the primary addressees in the introductory formulae (Leviticus 17.2a; 21.1a; 22.2aa); and 3. the references to the members of Israel as the primary addressees (Leviticus 18.2a; 19.2aa; 20.2aa; 23.2aa; 24.2aa; 25.2aa).

The first two observations present the Levites in a position that is subordinate to the sons of Aaron, suggesting that the Aaronite priests are in power. The latter observation reveals a structural connector for the respective units (Leviticus 18–20; 23–25). Throughout each unit the intended final recipients are the same, changing only beyond these sections, and thereby bracketing them. Third, further similarities may be seen in Leviticus 19 and 23, 24.

In spite of mixed concerns that relate to other sections, these chapters contain passages that regulate the participation of the people in worship, such as eating (cf. 19.5-10, 23-25; 23; 24.5-9) and worship practices (cf. 19.3, 4, 26-32; 23; 24.2ab-9), which are also handled in the central section (21.16-23; 22). The distinguishing feature is the primary addressees, that is, the intended final recipients, for whom the instructions are presented. The difference between these two audiences is the direction of their responsibilities: the priests are primarily responsible *for* the people, while the people are to be accountable to the priests. So, the similarities between Leviticus 18–20 and 23–25 also reveal identical parties that are responsible, as distinct from those in Leviticus 21, 22.

Though all of the material within each unit is not substantially related, the major portions are. Thus, Leviticus 18–20 and 23–25 have a common focal point (i. e., Leviticus 21, 22) that projects the priests as the center, and suggests that these priests are the proponents of all three units of instructions. Though the instructions are purportedly for the laity as the intended final recipients, the written collection is primarily designed for use by the priests in the form of catechism or professional training. In light of the discussions about holiness-unholiness, and the insights from examination of its structure, Leviticus 17–26 is best classified as a *manual of discipline* for some faction of the Aaronite priests.

The Theme of Holiness in Leviticus 17–26: Its Use

As noted above, Leviticus 23–25 is laterally related to Leviticus 18–20. Because of this, the concern with holiness in Leviticus 23–25 develops the themes that are found in Leviticus 18–20. The dominant concern in Leviticus 23–25 is the establishment of the economy of the community which involves regulation of communal life (23.1—24.9; 25.1-12), control of deviant behavior (24.10-16), legislation of discrepancies in legal affairs (24.17-23), and redemption of property and persons (25.3-55). The underlying focus is management of the communal resources. The deprivation that had ensued due to exploitation had materialized in indentured servitude and loss of land (cf. Nehemiah 5.1-13).

Regardless of whether or not the sabbatical years and Jubilee (25.1-13) were observed, the regulations regarding these times aim toward redemption of property, and persons, and prevention of permanent land-sales (25.23a). In response to poverty and debt-slavery, a traditio-literary context for its cases of redemption is created, that is, Jubilee, and the primary goal is reacquisition of land and relief from debts. Positing that the land is holy because it is the LORD's (25.23a), the different cases are adjudicated: 1. redemption of property/crops (25.14-18); 2. securing of the land (25.19-24); 3. redemption of property in general (25.25-28); 4. redemption of a house in a walled city (25.29, 30); 5. redemption of houses in unwalled villages (25.31); 6. redemption of the property of the Levites (25.32-34); 7. maintenance of the poor Israelites (25.35-38); 8. redemption of an Israelite from an Israelite (25.39-46); and 9. redemption of an Israelite from a non-Israelite (25.47-53).

These stipulations, then, presuppose that their proponents claim the political authority to enforce them. In other words, the cases of redemption assume the legalization of holiness, whereby their composers addressed the legal inconsistencies (24.17-23), and the deviant behavior (24.10-16), that had occurred due to the mixed population. This use of the theme of holiness marks an effort to establish uniformity in jurisprudence (24.22). These chapters and themes culminate in another dimension of holiness. Here, holiness is the "traditio-spatio-temporal boundary-marker" for the community, which regulates its occasions for worship and business, as well as legal affairs. The view is fostered that the politics, and the economics of the community are to be premised upon the understanding that the land, and therefore time in the land, is holy.

In sum, the logical progression of the development of the holiness theme is: the personification of holiness by the priests (Leviticus 21–22) initially led to the parochialization of holiness (Leviticus 18; 19.19-32; 20) and the legalization of holiness (Leviticus 18; 19.11-18, 33-37; 24.10-23; 25; 26), by which the localization of holiness (Leviticus17) and the periodization of holiness (Leviticus 19.5-10; 23.1—24.9) occurred. The goal of the whole effort, or the most essential development, is the parochialization of holiness as the mechanism for the definition, and the demarcation, of the post-exilic Jewish community.

The Concern with Survival in Leviticus 17–26

The composition of Leviticus 17–26 is located in post-exilic Judah, specifically during the late Persian Period (350-300 B.C.). It addresses several local problems that had persisted from the beginning of the period when Cyrus instituted his administration: 1. the weakened socioeconomic fabric of Judah which was reflected in indentured servitude of Jews to Jews due to loss of land and debts (Nehemiah 5.1-15); 2. the conflicts of interest between the Palestinian Jews that remained in the land and the Jews that returned, that were reflected in the interference of the Samaritans (Nehemiah 3.10, 19; 4.1-3, 7, 8; 6.1, 2, 6, 7), the interference of "adversaries" of Judah and Benjamin (Ezra 4.1-5), and the rivalry among the priesthoods (i. e., the Levites and the Aaronites); and 3. the thin population of Judah.

Specifically, at the time of Nehemiah and Ezra, Judah was still internally disorganized, reflecting: 1. loss of identity and rights to land due to uncontrolled syncretism caused by marriage to foreign women (Nehemiah 10.30; 13.23, 24; Ezra 9, 10); 2. unregulated market practices such as selling on the Sabbath (Nehemiah 10.31; 13.15-18); 3. neglect of the seventh-year land-rest (Nehemiah 10.31); 4. neglect of the Levites and the sanctuary (Haggai 1.1-11; Malachi 2.4-9; Nehemiah 10.32-39; 13.10); 5. abuse, or misuse, of the sanctuary and offerings (Malachi 1.1-14; 3.6ff; Nehemiah 13.4, 5); and 6. infidelity among the priests (Malachi 2.13-17).

These features were caused by: 1. the termination of the Davidic monarchy which had provided economic and political structure, including its royal officials and the temple; 2. the rivalry among the leaders that remained in the land, particularly the priests; 3. the lack of a politically-endorsed ideology for the community; and 4. the increased de-urbanization of the Jewish population. To address these matters, Aaronite priests composed Leviticus 17–26, employing the theme of holiness as a mechanism for survival.

Series Musical Instruments Horn. © Copyright dieKlinert/ Superstock.

The primary concern of the post-exilic community, as throughout Israelite-Judean history, was survival, particularly since their community constituted a "minority culture" that was not politically self-determinant. The community, headed by its leaders, sought to address this concern in seven ways, which constitute categorically principles for survival. In this respect, both Ezra-Nehemiah and Leviticus 17–26 are reflections of the efforts of these post-exilic leaders.

First, survival required some administrative structure. This structure would account for the leadership, and provide the details of their positions and responsibilities. Ezra-Nehemiah shows that the Aaronite priests as well as non-priestly members of the exilic community were employed. While Nehemiah served as a governor, overseeing religious, political, and military affairs (cf. Nehemiah 8, 10, 11), Ezra's assignment was restricted to investigation of the central administration, which he scrutinized according to a Persian-endorsed version of Israelite laws (cf. Ezra 7.6, 11-21). The stylistic features of Ezra-Nehemiah betray two tendencies (i.e., that of the Aaronites, and that of the Levites), which reflect competing biblical traditions (i.e., some versions of the Priestly traditions and the Deuteronomic traditions). However, Leviticus 17–26 does not allude to such a tension, but assumes that the Aaronites are in control (cf. Leviticus 24.10-23), making only one reference to the Levites (Leviticus 25.32, 33), and building upon the extant traditions.

The second requirement for survival is ideological standardization, that is, establishment and determination of the policies for intra-communal organization. This was necessary because of the mixed composition of the community. These Israelite traditions, including possible law collections, that Ezra purportedly taught (cf. 9.1, 2, 10-15; 10.2, 10-14, 44), and that Nehemiah enforced (cf. 13.23-31a), provided the rules that regulated the life of the community. Similarly, the whole of Leviticus 17–26 instructs a priestly faction that would have been operative in a society like that of Nehemiah and Ezra, that is, a society that resembles that of Ezra-Nehemiah.

Leviticus 17–26 projects a heterogeneous society in which power struggles were occurring, that included concern over land-rights. This mixture is especially evident in the concern with morality and exogamy (cf. Leviticus 18, 20, 21, 24), suggesting that cultural clashes ensued in which conflicting standards were propagated.

Though the Aaronite priests were in power, they suffered from internecine struggles. However, that faction of their group that composed Leviticus 17–26 offers a more conciliatory view to the two polarized positions of the Levites (represented by Nehemiah) and the Aaronites (represented by Ezra).

The third requirement for survival is economic independence. This concern with acquisition and management of intra-communal resources is the underlying purpose behind Nehemiah's, and Ezra's, abolition of intermarriages, and the focus upon observance of Sabbath (cf. Nehemiah 5; 10; 13.15-22). Similarly, Leviticus 17–26 endorses the Sabbath, establishing its priority in the cultic calendar (cf. Leviticus 23.3), and Jubilee (cf. Leviticus 25.10-55), which appears as a development of the Sabbath-year (Leviticus 25.1-9). There, the rules pertaining to intermarriage, particularly those regarding familial relations (chapters 18, 20), are on the same structural level as those pertaining to worship matters (chapters 23–25).

By means of structural association, the rules concerning the social behavior of its community are related to those regarding its economic status and prevalent problems. The focus upon the worship-system, then, reveals the concern with establishment of the rules for the community, and the regulation of the life of the people. This, inevitably, included the effort to control the economics of the community (cf. Leviticus 17, 22, 23, 25). However, Leviticus 17–26 goes further than Ezra-Nehemiah by defining the familial relations, and detailing the cases of land-rights disputes, including their respective, legal decisions. Its focus upon purity constitutes its effort to preserve the solidarity and the identity of the Judean community, that is, to create a "culture of resistance," and thereby completes the missions of Ezra and Nehemiah.

The other four requirements for survival are implicit in the previous ones. They are: 1. selective appropriation; 2. common language; 3. population; and 4. land. The concern with land, especially maintenance and protection of land-rights (cf. Nehemiah 5; Leviticus 25), has been discussed. This preoccupation is understandable since agriculture was the basis for the economy of the community. Also, having a common language within the community was an obvious necessity for perpetuation of the governing and founding traditions of the community (cf. Nehemiah 13.23, 24). The concern with promotion of Israelite traditions inevitably included, and required, the preservation of the "mother tongue." This requirement is, thus, an ingredient of ideological standardization.

Regarding selective appropriation, the community had to balance the extra-communal influences and the intra-communal accommodation. In other words, they had to assimilate carefully the features of the dominant culture that they could adopt (cf. Nehemiah 7.6-72; 10.1, 2; Leviticus 18.1-5, 24-30; 20.22-26). This concern is particularly at stake in the area of ideological standardization, in which the norms for the community are determined. However, as a dominated culture, this concern was most acute. It is noteworthy, then, that Leviticus 17–26 addresses this concern that is prevalent in Ezra-Nehemiah, and promulgates legal decisions regarding cases of violation (cf. Leviticus 18, 20), of which Ezra and Nehemiah (and the writer of their work) were ignorant. Lastly, and most obvious, population was a primary concern. Nehemiah's efforts at debt-release, whereby land could be regained, served the purpose of relocation of the people to Jerusalem (cf. Nehemiah 5). Also, the efforts of both Nehemiah and Ezra entailed the fortification of Judah, which required the numbers of the people in the area to be increased.

Besides the concern with land-rights and familial relations, Leviticus 17–26 indirectly encourages (re)population in its definitions of inter-personal relations. For example, that homosexuality is forbidden (Leviticus 18.22; 20.13) suggests that, not only was it regarded as a "confusion" or an "unnatural mixture," it was unproductive; it did not contribute to the biological perpetuation of the community. Thus, Leviticus 17–26 is a comprehensive statement of the rulings that implicitly addresses the situation that is described in Ezra-Nehemiah, and is best seen as a law collection that is directed toward resolution of the lingering problems that the missions of Nehemiah and Ezra sought to handle. In this light, Jubilee is best understood.

The Message of Leviticus 17–26

Leviticus 17–26 has two general categories of addressees: the primary addressees and the intended final recipients. The Aaronite priests are the primary addressees in Leviticus 17.2a; 21.1a; and 22.2aa, while the members of Israel are the primary addressees in Leviticus 18.2a; 19.2aa; 20.2aa; 23.2aa; 24.2aa; 25.2aa. Also, the people are the intended final recipients in those chapters, where the priests are the primary addressees. Notice that the instructions are always initially directed to the Aaronite priests, who are charged with the responsibility of conveying the message to the people. This is understandable by virtue of the position of the priests who were numbered among the leadership of the community, and probably drafted the laws for the community.

▸ Shofar. Carved dark brown ram's horn with Hebrew inscriptions. Mid-18th century, from Germany. Judaica Collection, Max Berger, Vienna, Austria. Photo credit: Erich Lessing/ Art Resource, New York, NY

As a manual of discipline for its priests, Leviticus 17-26 was designed to establish uniformity in theory and practice regarding the governance of the cult and the community, specifically in the aftermath of the missions of Nehemiah and Ezra, which is reflected in Samaritan Yahwism (cf. Nehemiah 3.10, 19; 4.1-3, 7, 8; 6.1, 2, 6, 7) and Zionistic Yahwism (cf. references to "Jew[s]"-- Ezra 5.1, 8; 7.14; Nehemiah 1.2; 2.16; 3.33, 34; 4.6; 5.1, 8, 17; 6.6; 13.23), respectively.

The situation that Leviticus 17–26 addresses was further complicated by those who may have been non-Israelites, or non-believers, and were categorized as: 1. "nation" (cf. Leviticus 18.24, 28; 20.23); 2. "stranger" (cf. Leviticus 22.10, 12, 13); 3. "native" (cf. Leviticus 17.15; 19.34; 24.22); 4. "resident" (cf. Leviticus 25.6, 23, 35, 40, 45, 47); 5. "day-laborer" (cf. Leviticus 22.10; 25.6, 40); and 6. "resident alien" (cf. Leviticus 17.8, 10, 12, 13, 15; 18.26; 19.33, 34; 20.2; 22.18; 23.22; 24.22 [cf. vv. 10-16, 23]; 25.23, 35, 45, 47 [cf. v. 6]).

"One of the nations" signifies "a political entity that is different from Israel," while "stranger" denotes "an individual who is not a member of Israel." These are used to refer to outsiders. "Native" is a generic term for "one who is born among (i.e., within the territory of) the member group," while "resident" indicates "one who resides in the vicinity of the member group" but is not necessarily a member of the group, such as a "day-laborer." In this sense, the "resident" is a foreigner, or non-Israelite, that is, one who is

▸ Stained glass window in a synagogue. © Fotosearch/ Superstock.

"Jubilee" may be understood in terms of economic equality, that is, economic fairness, commitment to the equal life chances and redistribution of material resources, such as land, regardless of identity, race or class.

uncircumcised and thereby a non-proselyte. Now, the most frequent references are to the "resident alien." Its frequency reflects a concern with the welfare of the persons in this category. This label denotes "one who is fully integrated into Israel," that is, "a proselyte who has been circumcised, and thereby has obtained rights equal to any Israelite."

The various possible strands of Israelite faith, including their respective proponents, and the mixed composition of the community combined to create a situation in which confusion persisted regarding the aims of the Persian overlords, as presented by the local leaders, and the identification of the legitimate leaders. Specifically, the competing Israelite groups evidently differed regarding the degree of inclusivity that would be operative for determining the Israelite (here, Judean) community. So, Leviticus 17–26 informs the priests and the people, particularly the "newcomers" or proselytes, of the standards that are regarded as the administrative policy for the community. It is intended to enhance its support from the priests, and to solicit allegiance to its sponsoring priests from the populace, particularly the "resident aliens."

Leviticus 17–26 addresses the problem of confusion regarding the standards for the community that is due to competing priestly factions within the community. The mixed composition of the community fostered internecine struggles between competitors for control. In this context the identity, and the existence, of Israel were threatened due to unqualified accommodation of foreigners by the majority of the Aaronite priests.

Regionally, the Samaritan worshipers and the Judean worshipers — representatives of two forms of Israelite faith/Yahwism—argued for the legitimacy of their respective worship traditions and sites. Locally, the Aaronite priesthood was divided regarding a temple-focused worship-system as opposed to a popular-oriented one. The key issue was the degree of inclusion of outsiders, that is, to what extent the resident aliens were to be involved in the Judean community. This matter was, then, addressed through the theme of holiness. Leviticus 17–26 was compiled to train its priests in facilitating the education of the resident aliens, along with the other Israelites within the community, who suffered at the hands of the Aaronite priests who contended with the priests who composed it.

The solution that Leviticus 17–26 offers has several premises. First, it assumes that one's level/degree of holiness is commensurate with that of one's political power and status. In this respect, the high priest held the highest level/degree of holiness, since he permanently remained within the sanctuary confines (Leviticus 21.10-13) and headed the Aaronite priests. The Aaronite priests, then, constituted the second level. On the third, and lowest, level of holiness were the people of Israel, whose status as holy was contingent upon compliance with the regulations, and thereby maintenance of the purity of the land. Thus, it is posited that one's state of holiness is equivalent to one's social standing. The corollary, then, to the first premise is that the purity laws of Leviticus 17–26 are its norms for the community.

The central message of Leviticus 17–26 relates to the issue of survival, particularly in regard to the inclusion of the resident aliens. Through use of holiness as a multi-faceted boundary marker, in which the purity laws are utilized as the norms for the community, it argues that Israelite-monitored inclusivity is mandatory for Jewish existence. It perceives that foreigners, especially the resident aliens, are indispensable for the economic well-being of the Jewish community. However, these foreigners could not be unconditionally permitted to participate in the community, since they had acquired land and status within the community.

By means of parochialization of holiness, the legal mechanism to include and supervise the resident aliens is drafted. This stance is conciliatory: a line is drawn between the right-wing view of the Aaronite priests who advocated a temple-focus, and the left-wing view of the popular culture, which included the Samaritan worshipers of the Lord and the Levites, who advocated forms of Israelite faith that were different. This inclusion of the resident aliens, and the conciliatory stance, permitted the priests who composed Leviticus 17–26 to gain the dominance that was needed to control the community. Thus, the Judean community was redefined. Now, anyone, regardless of origin or prior affiliations, who lived in the province of Judah, and followed Leviticus 17–26, the rulings of a conciliatory faction of the Aaronite priests, was a legitimate member of Israel (i.e., a Yahwist), and thereby holy. The consequence of this movement was the survival (i.e., the establishment and the expansion) of the Judean community through the end of the Persian period.

Conclusion: The Implications of Jubilee according to Leviticus 17–26

This examination of Leviticus 17–26 has uncovered several things about Jubilee. First, the Jubilee regulations are developments of the principle of Sabbath, which is designed for control and management of the economics of the community. Second, the Jubilee regulations have several interrelated premises: 1. the land is the basis of the economy; 2. the land is the LORD's and thereby not marketable; and 3. the land is holy, and therefore time in the land is holy. Third, the Jubilee regulations have a two-fold design: 1. to prevent latifundialization, that is, the accumulation of land in the hands of a few landowners to the detriment of peasant farmers; and 2. to redeem land and people. These foci serve the larger goal of protecting and maintaining land-rights. Fourth, the Jubilee regulations directly counter the situation, mainly status, of the resident aliens, who owned land that had been confiscated due to debts, yet whose participation in the community was indispensable for its economic well-being. These resident aliens were the creditors, to whom the indebted Israelites, probably Jews, had been indentured slaves. The inclusion and the conversion of the resident aliens, then, served to facilitate reconstruction of the community by means of debt-release.

Several implications emerge for modern appropriation and practice of Jubilee. First, *people should not profit at the expense of others' integrity*. Economic exploitation is tabooed! Jubilee and Leviticus 17–26 as a whole employ a "principle of fairness/equality," which highlights the "connectedness" of all members of society. When the well-being of one is meaningfully tied to the well-being of another, welfare systems and government medical assistance become superfluous, for these programs would be supplied by the "grassroots movement"of the families. In other words, the "Social Security" commandment (Exodus 20.12; Deuteronomy 5.16) must constitute the basis for family life. On a larger scale, Jubilee demands economic cooperation between the suburbs and the inner cities, the rural areas and the urban areas!

Second, *integration must be integritous.* The lack of success of the prevalent attempts at integration, the various efforts at cooperation, and the diverse projects for reunification is due to the approaches that are taken, that is, the standards and the policies are not integrated, but the cards of color, race, and status as reflected in the people are shuffled, while the rules of the game remain the same! True integration, as suggested by Leviticus 17–26, requires genuine and mutual appreciation of others (i.e., peoples, races, ethnic groups. etc.). Just like the returning descendants of the exiled Jews needed the resident aliens, so do all the diverse facets of our citizenry need each other, not as political pawns but as partners! Those who are most socio-politically self-determinant must be compassionate and sensitive to those who are not, as expressed through thorough inclusivity, which cannot be legislated but must be self-motivatedly orchestrated at the nuclear (i.e., individual, personal, or family) level.

Third and final, *a sense of awe and wonder must be reembraced*, such that life and land are primary. Survival is simply people in some place with some sacred purpose. Jubilee is based upon the premise that life is holy. In this respect, life must be consecrated—not "worship life" or some compartmentalized portions, but all of life! Such sanctification of life has to include intentional transformation of all spheres of society—family, job, neighborhood, schools, hospitals, businesses! The only way that one may know that the Lord is holy, even that the Lord is present, is through holy living! In other words, holy—"holistic"—living *re-presents* the Lord's holy presence.

Selected Bibliography

Gerstenberger, Erhard S. *Leviticus. The Old Testament Library Series,* translated by Douglas W. Stott. Louisville: Westminster/John Knox Press, 1996.

Knohl, Israel. *The Sanctuary of Silence: The Priestly Torah and the Holiness School.* Minneapolis: Fortress Press, 1995.

Ross, Jerome C. *The Composition of the Holiness Code* (Lev. 17–26). (Dissertation: University of Pittsburgh, 1997) [UMI 9816816].

Wright, Christopher J. H. *"Jubilee, Year of"* in *The Anchor Bible Dictionary, Volume 3,* edited by David Noel Freedman and others. New York: Doubleday, 1992.

Wright, David P. *"Holiness (OT)" in The Anchor Bible Dictionary, Volume 3,* edited by David Noel Freedman and others. New York: Doubleday, 1992.

Three

The Message of Salvation

Thomas L. Hoyt, Jr.

The article on Luke 4.16-30 is written with the original readers in mind and with the realization that the re-enactment of traditions creates through the Spirit of God an ever new event in the life of new believers. This text is shown to be programmatic for the whole of Luke's Gospel. It connects Jesus' ministry to the Year of Jubilee, a time of care, redemption, and release. It shows how the ministry of Jesus epitomized a rejection-acceptance theme: Gentiles accept Jesus, Jewish religious leadership does not; poor, sinners, outcasts accept Jesus, but so-called rich, righteous ones, religious leaders, and others do not.

This message of salvation, so dear to the Lukan congregation, has functioned in the lives of African Americans, giving impetus for hope and motivation for positive action against oppression.

◂ Young woman reading the Bible, ca. 1937. Courtesy of American Bible Society Archives, New York, NY

Luke 4.16-30

Jesus and those who originally interpreted his mission were influenced by the prophetic tradition of Hebrew scripture. This Bible Study lifts up the salient features of the prophetic ministry of Jesus as described by one trajectory of the biblical text, Luke 4.16-30.

Importance of the Lukan Text

Luke 4.16-30 has been called the entire Gospel in a nutshell. It is the prelude to all that will come after. Robert C. Tannehill describes the event at Nazareth as having "typical and programmatic significance for the whole of Jesus' ministry as Luke understands it." [1] The introduction of themes which re-occur elsewhere in Luke-Acts is one major indication of the programmatic nature of Luke 4.16-30.

The importance of this text is further shown by the manner in which Luke borrowed the original story from Mark and determined its form and position within his Gospel to create his original version. In my opinion it seems reasonable to be allied with those scholars (Creed, Tannehill, Fitzmyer) who maintain, with Bultmann, that while vv. 25-27 have come to Luke from one tradition and v. 23 has been incorporated from another source (with its mention of Capernaum and the proverb), Luke has constructed the scene at Nazareth rewriting the Markan account (cf. the much shorter Mark 6.1-6). Verses 17-21 and 28-30 are probably from Luke's own pen.[2] In the words of Tannehill, "the most convincing view of the origin of this pericope is that Luke has rewritten the Markan account, supplementing it with fragments of tradition and with material of his own composition."[3]

Locating the story at this point has a programmatic character. Regardless of one's opinion concerning the origin of Luke's account, one thing is clear: the point of the Lukan pericope is no longer simply the rejection at Nazareth; it has been expanded to introduce what Jesus' ministry is all about. This passage is Jesus' kerygmatic announcement, substituted for Mark 1.14b,15, which Luke omits.

[1] Robert C. Tannehill. "The Mission of Jesus according to Luke 4.16-30," in *Jesus in Nazareth*, Walther Elthester. ed. (Berlin: de Gruyter, 1972), 51.

[2] Joseph Fitzmyer, "Luke," *Anchor Bible* (New York: Doubleday, 1981, 526-27).

[3] Tannehill, op. cit., 52.

The Inaugural Sermon

Luke uses 4.16-30 as a launching pad for the further development of the story of Jesus and compels the reader to become arrested by that fact by utilizing it as the inaugural address of Jesus as he begins his public ministry. There seems to be scholarly unanimity that this passage is programmatic for Luke's two volumes.[4]

As Luke's plan develops, the sequence seems to be deliberate as seen in the cry of John the Baptist, the Baptism of Jesus, the establishment of Jesus' divine and human ancestry, aborted attempts of "Satan" to impede the divine plan of salvation, and Jesus travels from Jerusalem to Galilee (4.14a). Jesus has now come to the discovery of who he is and recognizes that the Spirit of God is upon him. His fame spreads throughout the entire region (4.14b) and his teaching is universally acclaimed (4.15). The next step seems obvious: the public announcement of his mission which takes place in the synagogue at Nazareth (4.16-30).

Luke emphasizes four major points which I shall discuss separately. First, the announcement of Jesus' ministry as the fulfillment of God's salvation time; second, a statement about the nature of fulfillment of Jesus' ministry based on the quotation from Isaiah; third, the foreshadowing of Jesus' final suffering and rejection; and fourth, the foreshadowing of the movement of the Gospel from Jew to Gentile.

The Today of God's Salvation

The opening section of this text emphasizes rather dramatically the "today" of Jesus appearance. Today is "salvation-time." The "today" is intended to emphasize the fact that the fulfillment of the Scriptures has actually come to pass. This appears to be the most prevalent meaning of this term in Luke's usage.[5] Today, the Old Testament prophecies reach their goal. Thus, the text does not seem to sustain the thesis of some interpreters that "today" indicates that Luke thought of it as belonging to past history in terms of fulfillment of hope for a future kingdom.

[4] Walter E. Pilgrim. *Good News to the Poor: Wealth and Poverty in Luke-Acts.* (Minneapolis: Augsburg, 1981), 64. See Howard Marshall, *The Gospel of Luke: A Commentary on the Greek Text.* (Grand Rapids: Eerdmans, 1978), 178.

[5] See William F. Moulton and A.S. Geden, *A Concordance to the Greek Testament*, 2nd ed. (New York: Charles Scribner's Sons, 1960), 891-2.

In fact, it appears that a basic element of Luke's belief about the end of the age is the documentation of the present as the fulfillment of the promises made long ago. The time of fulfillment of Luke 4.18,19 is now.

Since the time of salvation is here, the kingdom of God has begun, and the setting of this word "today" is within the context of Isaiah 61.1,2a, describing that in which the kingdom consists, it is important to study the quotation 4.18,19 to see how the ministry of Jesus is portrayed.

The Nature of Fulfillment in 4.18,19

Jesus, on the Sabbath, went in the synagogue of his hometown of Nazareth. He was following both his own and the Jewish custom (4.16). He stood to read the scripture from the scroll of the prophet Isaiah. He opened the scroll and sought the passage which says:

> "The Spirit of the Lord is upon me, because he has anointed me to preach good news to the poor. He has sent me to proclaim release to the captives and recovering of sight to the blind, to set at liberty those who are oppressed, to proclaim the acceptable year of the Lord." 4.18,19 (*RSV*).

The Greek word, *heuren* of verse 17 does not mean "he found," but "he sought till he found," a fact many commentators and translators have overlooked. The text which Jesus read, Isaiah 61.1,2, is so central to Jesus' teaching (and to the themes of Luke's

▸ "Banquet given by Solomon for the Queen of Sheba," 19th century Ethiopian. © The Art Archive/ Superstock

Gospel) that it is unacceptable to ascribe its selection to a coincidence. No, when Jesus was handed the Isaian scroll, he deliberately searched for this passage. This must have taken some time. If we remember that the scroll was probably 30 feet long and that it had to be unwound from the left spindle on to the right one, that Isaiah 61.1,2b is almost at the end of the book, and that in Jesus' time the text had not been sub-divided into chapters, verses, or paragraphs, we may well imagine that it took Jesus some minutes before he located the text he wanted! If indeed Jesus delivered this sermon, one does not wonder that Luke remarks: "All eyes in the synagogue were fixed on him"! Luke (or Jesus) wanted this text and no other, because in his search of the Scriptures he had identified this text as central to the message of Jesus.

Essentially, verses 18 and 19 are a loose quotation of Isaiah 61.1,2a (LXX) and an additional clause from Isaiah 58.6. Since Luke probably had a fondness for the Septuagint (the Greek translation), we would expect a great deal of agreement with it. Luke 4.18,19 follows closely the Septuagint, including its word order and its variations from the Hebrew text; nevertheless, there are some significant differences between the Septuagint and the Lukan version of Isaiah.

Luke substitutes "proclaim" for "call" in two instances in verse 19. After "he has sent me," Luke omits "to heal those who have been brokenhearted." Luke adds a phrase from Isaiah 58.6, "to set at liberty those who are oppressed."[6] Finally, the quotation ends abruptly in the midst of Isaiah 61.2 and, consequently, omits the phrase, "and the day of vengeance." The omission of this latter phrase from the quotation of Luke implies that Jesus spoke words of mercy and grace, which probably accounts for the reaction of the Jews to Jesus' works, and which might even have prompted John to inquire of Jesus' identity (7.22).

The differences between the Lukan version and the texts from which he quotes may be the result of combined or isolated factors. First, the quotation in Luke may have been taken from a tradition of the Septuagint that no longer exists; second, some or all of the variations may be due to an attempt by either Luke or the church to recall the Old Testament passages from memory; or third, the

[6] G. W. Lampe, "Luke," in *Peake's Commentary on the Bible*, ed. M. Black (rev. ed., London: Thomas Nelson and Sons, 1962), 828, stipulates that the clause added from Isaiah 58.6 enables Luke "to introduce his favorite theme of 'release,' a word generally used in the sense of 'forgiveness' (of sins), which for him is the essence of the gospel."

"The Righteous Path," by John Holyfield. Courtesy of John Holyfield, Holyfield Studios

quotation may reflect evangelistic editorializing. A closer look at these Septuagintal changes suggests that Luke 4.18,19 is an interpretive rendering of the Isaianic passages designed to emphasize a particular point. Otherwise, how does one explain how Jesus, while reading, or Luke while composing, could omit two particular phrases? Even more important, how could he have added a phrase (58.6) that was not even in the text that he is purported to have read? Apparently, the quotation merely helps us see that early church tradition depicted Jesus' ministry in the light of Isaiah 61.1, 2. Whatever may be the reasons for the variations of the Septuagint,

those variations confirm that an interpretation of the use of the quotation must be done in the light of the messianic implications of the passage.[7]

"The Spirit of the Lord GOD is upon me." The opening line of Isaiah touches on a special theme of importance to Luke. In both the Gospel and Acts, the role of the Spirit is crucial. Jesus is conceived

[7] Cf. James Muilenburg, *The Book of Isaiah, Chapters 40-66: Introduction and Exegesis*, IB, V, 708-709. He sees that the Isaianic passages are descriptive of the anticipated mission of the Servant of Yahweh during the Messianic era.

by the Spirit, baptized by the Spirit, empowered by the Spirit, the bearer of the Spirit, and anointed by the Spirit; and the entire story of the Church in Acts is a continuation of the work of the Spirit.

Not only in this episode, but throughout the Gospel, Luke points out the effect of the Spirit in the people when Jesus is present. The people are astonished, filled with awe, and obedient to his commands as they see signs of the inbreaking of the kingdom and the Spirit's manifestation. One notes that where there is movement of the Spirit, there is always movement toward the neighbor (Luke 4.22; 5.25; 7.16; 13.13; 17.15; 18.43).

The Greek word for poor in 4.18 is *ptochos*. The Hebrew word that lay behind the Greek of Isaiah 61.1 is *anawim*. This latter word usually means pious, God-fearing fold. Probably the word used in 4.18 has religious significance. Manson postulated that "poor," as well as "captives," "blind," and "oppressed," meant victims of inward repressions and spiritual ills. Hence, Jesus was offering spiritual deliverance.[8] This observation appears to be only partially correct. It minimizes both the historical occasion and the Lukan context of the text. As the evangelist used this passage, the religious import is certainly less clear.

The nature of Isaiah 61.1 must be remembered in any interpretation of 4.18, 19. Gilmour says, "The original expressed some post-exilic prophet's consciousness of mission."[9] The mission was to herald a joyous return from Babylonian exile, with the imagery of the year of Jubilee saturating the whole. The phrase, "to proclaim the acceptable year of the Lord" (4.19), suggests the imagery of the Old Testament's year of Jubilee. The year of Jubilee included the following four prescriptions: (1) leaving soil fallow, (2) the remission of debts, (3) the liberation of slaves, (4) the return of family property to each individual.

Paul Hollenbach offers a striking summary of this Sabbath-Jubilee tradition in other Torah texts. He summarizes as follows: There are to be no poor, i.e., disinherited, in Israel according to her covenant with Yahweh; however, if Israel breaks the covenant and Israelites wrong (i.e., dishonor) each other and Yahweh, and poor appear, their needs are to be met generously in three time frames—

[8] William Manson, *The Gospel of Luke* (New York: R.R. Smith, 1930), 41-42.

[9] S. M. Gilmour, "*The Gospel According to St. Luke*," IB, VIII (1952), 91.

their immediate need for food and clothing, their short-term need for family restoration, and their long-term need for total social reconstruction; in these ways the honor of the disinherited and of Yahweh will be restored.[10]

After this summary, Hollenbach sets up a schema which stems directly from the Sabbath-Jubilee tradition for understanding the thinking and deeds of Jesus. He says:

> The purpose of SJ (Sabbath-Jubilee) provisions is to prevent the permanent degradation of the poor by meeting their needs in these three time frames and in two social settings. Meeting needs in immediate, short-term, and long-term frames we may call care, redemption, and release. The social settings are kinship and politics. The first two time frames concern the kin of those in need, while the third concerns the total community. This is so because the first two kinds of need are largely individual, while the third is a matter of the structure of the whole society. The first two needs can be met by philanthropic acts, while the third can be met only through a reordering of the whole social structure. The first two are designed to prevent the need for the third, but the third is necessary because the first two do not do the job. In short, the SJ legislation is designed to prevent the development of an aristocratic-peasant society out of a covenantal egalitarian society, but should such a shift occur, the legislation also is designed to prevent its being permanently established.[11]

Claus Westermann agrees with the basic analysis of Hollenbach when he suggests that the passage from Isaiah refers, not to the exiles, but to persons imprisoned for indebtedness. Furthermore, he sees the suffering as actual in nature.[12] Thus, if Luke relates to the Isaianic text with the meaning as projected by Westermann, the year of Jubilee saturates the whole and speaks to physical destitution, possibly signifying the new age. Salvation is, therefore, not just spiritual, but also physical.

The question can be asked: Do we find in the ministry of Jesus the three responses of care, redemption, and release as displayed in the Sabbath-Jubilee? A brief look at each may show the following:

10 See "Liberating Jesus for Social Involvement," *Biblical Theology Bulletin* Vol. XV, 153.

11 Ibid.

12 Claus Westermann, *Isaiah 40-66*, trans. David M.G. Stalker (Philadelphia: Westminster Press, 1969), 366-7.

Care, Redemption, and Release

While care for the poor was the basic character of the actions and teachings of Jesus, redemption and release certainly would flow from his compassionate ministry.

In the conversation with John's disciples, Jesus makes known the nature of his ministry which was in doubt by John. "Are you the one who is to come, or shall we look for another?" *(RSV)* The several tasks to be carried out by the one anointed by the Spirit are suggested in Luke 7.21,22 as presently being carried out in the ministry of Jesus.

> In that hour he cured many of diseases and plagues and evil spirits, and on many that were blind he bestowed sight. And he answered them, "Go and tell John what you have seen and heard: the blind receive their sight, the lame walk, lepers are cleansed, and the deaf hear, the dead are raised up, the poor have good news preached to them." *(RSV)*

This quotation fits perfectly the theme of the opening sermon of Jesus. What could it mean that the "blind receive their sight?" Allan Boesak of South Africa has some wonderful images of what these phrases in Luke really mean. The blind received their sight:

> What else can it mean but that people can now see themselves as God sees them. They can see their human possibilities as well as they see their present situation. They can see a future of freedom and human dignity to which they have been blind before.

The lame walk:

> What could it mean for those who for so long were lying by the wayside crippled by feelings of inferiority, fear and lack of vision?

Boesak says of his poor and oppressed fellow pilgrims:

> We got so used to our lowly position, we accepted our suffering as God's will. We stared ourselves blind against the white man's power and his guns. We were lame! Jesus is saying to us: the kingdom is yours. Get up and walk. Its power is yours: stand up and be strong.

Lepers are cleansed:

> Means that God has touched the poor in Jesus the Messiah. God has given "untouchables" a new self image of "worthfulness".

The deaf hear: What do they hear?

> They hear good news. No longer a pseudo-gospel designed to justify oppression and comfort for the oppressor. No longer a gospel so spiritualized that it has become anemic and incapable of dealing with the harsh realities... , but a word of liberation and freedom and human dignity.[13]

The dead are raised up:

> There are various kinds of death. There is physical death; there is death which one experiences outside of the human community. This latter experience is the death of a person who is merely property and is not accepted by others. More importantly, there is a death in which one is not at peace with oneself, when one does not accept oneself as a vital link in the human community. Such has been the case of so many in the Third World and those in the first world living under Third World conditions.
>
> To all these people Jesus preaches the good news that God, in Messiah Jesus, has seen the condition of the people, has taken upon God's self the condition of the people, and taken their cause as God's own. That is the good news: He filled the hungry with good things, and the rich he will send empty away (Luke 1.53, *RSV*). The Sovereign One "works vindication and justice for all who are oppressed" (Psalm 103.6, *RSV*). The good news is that the Sovereign One is here to execute justice for the oppressed, to give food to the hungry, to uphold the widow and the fatherless, and to bring to ruin the way of the wicked.

Rejection at home (4.22-30)

This announcement of a new age in 4.18,19 contained an inherent criticism of all those powers and agents of the present order. This was the time of release announced by Jesus. Walter Brueggemann summarizes concerning the ministry of Jesus:

[13] Allan Boesak, "Shall We Look For Another?" *The Reformed Journal* Vol. 31 (June, 1981), 19.

> His message was to the poor, but others kept them poor and benefitted from their poverty. He addressed the captives (which meant bonded slaves). But others surely wanted that arrangement unchanged. He named the oppressed, but there are never oppressed without oppressors.[14]

We are surprised, therefore, by the initial reaction of the crowd: "They marvelled at the words of grace which proceeded out of his mouth" (v. 22, *RSV*). The record of Matthew 13.57 and Mark 6.3 state that the crowd took offense at him. The initial reaction of the crowd in Luke later turned into the same reaction as recorded in Matthew and Mark.

The final rejection by the crowd ensued because Jesus continued to talk about prophets lacking honor in their own country (v. 24). He also recounted in a second sermon (vv. 25-28) the Old Testament stories of Elijah and Elisha. These two prophets, in their ministry to Gentiles, were used to illustrate the proverb: "No prophet is acceptable in his own country" (v. 24, *RSV*). Both prophets were more successful with Gentiles (strangers) than with Jews. Elijah ministered to the widow at Zarephath, a Sidonian town and Elisha healed Namaan, a leper at Syria.

The implications are two-fold: (1) Those of Jesus' territory will not understand, and the Gentiles will. Luke once again stresses his universalism. (2) Jesus' way of salvation did not sustain the idea of preference, which some Jews had derived from their belief in God's election of them. God's love and redemption was on behalf of all. Poor and outcasts in one place were loved alike in another place by the God of Abraham, Isaac, and Jacob. God was free to love and choose whomever God desired. "The acceptable year of the Lord" was for all people. Israel is called to be a light to the nations, and in Jesus that calling has become a reality.

In this second sermon (4.25-28), if Israel rejects the gospel, the good news is preached to those who will hear, i.e., the Gentiles, the poor and outcast. In the first sermon, 4.18,19, Jesus' ministry was described in terms of a program in obedience to his calling, which had been sealed at baptism. The first sermon established a program for the whole of Luke's Gospel, and the second sermon laid out a basis for Acts.

[14] Walter Brueggemann, *The Prophetic Imagination.* (Philadelphia: Fortress Press, 1978), 83.

The Scene Ends

The hometown folk rejected Jesus because they refused to believe that the village boy, the son of a carpenter, whom they had known from infancy, had a right to talk with them as a prophet. The crowd became incensed and wanted to cast him out of their village. They held his background against him, but, more importantly, their pride and prejudice stood in the way of their acceptance of his message and the universality of the good news that God had visited God's people.

▸ Elderly man reading the Bible, ca. 1949. Courtesy of American Bible Society Archives, New York, NY

In this section, we have attempted to show that Luke modified the tradition in order to accent the present fulfillment of scriptures. The less-clear Markan summary of Jesus' beginning is replaced by a dramatic scene in which Jesus announces the presence of the messianic age, which is also described by Mark as "the Kingdom of God." The present kingdom is understood to be the coming of the anointed one in Jesus and his proclamation or evangelization of the physically and spiritually poor. Yet this present fulfillment in no way negates the consummation of the kingdom, which is characterized as "The End" (21.9). The kingdom is present and yet to come. We live between an "already" and a "not yet." In its present form, the poor are being evangelized. The deed and the word have combined to give power to the proclamation on behalf of the poor. There is release for the captives, sight for the blind, and liberty for the oppressed. They only have to receive what is being offered.

Four

The Relationship between Hebrew and African Languages

Edwina M. Wright

Very explicit linguistic connections can be made between the original language of the Old Testament, Hebrew, and certain African languages. Hebrew is a language of the Semitic family, as are certain languages of ancient and modern Ethiopia: Ancient Ethiopic and modern Ethiopian languages such as Amharic, Tigré and Tigrinya.

Another more fundamental linguistic connection between Hebrew and African languages is demonstrated by the fact that the Semitic language family itself is part of a larger language superfamily known as Afro-Asiatic. The Afro-Asiatic phylum is comprised of languages from the following language groups: Semitic, Berber, Egyptian, and the distinctly Black African language groups, Chadic and Cushitic.

◂ Ethiopian psalter. Courtesy of American Bible Society Rare Book Collection

This linguistic interrelationship between Hebrew and African languages allows for the discussion of further cultural linkages between the Old Testament and African reality.

The Hebrew language is the original language in which almost all of the Old Testament was written. Classical Hebrew is written from right to left, with vowel points written primarily below and above consonants.

Hebrew was first recorded around 1200 B.C. These first writings are ancient poetry which are found in the Old Testament in Exodus 15.1-18 and Judges 5.2-31 (referred to as "The Song of the Sea" and "The Song of Deborah" respectively).

In order to understand the historical relationship of languages, linguists have classified them according to families. The primary family of which Hebrew is a part is the Semitic language family. Of interest to those familiar with biblical genealogies, the term Semitic is derived from the biblical name Shem, Noah's eldest son.

Over the years there have been various classifications of the Semitic languages. One prominent classification system has been developed by Robert Hetzron, with modifications by John Huehnergard. According to this classification system, Semitic languages can be divided into three major groupings: East Semitic, South West Semitic and Central West Semitic.

Hebrew is classified as a part of the Central West Semitic subdivision. This grouping includes Arabian dialects and those languages which are most closely related to Hebrew (the Northwest Semitic subgroup). The Arabic subgrouping includes modern and ancient dialects. The ancient dialects include Pre-classical North dialects (5th century B.C.-4th century A.D.) and Classical Arabic, the language of the Qur'an (ca. 4th century A.D.). The North West Semitic subgroup includes Aramaic, Ugaritic, Hebrew, and other languages related to Hebrew. Ugaritic is the language of ancient Ugarit, a city of about sixty square kilometers located in Northern Syria, just one kilometer from the Mediterranean Sea. Aramaic is a language also closely related to Hebrew and is found in passages in Ezra and Daniel in the Old Testament. From the 8th to 4th centuries B.C., Aramaic became the universal language of diplomacy in the Ancient Near East. Certain Aramaic phrases are also found in the New Testament (e.g. Mark 5.41; 15.34).

East Semitic languages include Akkadian and Eblaite. Akkadian is the language which was spoken by peoples of the same name who settled in Mesopotamia (generally described as the land between the Tigris and Euphrates rivers). Eblaite texts have been discovered in Syria and date from the 24th to the 23rd centuries B.C.

The third major Semitic subgroup, the South West Semitic languages, include South Arabian and Ethiopian languages. Recorded ancient South Arabian languages (called Old Inscriptional South Arabian) date from the 8th to the 6th centuries B.C. An example of a modern South Arabian dialect is the language Mehri, which is spoken in Yemen.

It is in the South West Semitic subgrouping that we find Ethiopian languages. In any discussion of the interrelationship of the Hebrew language with African languages, the most obvious linkage to be discussed is that with the Semitic languages found in the African country of Ethiopia. Edward Ullendorff writes regarding Ethiopia: "In its long history the country has always formed a bridge between Africa and Asia" (p. 23).

Most scholars suggest that South Arabians (sometime during the first millennium B.C.), motivated in great part by trade concerns, migrated to the northern area of Ethiopia and commingled with the existing African Agaw population. The original Semitic South Arabian tongue was influenced by the Agaw dialect; this influence resulted over time in the development of Ethiopian Semitic languages. However, it is the opinion of other scholars that Ethiopian Semitic is more original.

These Semitic languages are divided into northern and southern dialects. Northern dialects include Ge'ez, Tigré, and Tigrinya. Ge'ez, also referred to as Ethiopic, is an ancient Ethiopian language for which texts exist which date from the 4th century A.D. While it is no longer a spoken language, Ge'ez is used as the liturgical language of the Ethiopian Orthodox Christian Church. Tigrinya is primarily spoken in the northern part of Ethiopia, particularly in the area of the old Axumite Kingdom; Tigré is primarily spoken in the northern province of Eritrea.

Southern dialects include Amharic, Gafat, Gurage, Harari, and Argobba. Amharic is spoken in the central part of Ethiopia and is the national language. It has been written since the 16th century in the script of Ge'ez. Gafat, a largely extinct dialect is spoken in the region of the Blue Nile. Gurage is a cluster of dialects (including for example, Chaha, Ennemor, and Muher) which is spoken in the area to the southwest of Addis Ababa, Ethiopia's capital. Harari is spoken in the city of Harar in eastern Ethiopia; Argobba is spoken to the northeast of Addis Ababa, and like Gafat, is nearly extinct.

An even closer connection can be suggested between Hebrew and African languages than that which is provided by the linkage between Hebrew and Ethiopian languages as members of the same language family. This closer association is indicated by the fact that most linguists consider the Semitic language family to be one branch of the larger Afro-Asiatic superfamily (or phylum). In addition to Semitic, the Afro-Asiatic phylum encompasses at least four other branches. These branches are Egyptian, Berber, Chadic and Cushitic. Some scholars also include the Omotic languages as a separate branch; these languages are spoken in the Omo Valley in Ethiopia and were formerly understood as part of the Cushitic language family.

The Egyptian branch is the only branch which includes one language. It began as Old Egyptian which was recorded from the third millennium B.C. and continued through its latest stage, Coptic. Coptic is known from the 2nd century B.C. to the 17th century A.D., and is still used to a small extent in the liturgy of the Egyptian Monophysite church.

The Berber (or Berbero-Libyan) branch is divided into various subgroups: 1) a northern subgroup spoken in Morocco, Algeria, and Tunisia, including, for example Tamazight; 2) an Eastern subgroup found in Libya; 3) Tuareg in the Sahara and Sahel, in Algeria, Niger, Mali; and 4) a Zenaga subgroup in Mauritania and possibly Senegal.

The Chadic branch contains about one hundred fifty living dialects in Nigeria, Chad, Cameroun, and Niger. Chadic languages are divided into Western, Central, and Eastern Chadic. Western Chadic includes the well-known and widely spoken language Hausa, as well as the Bauchi and Ron language groups. Central Chadic includes Logone-Kotoko, Higi, and Wandala among others; Eastern Chadic includes, for example, Dangla and Sokoro.

Cushitic languages are spoken primarily by peoples in Ethiopia, Somalia, and northwestern Kenya. This branch is divided into Northern, Central, and Eastern (which is further subdivided into Highland East and Lowland East Cushitic). Northern Cushitic includes the Beja language which is spoken in eastern Sudan and northern Ethiopia. The primary language of Central Cushitic is Agaw. Highland East Cushitic, a primary example of which is Sidamo, is spoken around the Ethiopian Great Rift Valley. Low-

▸ Tcherqos church in the rock. Ethiopia. © age fotostock/ Superstock

land East Cushitic languages are the most numerous and include Oromo, Afar-Saho, and Somali, which is the official language of Somalia.

Discussions regarding the classifying of languages into families or superfamilies almost always are accompanied by some discussion of how and where the family (or superfamily) may have originated. Scholars who work with the Afro-Asiatic superfamily have put forth numerous hypotheses concerning its geographical and linguistic origins. Suggestions for the geographic origin of Afro-Asiatic include Arabia, North Africa and East Africa.

The fact that Ethiopian languages are a blend of Cushitic and Semitic and that these two branches of the Afro-Asiatic family intersect in an African setting is certainly very suggestive as to the location of the original Afro-Asiatic language family. Scholars have noted as much. (See, for example, Ullendorff, p. 118.)

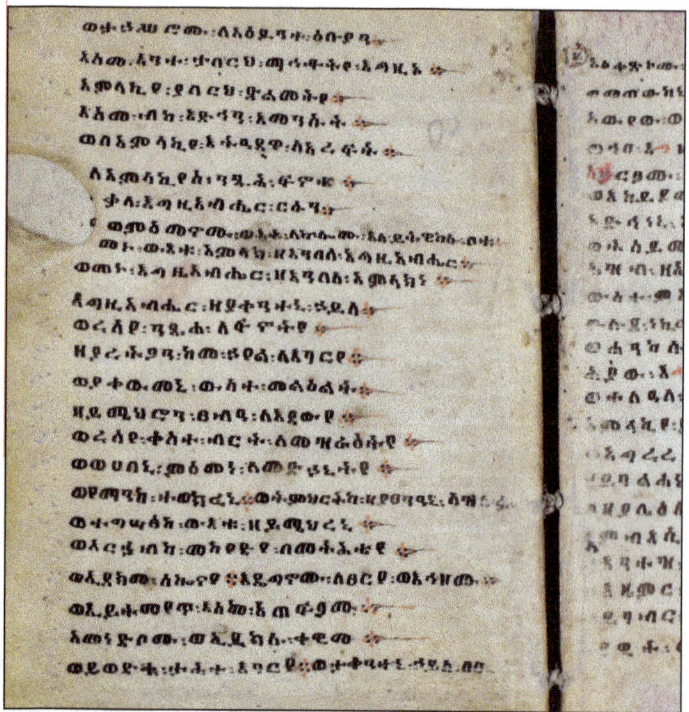

▸ Ethiopian psalter. Courtesy of American Bible Society Rare Book Collection

No final determinations about origins, however, can be made at this time. In fact, scholars are not yet fully agreed on the facts of this superfamily. In comparing the various languages of the superfamily not every language contains all the same features. Significant similarities, however, have been found among various branches in vocabulary, in some sound patterns, and in some grammatical forms (especially in some verbal forms, pronouns and gender referents). Historical linguists, aided by archaeological finds, will continue to investigate these languages and perform the tasks that will make comparisons more valid.

While such investigation continues, however, those of us in the Black Church can note with great interest the significant familial relationship which most scholars acknowledge exists between the Hebrew language of the Old Testament Scriptures and languages which are spoken by peoples of African descent.

Works Consulted

Diakonoff, Igor. *Afrasian Languages*. Moskow: Nauka, 1988.

Huehnergard, John. "Languages (Introductory)." in the *Anchor Bible Dictionary*, vol. 4, pp. 155-170. Edited by David Noel Freedman. New York: Doubleday, 1992.

_______. *"Remarks on the Classification of the Northwest Semitic Languages,"* in The Balaam Text from Deir, 'Alla Re-Evaluated: Proceedings of the International Symposium held at Leiden 21-24 August 1989, pp. 282-293. Edited by J. Hoftijzer and G. Van der Kooij. Leiden: E. J. Brill, 1991.

Ullendorff, Edward. *The Ethiopians: An Introduction to Country and People.* London: Oxford University Press, 1965.

INCOGNITA
Tartaria
Noruegia
Suedia
Bergen
Russia
Cracow
EVROPA
Buda
Danub. fl.
Ger.
Anglia
Paris
Gallia
Lion
Ausburch
Italia
Raguza
Grecia
Natol
Troia
Candia
Corsica
Sicilia
Brest
Hispania
Lisbona
Tunis
Bugia
Alger
Tripoli
Berdoa
Barbaria
Septa
AFRICA

Five

The Presence and Role of Africans in the Bible

Prince Vuyani Ntintili

There is a perennial and widespread misconception that the Bible is a White person's book and thus excludes other people; particularly those of African descent. This insidious fallacy is based on innocent ignorance on the part of some and on deliberate and calculated distortion on the part of others. This article cuts through this murkiness and demonstrates the conspicuous presence of African people on the pages of the Bible. But their presence does not make the Bible a Black person's book either. It is the Word of God (Ephesians. 6.17; Hebrews 4.12) which is written for the "teaching, rebuking, correcting, and training in righteousness" of all those who heed its precious instructions. THE BIBLE IS A BOOK FOR ALL HUMANITY. Let all freely drink from its fresh springs.

◂ Antique map. © Yagi Studio/ Superstock

Introduction

If one were to ask most people if Africans are found in the Bible, the common answer one would get would be that they are not. There are several reasons for such an answer. First, there is the prevailing belief that the Bible is a Caucasian person's book and, as such, people who are featured in it are Caucasians. This belief is attributable to many factors. It is the result of a confusion between the authors of the Bible and the characters featured in the Bible.

One reason why the Bible is assumed to be a Caucasian person's book is because it was brought to Africa by European, and later North American, missionaries. What complicates the matter is that the advent of Western missionaries coincided with the arrival of colonizers. Thus the two are associated and, in many instances, rightly so. It is for this reason that the Bible in many African/African American circles is viewed with suspicion because it is believed that it is a book that was brought to subjugate, colonize, and enslave African people.

The second reason often advanced for the belief of the absence of African people in the Bible is the mistaken but persistent belief that Africans, as descendants of Ham, are cursed. As such, they could not be featured in the Holy Scriptures. This view is based on innocent ignorance on the part of some and on deliberate distortion of biblical facts on the part of others. But it, unfortunately, this continues to feed the erroneous belief that there is no African presence in the Bible. This article seeks to demonstrate that there are African people who played very prominent roles in the Bible.

When one investigates the question of the presence and the role of African people in the Bible, one encounters two extremes. The first is the one already articulated in the preceding discussion, namely that there is no African presence whatsoever in the Bible. The other extreme is that of making almost every significant person in the Bible of African descent. This view is espoused by some scholars who are overly keen to prove that African people are featured in the Bible. In trying to achieve this, they overstate their point. Both extremes must be avoided if an investigation of the presence and role of Africans in the Bible is to remain objective.

This article purports, therefore, to do two things. First, it will prove that there is an African presence in the Bible. It will show that there are African countries and places that are actually mentioned in the Bible. Second, it will also show that there are places outside of Africa which were, nevertheless inhabited predominantly by African people. The presence of these territories in the Bible indicates the presence of African people who lived in them. This article will argue not only for the presence of African people in the Bible but also for the significant roles they played. The activities of Africans in the Bible, both positive and negative, reflect the strengths and frailties of humanity. The Bible is an account of the lives of those who obeyed God's commands and precepts and also those who flagrantly flouted them and the consequences they faced for doing so.

African Territories in the Bible

There are several territories geographically located in Africa that which are mentioned in the Bible. For illustrative purposes a few will be mentioned. First, Egypt is mentioned in many places in the Bible. In *Young's Analytical Concordance to the Bible*, Young explains that Egypt is "a country of the N[orth] E[astern] angle of Africa." There are more than 500 references to Egypt in the Bible. Egypt is mentioned from Genesis to Revelation (Genesis 12.10-14; Revelation 11.8).

Egypt is also referred to by other names. At times it is called Mizraim, which means "red mud." Mizraim was the second son of Ham (Genesis 10.6, 13; 1 Chronicles 1.8, 11). In Psalm 105.23 it is called "the land of Ham." Young points out that Egypt "was colonized by the descendants of Ham." He further explains that the word Mizraim is dual, and indicates the natural division of the country into an upper and lower regions—the plain of the Delta, and the narrow valley above."

When the singular form of Mizraim is used, it refers to lower Egypt only. When the plural form is used, it refers to the entire territory which extends from Migdol to Syene. The first king of Egypt was Menes. It is well known that Egypt enjoyed an advanced and thriving civilization for a long time and contributed much to the civilization of the world, particularly to the Greeks. Egypt and its people played a critical role, both positively and negatively, in the life of Israel (Exodus 1–15). It must not be forgotten that, according to Matthew 2.13-21, Joseph, Mary, and the child Jesus found refuge in Egypt when Herod was seeking to kill Jesus.

The second African territory mentioned in the Bible is Libya (Ezekiel 30.5; Daniel 11.43; Acts 2.10). Libya is a Greek word for this territory, which is situated west of Egypt along the African coast. *Young's Analytical Concordance to the Bible* states that "the

▸ Wood carving of African life. Courtesy of Dr. Joseph Crockett. Used by Permission

inhabitants of Libya [are] supposed to have sprung from Phut, the son of Ham [in] B.C. 2300." Josephus also concurs that Phut was the founder of Libya. People of Libya were known as valiant warriors (Jeremiah 46.9) who could "handle the shield." The country specialized in producing mercenaries and supplying other countries with them (see Ezekiel 27.10). The people of Libya played an important role in the Bible.

The third African territory that is featured in the Bible is Ethiopia (Genesis 2.13; 2 Kings 19.9; Esther 1.1; 8.9; Job 28.19; Psalm 68.31; 87.4; Isaiah 18.1; 20.3, 5; 37.9; 43.3; 45.14; Ezekiel 29.10; 30.5; 38.5; Nahum 3.9; Zephaniah 3.10; Acts 8.27). The Bible also speaks of Ethiopian(s) (Numbers 12.1; 2 Chronicles 12.3; 14.9, 12, 13; 16.8; 21.16; Isaiah 20.4; Jeremiah 13.23; 38.7, 10, 12; 39.16; 46.9; Ezekiel 30.9; Daniel 11.43; Amos 9.7; Zephaniah 2.12; Acts 8.27). The word "Ethiopia" is used by both the Greeks and the Romans and it is derived from two Greek words—*ethios* which means "burned" and *opes* which means "face." It is the Greeks who referred to people of Ethiopia as those of "burned faces" to indicate the complexion of their faces. The Hebrew word for Ethiopia is Cush, named after Ham's first son. *Young's Analytical Concordance to the Bible* explains that this country "comprehended, in its widest sense, the modern Nubia, Sennar, Kordofan, and northern Abyssinia, but in its more limited sense, only the kingdom of Meroe, from the junction of the White and Blue branches of the Nile to the [Southern] border of Egypt."

Concerning the country of Ethiopia, it is notable that it is one of the first countries mentioned in Scripture. Genesis 2.13 describes one of the rivers that waters the garden of Eden as Gihon which "winds through the entire land of Cush." It is for this reason that some scholars argue that Eden was in Africa.

The Bible also mentions certain cities found in Africa. One such city is Alexandria, and this city is mentioned in Acts 6.9; 18.24; 27.6; 28.11. Alexandria is a city in Egypt founded by Alexander the Great in B.C. 332 near the western branch of the Nile where it flows to the Mediterranean. Young notes that "it was long one of the most celebrated cities in the world, the metropolis of Egypt, as well as a grand seat of commerce and wealth." Certain people from this African city played a role in biblical history. For example Apollos who is described as "a learned man, with thorough knowledge of the Scriptures" was a native of Alexandria.

Another African city mentioned in the Bible is that of Cyrene, a city in Libya in Cyranaica, North Africa. It was the chief of the five cities called Pentapolitana. Young points out that, under the Romans, Cyrene was connected with Crete. This city is mentioned in Matthew 27.32; Acts 2.10; 11.20; 13.1. Certain persons of this city also played significant roles in the Bible.

Territories Inhabited by African People

Apart from territories that are actually found in the continent of Africa, there are other territories which are outside of Africa but which were inhabited by African people. People who lived in these areas were predominately African and significantly participated in the events that took place in the Bible.

First, there is what is known as the "land of Shinar," which is probably referred to in Hebrew as Sumer. Shinar is the place where God confounded and confused the languages of the people and the place was, as a result, called Babel. Shinar is a kingdom which was founded by Nimrod, Cush's son. R. K. Harrison, in his book, *Old Testament Times,* writes as follows: "About 4000 B.C., a people of superior intellectual caliber, known as Sumerians, occupied Sumer...They were a swarthy (black), non-Semitic group."

Second, there is the land of Babylon. Babylon is a city, together with Erech, Ahkkad, and Calneh, which was founded by Nimrod, Cush's son. It is believed that there was a strong presence of the Hamitic people among the Assyrian people of Babylon. Clem Davies, in his book,

The Racial Streams of Mankind, argues that there were many people of Hamitic descent in Babylon.

Third, there is the territory of Phoenicia. The Bible refers to this area as Sidon. Canaan's firstborn son was named Sidon. Canaan, himself, was Ham's first son (Genesis 10.15). Many scholars, including Young, Josephus, and Augustine, maintain that Ham's descendants occupied Sidon and that Phoenicians considered themselves Canaanites. Sidon is featured many times in the Gospels and in the Book of Acts (Matthew 11.21, 22; 15.21; Mark 3.8; 7.24; Luke 4.26; 6.17; 10.13, 14; Acts 12.20; 27.3). This shows that Christ ministered among people of African descent during his earthly ministry. It also speaks to Christ's attitude of inclusion toward people of other cultures and racial groupings.

Fourth, there are the territories of Canaan and Hebron which were occupied by the Hittites. The Hittites were of African descent because they were from Heth, Canaan's second son. R.K. Harrison, in his book, *Introduction to the Old Testament,* points out that Hittites "were in possession of advanced technological processes of smelting iron for all commercial purposes" and were also "renowned horsemen and were the first to manufacture chariots with iron fittings." These skilled people were all of African descent.

Fifth, there were the Jebusites, people of African descent who lived in Jerusalem. That explains why Jerusalem was called Jebus prior to David's conquest of that city (Joshua 18.16,28; Judges 19.10, 11; 1 Chronicles 11.4,5). Jebusites were descendants of Canaan, the son of Ham. The Jebusites, along with the Amorites and Girgashites, are described in the Bible as "families of the Canaanites" (Genesis 10.16-18). Since Jebusites came from Canaan, who was the son of Ham, it is correct to argue that they, too, were of African descent.

It must be noted that there are many other peoples who were fathered by Canaan, Ham's fourth son; peoples such as the Hivites, Arkites, and Sinites. The lineage of these people argues eloquently for the existence of a Black or African presence in the Bible.

People of African Origin in the Bible

In the preceding section, the African presence in the territories mentioned in the Bible was discussed. This section will highlight some people from these areas who are mentioned in the Bible.

The Old Testament

People of African Origin in the Pentateuch

In Genesis 10.6-14, Nimrod is mentioned as the son of Cush and a descendant of Ham. The Bible says that Nimrod was the first to be a *gibbor*, which means "a skilled warrior." He was "a mighty hunter for the Lord" (Genesis 10.8,9). He also built tremendous cities such as Babylon, Erech, Akkad, Calneh, Nineveh, Rohoboth-Ir, Calah and Resen.

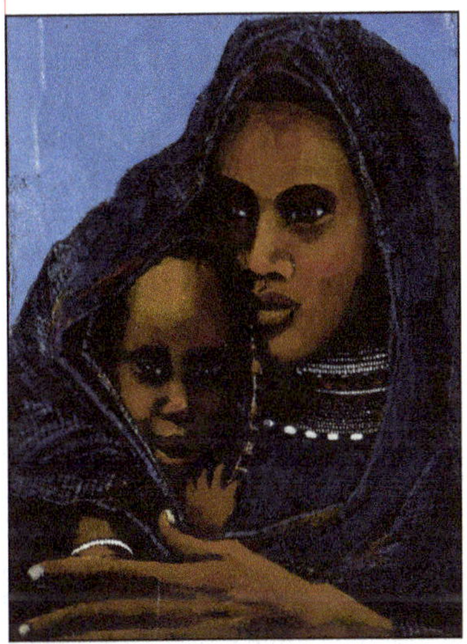

▸ "Black Madonna IV (Arab)," 1998. Elizabeth Barakah Hodges, (21st century American). © Elizabeth Barakah Hodges/ Superstock

Jethro, Moses' father-in-law, who was a priest from Midian was probably of African descent. Midianites are believed to have descended from Ham through the line of Cush, (Exodus 18.1). Some scholars purport that Moses' Cushite wife (Numbers 12.1) was probably Zipporah, the daughter of Jethro. As noted in Habakkuk 3.7, Midian and Cush are linked, and this could lead one to conclude that both Jethro and his daughter, Zipporah, were of African origin.

The Bible explicitly tells us that Hagar was "an Egyptian maid-serv-ant." It is notable that God promised, in Genesis 21.13, to "make the son of the (Egyptian) maidservant into a nation also, because he is your (Abraham's) offspring." In verse 18, God promises to make Ishmael, this African woman's son, "into a great nation." This shows that God is no respecter of persons. We, too, should emulate him.

Asenath, the wife of Joseph, was an Egyptian, and her father was Potiphera, the priest of On. On was the capital of Lower Egypt, about six miles northeast of Cairo and three miles north of modern Heliopolis. Asenath was the mother of Manasseh and Ephraim (Genesis 41.45; 46.20). These two sons played important roles in the history of the Israelites and became the eponymous ancestors of the tribes of Manasseh and Ephraim that inhabited the land of Canaan.

People of African Origin in the Historical Books

The queen of Sheba was of African descent. Sheba was the son of Raamah who was the son of Ham. Young, in his book, *Young's Analytical Concordance to the Bible*, explains that Sheba was "a land in the South West of Arabia, or in Africa near the Straits of Babel-mandeb." The queen of Sheba was a wealthy woman who played a prominent role in international trade and commerce. Thus, when she visited King Solomon, she was accorded the dignity and status of a head of state (1 Kings 10.10-13). This woman of African descent was bright, self-assertive, wealthy, and generous.

In addition, there is an unnamed soldier who brought David the news of the death of his son, Absolom. This soldier had the courage to tell David the truth concerning his son's death. According to 2 Samual 18.21, the soldier was a Cushite. Since it has already been established that Egypt is sometimes called Cush in the Bible, this brave soldier was undoubtedly an African.

People of African Origin in the Prophetical Books

In Jeremiah 38.7-13 there is the account of Ebed-melech, the Ethiopian, who saved the life of the prophet Jeremiah. In Hebrew, the name Ebed-melech means royal servant. Ebed-melech feared God more than men. He alone, among the palace officials, stood up against the murder plot. His intervention on behalf of Jeremiah could have caused him his life, but he was willing and courageous enough to take the risk. The Bible reports that God remembered what Ebed-melech had done for Jeremiah; and when Babylon conquered Jerusalem, God protected him from the Babylonians (Jeremiah 39.15-18). This Scripture states that Ebed-melech rescued Jeremiah because he trusted God.

Another person of African origin in the Prophetic Books is Zephaniah. He was the son of Cushi (Zephaniah 1.1). Zephaniah prophesied around 630 B.C., and his prophecies fostered a religious revival in Judah.

In the book of the prophet Amos, Ethiopians are described as worshipers with Israel: "Are you not like the Ethiopians to me, O people of Israel? says the Lord" (Amos 9.7a, *NRSV*). Similarly, the prophet Isaiah affirms that the blessings of God are extended to the people of Egypt (Isaiah 19.23-25).

People of African Origin in Wisdom or Poetic Literature

The Song of Solomon (also known as Song of Songs) is a collection of songs or poems in which a man and a woman express their love for each other. The woman describes her appearance as follows: "I am black and beautiful, O daughters of Jerusalem, like the tents of Kedar, like the curtains of Solomon. Do not gaze at me because I am dark, because the sun has gazed on me" (Song of Solomon 1.5, 6a *NRSV*).

In Psalm 68.31 the Psalmist says, "Let bronze be brought from Egypt; let Ethiopia hasten to stretch out its hands to God" (*NRSV*). In this Scripture passage, the Bible is not talking about individual Africans, but a group of people, and God is promising to save them. Also, in Psalm 87 there is a reference to a universal understanding that Africans are included among the people who know the Lord God and belong to Zion (Psalm 87.4-6).

The New Testament

People of African Origin in the Gospels

Simon, the one who helped Jesus bear the cross, was from Cyrene, a major city in North Africa (Matthew 27.32; Mark 15.21; Luke 23.26). This was a unique opportunity for Simon to be selected to help bear the burden of our Lord and Savior on his way to Calvary. In recognition of the role he played in our Lord's passion, it is significant that all three synoptic gospels mention his name.

People of African Origin in the Historical Book

African presence is also found in the only historical book of the New Testament; namely the Book of Acts. In Acts 2.10 we are told that some of the visitors in Jerusalem who witnessed the Day of Pentecost were from "...Egypt and the parts of Libya belonging to Cyrene," *(NRSV)*. On that eventful Day of Pentecost Africa too, had its representatives who were among the three thousand that responded to Peter's preaching. Cyrenians are also mentioned in Acts 6.9 as among those who belonged to the synagogue of Freedman (also known as Libertines). In Acts 13.1, Lucius of Cyrene is mentioned as being one of the leaders in the church of Antioch which commissioned the apostle Paul for his first missionary journey. Simeon of Niger was also one of the leaders of the church in Antioch. The word Niger, in Latin, means "black."

In Acts 8.26-39 we are told of the Ethiopian eunuch to whom Philip was sent by the Spirit of God. What is striking is that Philip was engaged in a thriving revival and awakening in Samaria and people were coming to the Lord in large numbers. But this Ethiopian official was so important in God's program that God asked Philip to evangelize this African individual. This man was "an important official in charge of all the treasury of Candace, queen of the Ethiopians" (Acts 8.27, *NIV*). He was a trusted and well-placed person in his nation's leadership. He was a highly learned man who could read the Scriptures in both Hebrew and Greek and who was able to converse with Philip. But more importantly, he was a devout man who not only attended the Jewish festivals but also read God's Word. He may have been a Gentile convert to Judaism. That day he became a follower of Christ.

People of African Origin in the Epistles

According to Mark 15.21, Rufus was the son of Simon of Cyrene who carried the cross of Jesus. In Romans 16.13, Rufus was chosen to do the Lord's work, and Paul said: "Greet Rufus, chosen in the Lord; and greet his mother—a mother to me also"(*NRSV*). He came from a good family with a father and a mother who were committed to the Lord.

People of African Origin in the Book of Revelation

In Revelation 5.9–10 the Bible speaks of Christ having "purchased [people] for God from every tribe and language and people and nation" and having "made them to be a kingdom and priests to serve our God, and they will reign on the earth" (*NIV*). Africans are among those who have been bought with the precious blood of Christ. Revelation 14.6b speaks of the Gospel which will be proclaimed to "every nation, tribe, language, and people." These Scriptures do include Africans even though they are not specifically mentioned by name.

Conclusion

There are several reasons why the issue of the presence of Africans in the Bible is of importance. Proving the presence of Africans in the Bible is not meant to prove that the Bible is a Black person's book; rather, it is meant to show that the Bible reveals the blessings God has for them. The Bible belongs to no particular race of people. It is God's book which unveils the plan that God has for all the peoples of the earth. No one is left out. Some groups may not be specifically mentioned by name but they are not excluded. The Bible says that God loved "the world"(John 3.16) and this means that everyone in the world is included. The Bible speaks of "whosoever" which includes every racial and ethnic group; every individual on earth (Revelation 7.9). But because people of African descent have been enslaved and oppressed, it is easier for them to believe that they are not included. This study refutes the misinterpretation that Ham and his descendants are cursed. The Bible does not teach that. (cf. "The Alleged Curse on Ham" by Gene Rice). Africans have always been included in God's redemptive plan. This is amply demonstrated by their inclusion in the holy history so ably explicated in the Bible. Finally, this study should help Blacks who may need to overcome a poor self-image which is caused by their sad history of oppression, slavery, and discrimination. The self-image of Blacks must be based on what God says about them which is supported by God's redemptive acts. They need to espouse a biblical view of ethnicity which does not change. All other fads will come and go but the truth of God's Word does not change. This study should prove to be helpful to both Black brothers and sisters as well as to White brothers and sisters. It ought to dispel myths which have been perpetuated for too many years.

Bibliography

Felder, Cain Hope, ed. *The Original African Heritage Study Bible, King James Version.* Nashville: The James C. Winston Publishing Company, 1993.

Harrison, R.K. *Introduction to the Old Testament.* Grand Rapids: Eerdmans, 1969.

McKissic, Sr., William Dwight and Evans, Anthony T. *Beyond Roots II: If Anybody Ask You Who I Am: A Deeper Look at Blacks in the Bible.* Wenonah, New Jersey: Renaissance Productions, 1994.

Tenney, Merrill C., ed. *Zondervan's Pictorial Encyclopedia of the Bible, Volume 2.* Grand Rapids: Zondervan Publishing House, 1975.

Unger, Merrill F. *Unger's Bible Dictionary.* Chicago: Moody Press, 1966.

Young, Robert. *Young's Analytical Concordance to the Bible.* Nashville: Thomas Nelson Publishers, 1982.

Six

The Presence of Blacks in Biblical Antiquity

Cain Hope Felder

The view of Africa, that has evolved in recent centuries has little or no historical integrity inasmuch as it reflects Eurocentric interpretations of the Bible. However, new light is shining on biblical antiquity, and layers of unfavorable biases are being peeled away. In their place is a more congenial basis for inclusiveness and reconciliation in conjunction with an emergence of critical studies on the Black presence in the Bible and the recovering of ancient African heritage in the Scriptures. Consequently, persons of African descent now have the opportunity to rediscover consistent and favorable mentioning of their forebears within the pages of the Bible. The Word of God shows itself to be a truly universal, inclusive, and multicultural message of salvation for the human race.

◄ "The Creation," by Aaron Douglas. Oil on canvas, 1935. The Howard University Gallery of Art, Permanent Collection, Washington, DC

"Then God said, Let there be light; and there was light. And God saw that the light was good; and God separated the light from the darkness." (Genesis 1.3, 4, *NRSV*)

This is the most exciting and intriguing time for Scripture study, especially by persons of immediate African descent. We, the people of the darker hue, are again at the turning point of a new millennium when God's ancient Word shows itself to be truly a universal, inclusive, and multicultural message of salvation for the human race. Evidence, ancient and modern, again and again confirms as fact that the human race began on the continent that is now known as Africa (a name derived from the Latin: "Africanus" –itself post-biblical). In the sweep of what has come to be called Western Civilization, Africa has often been dubbed "the Dark Continent," as if nothing good has ever, nor will ever, come out of this great land mass. The words of the ancient Psalmist resonate still in our ears: "Princes shall come out of Egypt; Ethiopia shall soon stretch out her hands unto God." (Psalm 68.31, *KJV*).

The view of Africa, that has evolved in recent centuries, has little or no historical integrity; rather it tells us much more about the ways that Europeans have re-interpreted the Bible along lines that have served mainly to affirm their own cultural identity and racial aggrandizement, particularly since the beginning of the seventeenth century at the onset of the Renaissance. Modern history has witnessed the painful consequences for Blacks in Africa and the African "Diaspora" (the "scattering"/dispersal from Africa through the slave trade or voluntary migrations). Sadly, the Black descendants of the continent have been too often stereotyped and even demonized. Nevertheless, thanks be to God, new light is beginning to shine on biblical antiquity.

Today, we are systematically peeling away layers of unfavorable biases that suggest that Black History consists only of the sad chapter of modern slavery. The latter-day negative overlays are disappearing; and in their place, one encounters a more congenial basis for inclusiveness and reconciliation. People of immediate African descent can see themselves once again in the Bible as an occasion for celebration, renewed spiritual motivation, and empowerment. Light is once more shining out of darkness. It can illumine the whole human race, if studied and taught with the right spirit— the spirit of love for all humanity.

The African Methodist Episcopal Church certainly has one of the more distinguished records for not only defending the dignity of

Black people, also for celebrating the existence of Blacks in biblical antiquity. Over the years, the denomination has taken strong stances on the protection of the rights of persons of African descent as human beings. This is well known. What is perhaps less familiar are the extraordinary ways in which leaders within this Protestant denomination have studied and systematically examined the Bible as a sacred record in which Africans have played a major role. Writing in 1895, for example, Daniel P. Seaton, D.D., M.D., a prominent leader in the A.M.E. Church, displayed considerable knowledge about ancient Blacks within the Bible as well as the locations of biblical lands and religious sites. Seaton made several field trips to Palestine at his own expense and documented his findings in a mammoth study published by the A.M.E. Church Publishing House containing 443 pages of texts, maps, illustrations and notes. In a remarkably careful manner he provided extensive descriptions of tombs, villages, and artifacts that suggested strongly influences of African heritage.

Everywhere Dr. Seaton visited in Palestine at the close of the 19th century, he encountered signs of "Hamites" or Hamitic influence. He wrote:

> "Because these Hamites were an important people, attempts have been made to rob them of their proper place in the catalogue of the races. The Bible tells us plainly that the Phoenicians were descendants of Canaan, the son of Ham, and anyone who will take the time to read the Bible account of their lineage must concede the fact." (p. 377)

It is indeed noteworthy that Seaton was profoundly aware of scholarly racial bias on the part of the so-called bona-fide Bible scholars (i.e., products of the European academy and its American offshoots) of his day. Nevertheless, as much as we may applaud Dr. Seaton's constructive intent, he could clearly have benefited from the historical-critical methods of biblical study and a more substantial understanding of the evolution of race topologies, pseudo-scientific theories, and ideologies of racial supremacy in modern Western Civilization. Today, in the United States of America, other parts of the global African diaspora, and increasingly even on the continent of Africa herself, there is developing a proliferation of critical studies on the Black presence in the Bible together with Afro-sensitive versions of the Bible with maps of the Holy Land in relation to the African land mass. These resources are often accompanied by study guides, illustrations, and supplemental essays designed to underscore the importance of African connections with the ancient biblical record. Even so, caution must be urged for anyone who might tend to construe the sons of Noah (Genesis. 9.18-29)—Ham, Shem, and Japheth—as somehow representing three different "races." Any conclusion of this type is highly flawed and moves in the opposite direction of the "Curse of Canaan" narrative. The intent of the story is really to provide the ancient Hebrews with a kind of theological justification for taking over the land of the Canaanites. The "Curse of Canaan" passage, after all, speaks of three brothers from the same family.

The Bible emerges out of the ancient world that knew nothing of racial types like Caucasoids, Mongoloids, or Africaoids. These arbitrary and pseudo-scientific categories are actually quite modern. They constitute little more than fraudulent mythologies created to further the social construct of racism and the dubious notion of Aryan supremacy and so-called Africaoid inferiority. African American and other scholars from Ashley Montague (*Man's Most Dangerous Myth*) to Martin Bernal (*Black Athena: The Afro-Asiatic Origin of Western Civilization*) have demonstrated that white racism is essentially a European by-product after 1492.

With the Renaissance (16th and 17th centuries) and the so-called European Enlightenment that followed (A.D. 1700-1899), we begin to see a carefully orchestrated pattern of European racially biased "scholarship," claiming to have an objective, empirical basis, but in fact having nothing of the sort. Still there emerged a Western "scholarly" consensus from Francois Bernier (1685), Carolus Linnaeus (1735), to the German social anthropologist Johann Blumenbach (1775-1795). The new consensus was that North Africa was to be seen as Caucasoid or non-Black; this was clearly a subtle political decision. In this way, European scholarship literally de-Africanized the entire Nile Valley civilization! This woeful development still dominates the way in which American and European universities regard the people of North Africa. Despite even the color of these people (invariably shades of Brown to Black), the Western official race category for them is "honorary" Caucasians.

Revelations of this kind lend a certain urgency to recovering the ancient African heritage in Scripture. African Americans are fundamentally people of the Book even as they have adapted remnants of their traditional African religions with Hebraic/Jewish, Christian, or Islamic thought and practice. More Black pastors today need to realize that Islam or the Muslim religion begins formally with Muhammad of Arabia in the mid-seventh century A.D., 600 years *after* Jesus of Nazareth, and that Muhammad had great respect for the Book on which his own Qur'an depended to some extent. That "Book" was the Holy Bible; and it is crucial for each generation of spiritual leaders, to people of immediate African descent, to celebrate the fact that they, by no means, are an "afterthought" in the plan of God.

On the contrary, the Bible constantly reminds us that not only did God bring light out of darkness, but that God also has made it clear that "out of Africa (Egypt), I have called my child." This applies not just to the quotation in Hosea 11.1 and Matthew 2.15, but also to the Garden of Eden, which begins with the Nile (Gihon) River (Genesis 2.10-14), and extends through the Exodus Saga. Indeed it continues with notices from both the Old Testament prophetic literature and the Psalms that African people hasten to extend their hand to God (Psalm 68.31) or that they will bring offerings from "beyond the rivers of Ethiopia" (Zephaniah 3.10). Here, doubtless, is a reference to the Blue and White Nile Rivers which together make up the longest river in the world.

With the foregoing observations as general background, let us establish a basis for two propositions that will guide a six-fold survey of discrete segments of the Bible. The first proposition is that much of the material in the Old Testament or Hebrew Bible arises against the backdrop of ancient pre-historic Africa primarily, and Mesopotamia or the Fertile Crescent, secondarily. This claim opposes that championed by European scholarship which has so rigorously sought to de-Africanize not only Egypt but also Ethiopia. Consider, however, the simple preponderance of references in the Old Testament to Egypt, Ethiopia, Put, Punt, Libya and other lands known to be associated with the African continent, including Sheba and Havilah. (There are well over 1,500 such references in the Old Testament. This is far more than mentioning of lands in Mesopotamia.) Then too, whenever there was famine within or the threat of military invasion to Ancient Palestine/Israel, invariably the patriarch, including Abraham, would flee or otherwise seek relief in Africa – not Mesopotamia.

Of course, there were interactions between the peoples of Africa and Mesopotamia in the biblical world, and these were of a commercial, military, and cultural nature yielding similarities in language, folklore, and religious customs. It is for precisely this reason that we emphasize a second guiding proposition for our survey, namely that the best refer to the people of the Old Testament as being of Afro-Asiatic stock. Hebrew as well as Ethiopic are technically Afro-Asiatic languages. Thus, it should not be surprising that behind many of the Old Testament ways of life are architectural and cultural influences that originate in Africa, from the idea of an Ark/sacred boat to the "holy of holies" within the Temple. If the Hebrews spent as much as 400 years in Egyptian bondage, one would only naturally conclude that, despite a relatively brief interlude in the wilderness of Sinai, they would retain an enormous amount of cultural and social mores from the hundreds of years in Africa once they entered the Promised Land.

Once we understand the centrality of the ancient African ethos to the development of the Old Testament, the biblical world truly emerges as a world not only before any "color prejudice," but also as a world that had no notion of "race" based on the physical make-up of a person. The biblical world certainly practiced gender, class, tribe, and even religious bias, but not racial discrimination in any way comparable to that found in Western societies within the past few centuries after the rise of modern European imperial powers. As a consequence, persons of African descent have the opportunity to rediscover and recover today consistent and rather favorable mentioning of their forebears within the pages of the Bible, despite the fact that others have intentionally tried to obscure this important fact.

Part I. The African Heritage in the Old Testament

The Old Testament or Hebrew Bible may be divided into three parts. It is customary to divide the traditional Old Testament narratives into groupings known as the Law, the Prophets, and the Hagiographa (including the Psalms and the Wisdom Literature). Normally, the Law refers to the "Five Books of Moses" or the Pentateuch, although Moses did not literally write these books, any more than King David composed all of the Psalms. The Law, when seen as Genesis, Exodus, Leviticus, Numbers, and Deuteronomy, is merely a traditional way to recognize the opening Books of the Bible as having the giving of the Mosaic Law as a central feature. Moreover, these books provide the literary and quasi-historical context for the giving of the Law on Mount Sinai (some Hebrew sources say on Mount Horeb). After all, the Law epitomizes ancient Hebraic, and later, Jewish faith. The two other

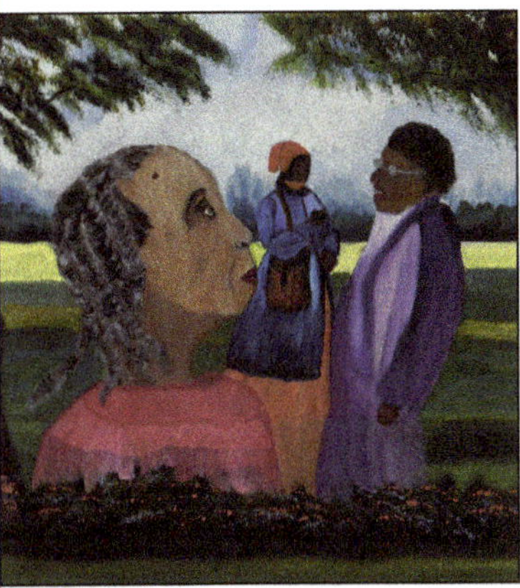
"Three Freedom Fighters: Sojourner Truth, Harriet Tubman, Rosa Parks, 1992. by Anna Belle Lee Washington (1924–2000/ American). Oil on Canvas © Anna Belle Lee Washington/ Superstock

segments of the Old Testament are the Prophetic Literature (including the Major and Minor Prophets) and the Hagiographa ("holy writings"). In each of these three parts of the Old Testament, one encounters numerous favorable references to the lands and people of what later came to be called "Africa" by the Romans. Since the term Africa is not found in the Bible, one will need to become familiar with the biblical names of those areas within Africa, but too often construed to be somewhere other than in that continent to which we today routinely refer as Africa.

The presence of Blacks in the Old Testament/Hebrew Bible is rather substantial; fortunately, ours is an age that increasingly allows such an important fact to be acknowledged more widely than perhaps ever before. Since this specific topic has long been studied by Dr. Gene Rice, Professor of Old Testament, he has supplied a representative listing of key Old Testament passages that mention, indeed often celebrate, the Black biblical presence. He has graciously offered the following:

Nimrod, son of Cush, "the first on earth to become a mighty warrior." Nimrod is also credited with founding and ruling the principal cities of Mesopotamia (Genesis 10.8-12).

Hagar, the Egyptian maid of Sarah (Genesis 16; 21.8-21). If Abraham had had his way, Hagar would have become the foremother of the covenant people (Genesis 17.18).

Asenath, daughter of Potiphera, priest of On (Heliopolis), wife of Joseph and mother of Ephraim and Manasseh (Genesis 41.45, 51,52; 46.20), whom Jacob claimed and adopted (Genesis 48.38).

Moses' Cushite wife (Numbers 12.1). She was probably Zipporah of the Kenite clan of the Midianites (Exodus 2.21-23). If Moses' Cushite wife is indeed Zipporah, then her father Jethro, (also called Reuel), would also have been an African. Since Jethro was the priest of Midian (Exodus 2.16; 3.1; 18.1) and the mountain of God where Moses was called was located in Midian (Exodus 3.1; 18.5), and Jethro presided at a meal where Aaron and the elders of Israel were guests (Exodus 18.12), the Kenites may have been the original worshipers of God by the name of the LORD, that is, Yahweh (YHWH). Jethro also instructed Moses in the governance of the newly liberated Israelites (Exodus 8.13-27).

Phinehas, the grandson of Aaron and a high priest (Exodus 6.25). The name, Phinehas, is Egyptian and means literally, "The Nubian," or "The Dark-skinned One."

The "mixed multitude" that accompanied the Israelites when they left Egypt undoubtedly included various African and Asian peoples (Exodus 12.38).

The unnamed Cushite soldier in David's army. He bore the news of Absalom's death to David and, in contrast to Ahimaaz, had the courage to tell David the truth about Absalom (2 Samuel 18.21, 31, 32).

Solomon's Egyptian wife. She was an Egyptian princess and by his marriage to her, Solomon sealed an alliance with Egypt (1 Kings 3.1; 11.1).

The Queen of Sheba. She ruled a kingdom that included territory in both Arabia and Africa. When she visited Solomon, she was accorded the dignity and status of a head of state (1 Kings 10.1-13).

Zerah, the Ethiopian. He commanded a military garrison at Gerar in SW Palestine and fought against King Asa of Judah and almost defeated him (2 Chronicles 14.9-15). After Egyptian influence ceased in Palestine, the Cushite soldiers stationed at Gerar settled down and became farmers. Some two centuries after the time of Zerah, the Simeonites took over Gerar "where they found rich, good pasture, and the land was very broad, quiet, and peaceful; for the former inhabitants there belonged to Ham." (1 Chronicles 4.40).

Cush, a Benjaminite (heading to Psalm 7). He is identified as Saul in the Talmud.

The Ethiopian ambassadors who came to Jerusalem to establish diplomatic relations with Judah (Isaiah 18.1,2). They represented the Ethiopian Pharaoh, Shabaka (716-702) of the Twenty-fifth Dynasty of Egypt.

The Ethiopian, Taharqa, spelled Tirhakah in the Bible. When Hezekiah revolted against Assyria in 705 B.C., he did so with the support of Shaboka and Shebitku (702-690), rulers of the Twenty-fifth Dynasty of Egypt. Tirhakah led an army in support of Judah during Hezekiah's revolt against Assyria (2 Kings 19.9; Isaiah 37.9). Tirhakah later ruled Egypt from 690-664.

The Prophet Zephaniah. Zephaniah's father was Cushi, his grandfather Gedaliah, his great-grandfather Amariah, and his great-great-grandfather (King) Hezekiah (Zephaniah 1.1). Zephaniah was active about 630 B.C. and sparked a religious revival in Judah.

Jehudi ben Nethaniah ben Shelemiah ben Cushi. The context in Jeremiah 36 indicates that Jehudi was a trusted member of the cabinet of King Jehoiakim of Judah (Jeremiah 36.14, 21, 23).

Ebed-melech ("Royal Servant"), the Ethiopian. He was an officer of King Zedekiah who, at great risk to himself, saved Jeremiah's life (Jeremiah 38.7-13), and was blessed by Jeremiah (Jeremiah 39.15-18).

Africans as Worshipers with Israel

Among those who know me I
　　mention Rahab [Egypt] and Babylon;
Philistia too, and Tyre, with
　　Ethiopia–
"This one was born there,"
　　they say. (Psalm 87.4, *NRSV*)

Let bronze be brought from
　　Egypt;
let Ethiopia hasten to stretch
　　out its hands to God. (Psalm 68.31, *NRSV*)

At that time gifts will be brought to the LORD of hosts from a people tall and smooth, from a people feared near and far, a nation mighty and conquering, whose land the rivers divide, to Mount Zion, the place of the name of the LORD of hosts. (Isaiah 18.7, *NRSV*)

On that day there will be a highway from Egypt to Assyria, and the Assyrian will come into Egypt, and the Egyptian into Assyria, and the Egyptians will worship with the Assyrians. (Isaiah 19.23, *NRSV*)

On that day Israel will be the third with Egypt and Assyria, a blessing in the midst of the earth, whom the LORD of hosts has blessed, saying, "Blessed be Egypt my people, and Assyria the work of my hands, and Israel my heritage." (Isaiah 19.24,25, *NRSV*)

At that time I will change the
speech of the peoples
to a pure speech,
that all of them may call on the
name of the LORD
and serve him with one accord.
From beyond the rivers of
Ethiopia
my suppliants, my scattered ones,
shall bring my offering. (Zephaniah 3.9, 10, *NRSV*)

Are you not like the Ethiopians to me,
O people of Israel? says the LORD. (Amos 9.7a, *NRSV*)

Africa as the Home of the Jewish Diaspora

On that day the Lord will extend his hand yet a second time to recover the remnant that is left of his people, from Assyria, from Egypt, from Pathros, from Ethiopia, from Elam, from Shinar, from Hamath, and from the coastlands of the sea. (Isaiah 11.11, *NRSV*)

Lo, these shall come from far away,
and lo, these from the north and
from the west,
and these from the land of
Syene [Aswan]. (Isaiah 49.12, *NRSV*)

The word that came to Jeremiah for all the Judeans living in the land of Egypt, at Migdol, at Tahpanhes, at Memphis, and in the land of Pathros,... (Jeremiah 44.1, *NRSV*)

Part II. The African Heritage in the New Testament

As with the Hebrew Bible, the New Testament may be divided into three parts, namely the Gospels (including the Acts of the Apostles, as Luke's second volume), the Epistles, and the unique apocalyptic book, the Revelation to John, that closes the New Testament canon. Romans and Greeks are certainly part of the New Testament which frequently mentions them by name, military rank, or political title. Yet, Africans, and persons of African descent, are fully represented as well. For years, persons of African descent have taken heart upon reading the celebrated passage in Psalm 68.31, KJV–"Princes shall come out of Egypt; Ethiopia shall soon stretch out her hands unto God." But today there is a much greater basis upon which Blacks may celebrate and otherwise take seriously their rich ancient heritage with sacred Scripture, showing that long ago, their outstretched hand was fully accepted by God, despite what has happened to them in the intervening centuries. The substantial African presence in Scripture is by no means limited to an isolated verse here and there.

The African presence in the Bible is also by no means limited to the Old Testament. Indeed many Jews of the first century lived in regions where Africans intermingled freely with other racial and ethnic types. We too easily forget today that miscegenation or interracial marriage was an explicit part of Alexander the Great's policy; he wanted all subjects to have Greek blood flowing through their veins! Of course there was no notion of the modern idea of "race" during that time, but suffice it to say that the ancients had no problem with Black people nor did the Greeks and Romans consider them to be inferior.

Consider a few inescapable factors that challenge the traditional Western perception of the Madonna and Child. In the Gospel of Matthew, we find the quotation from Hosea 11.1 which reads "out of Egypt I called my son." The passage is part of the notorious "Flight into Egypt" that describes the way in which Mary and Joseph fled to Egypt to hide the one that King Herod feared would displace him. Assuming that we can lend some historical credence to this report, it is difficult imagining, if the holy family were indeed persons who looked like typical "Europeans," that they could effectively "hide" in Africa. One must remember and take most seriously the fact that Egypt has always been and remains part of Africa. Her indigenous people are noticeably different from the European types, notwithstanding the Hellenistic cultural incursions, beginning in earnest just over 300 B.C. In fact, it has only been in recent centuries that the Egyptians and other North Americans have been officially racially classified as somehow "Caucasians" (similar to the manner in which Western Civilization has come to regard all of the indigenous Africans north of the Sahara). Nevertheless, for thousands of years, Africans have migrated out of biblical Ethiopia and Egypt and have passed through Palestine en route to the Fertile Crescent or Mesopotamia. Thus the term

▸ "Black Madonna and Child," by Joe Cauchi. Oil on canvas. Courtesy of Superstock

Afro-Asiatic emerged, and it is a fitting description of persons from Abraham to Jesus and his disciples.

Beyond this, we must also consider the hundreds of shrines of the Black Madonna that have existed in many parts of North Africa, Europe, Meso-America and Russia. These are not some weather-beaten misrepresentations of an original White Madonna. Rather, as recent studies of the oldest such Madonnas in Italy have shown, they are uncanny reminders of the diverse ethnography of those who inhabited Palestine at the time of Jesus of Nazareth and earlier. Today, in Western Civilization, many avoid the term Afro-Asiatic, due to negative modern attitudes that have been associated with Africa over the past three or four hundred years. Yet, it may not be going too far to suggest that the "Sweet Lil' Jesus Boy" of the negro spiritual is probably most accurately described as an Afro-Asiatic or "person of color." While the Negro Spiritual intones: "we didn't know who you was," it paradoxically reminds many modern Christians that what Jesus actually looked like may come as a surprise.

As long as one keeps in mind that, for the most part by modern standards of ethnicity, first-century Jews could be considered Afro-Asiatics. This is to say that Jesus, his family, his disciples and, doubtless, most of the fellow Jews that he encountered in his public ministry were persons of color. They would certainly not be Europeans. We stress this point only because it has become virtually axiomatic for people today to envision that somehow the ancient people of the New Testament were all Europeans. Without much reflection or critical analysis, people tend to project modern Jews back into antiquity as if two thousand years of assimilation never occurred. Having established this important interpretive principle, we can identify a few New Testament passages where there is an explicit African presence.

Matthew 1.1-14	The genealogy of Jesus in which four Afro-Asiatic women are included, viz. Rahab, Tamar, Ruth, and Bathsheba.
Matthew 2.13-18	Out of Egypt (Africa) I have called my son (see Hosea 11.1).
Matthew 12.42	The Queen of the South, meaning "the Queen of Sheba" (parallel reference in Luke 11.31; compare 1Kings 10.1-10 and 2 Chronicles 9.1-9).

Matthew 27.32	Simon of Cyrene compelled to carry the cross (parallel accounts in Mark 15.21 and Luke 23.26).
Mark 1.3	Note the mentioning of "the wilderness" or desert as a reminder of the geographical context for the gospel and most of the biblical narratives.
Luke 13.29	Luke instructs us through his more inclusive editing of Jesus' sayings found in Matthew 8.11. Here, Luke adds "north and south," thereby underscoring the Lukan universalism of both the gospel and the plan of salvation.
Luke 19.41-44	Jesus weeps over the city and initiates change.
Acts 2.9, 10	The Jewish pilgrims gathered at Pentecost included persons of African descent, notably the Elamites of Mesopotamia and those from Egypt, Libya, and Cyrene.
Acts 8.26-40	The Ethiopian Finance Minister on a mission for the Queen of the Ethiopians, the Kandake or Candace; he is baptized as perhaps the first non-Jew (an early tradition that rivals the baptism of Cornelius).
Acts 13.1	Two of the four prophets and teachers at Antioch (where persons of the Way were first called Christians—11.26) were Africans, namely Lucius of Cyrene and Simeon who was called Niger, a Latinism for "the Black Man."
Acts 18.24, 25	Apollos, the Jew of Alexandria in North Africa, becomes converted (1 Corinthians 3).
John 4.7-39	The Samaritan as ancient outcast and here metaphor for victims of racial, ethnic, and gender bias today.
John 8.32	"You will know the truth, and the truth will make you free." *(NRSV)*

Galatians 5.1	"For freedom Christ has set us free. Stand firm, therefore, and do not submit again to a yoke of slavery." *(NRSV)*
1 Corinthians 3.11	Apollos, the African Preacher (He was from Alexandria on the Nile Delta.)
1 Corinthians 7.21c	Further evidence of Paul's dislike of slavery: If you are able to gain your freedom, avail yourself of the opportunity (2 Corinthians 11.20 and the Epistle to Philemon).
James 2.1-8	Outward appearances can lead to fraudulent judgments about people. (Although James principally has in mind class distinctions, the principle supports a wider application.)
1 Peter 2.4-10	Those who believe and do the will of God through humble service and self-sacrifice are the "Chosen People" and the true "royal priesthood" and the recipients of God's mercy. No racial or ethnic basis for divine election!

▸ Detail, "The Creation," by Aaron Douglas, Oil on canvas, 1935. The Howard University Gallery of Art, Permanent Collection, Washington, DC

As the Holy Scriptures testify, all people of faith are "one in Christ Jesus" and "heirs according to the promise" (Galatians 3.28, 29). And as the apostle Paul stated, "From now on, therefore, we regard no one from a human point of view; even though we once knew Christ from a human point of view, we know him no longer in that way. So if anyone is in Christ, there is a new creation: everything old has passed away; see, everything has become new! All this is from God, who reconciled us to himself through Christ, and has given us the ministry of reconciliation; that is, in Christ God was reconciling the world to himself, not counting their trespasses against them, and entrusting the message of reconciliation to us" (2 Corinthians 5.16-19, *NRSV*).

Bibliography

Bernal, Martin. *Black Athena: The Afroasiatic Roots of Classical Civilization, Vol. I.* London: Free Association Books, 1987.

Birnbaum, Lucia Chivola. *Black Madonnas: Feminism, Religion & Politics in Italy.* Boston: Northeastern University Press, 1991.

DeCoy, Robert H. *The Blue Book Manual of Nigritian History: American Descendants of African Origin.* New York: Nigritian, Inc., Publishers, 1969.

Featherman, A. *Social History of the Races of Mankind: First Division; Nigritians.* London: Trubner & Co., 1985.

Felder, Cain Hope, ed. *Stony the Road We Trod: African American Biblical Interpretation.* Minneapolis: Fortress Press, 1991.

____________. *Troubling Biblical Waters.* Maryknoll, New York: Orbis Books, 1989.

Harris, Joseph E. *Pillars in Ethiopian History: The William Leo Hansberry African History Notebook, Vol. I.* Washington, DC: Howard University Press, 1974.

Hughley, Ella J. *The Truth about Black Biblical Hebrew-Israel.* Springfield Gardens, NY: Hughley Publications, 1982.

James, George G. M. *The Stolen Legacy: Greek Philosophy is stolen Egyptian Philosophy.* New York: The African Publication Society, 1980.

Leslau, Wolf. *Falasha Anthology: The Black Jews of Ethiopia.* New York: Schocken Books, 1951.

Martin, Clarice J. *"A Chamberlain's Journey and the Challenge of Interpretation for Liberation," Semeia.* Vol. 47, 1989.

McKissic, William Dwight., Sr. *Beyond Roots: In Search of Blacks in the Bible.* Wenonah, NJ: Renaissance Productions, 1990.

Montagu, Ashley M. F. *Most Dangerous Myth: The Fallacy of Race.* New York: Harper & Brothers Publishers, 1952.

Mosley, William. *What Color was Jesus?* Chicago: African-American Images,1987.

Nantambu, Kwame. *Egypt & Afrocentric Geopolitics: Essays on European Supremacy.* Kent, OH: Imhotep Publishing Company, 1996.

Onyewuenyi, Innocent C. *The African Origin of Greek Philosophy: An Exercise in Afrocentrism.* Nsukka, Nigeria: University of Nigeria Press, 1993.

Seaton, Daniel P. *African People of Bible Lands.* Nashville: The A. M. E. Church Publishing House, 1895.

Snowden, Frank M., Jr. *Blacks in Antiquity: Ethiopians in the Greco-Roman Experience.* Cambridge, MA: Harvard University Press, 1970.

_____________. *Before Color Prejudice: The Ancient View of Blacks.* Cambridge, MA: Harvard University, 1983.

Ullendorff, Edward. *Ethiopia in the Bible: The Schweich Lectures, 1967.* London: Oxford University Press, 1968.

In omni tribulatione et angustia: suc-
currat nobis virgo maria. Amen.

Et sic in Syon firmata sum: Et in civi-
tate sanctificata similiter requievi:
et in Jherusalem potestas mea: Et radicavi in po-
pulo honorificato: Et in partes dei mei he-
reditas illius et in plenitudine sanctorum
detentio mea. Tu autem domine miserere nobis.
Deo gratias. Beata es virgo Maria que
dominum portasti Creatorem mundi. Genuisti
qui te fecit et in eternum permanes virgo. Ave maria gratia plena dominus tecum. Genuisti. Iube domne be-
nedicere. Per virginem matrem concedat nobis dominus salutem et pacem. Amen.

Seven

The Alleged Curse on Ham

Gene Rice

Genesis 9.18-29 has been popularly understood to mean that Ham was cursed, and this understanding has often been used to justify oppression of African people, the descendants of Ham. The text gives the impression that Ham offended his father Noah and because of this was cursed, but a careful reading of the passage reveals that this is not so, but rather that Canaan was the offender and was the one cursed. Confusion has arisen because Genesis is not a book in the modern sense, but an editorial synthesis of different traditions of Noah's family. Genesis 9.18-29 is concerned with giving an account of the political relationships between the Israelites, the Philistines, and the Canaanites in biblical times and has nothing to do with race. In fact, the Bible knows nothing of a curse on Ham and nowhere does it have anything negative to say about Africans because of their race. The theological heartbeat of the Bible is that we are all sons and daughters of God, that we are all related to one another as members of a family, that each one of us, whatever our race, ethnicity, and nationality, is special and precious to God, and that we were created for companionship with God—and fellowship with one another.

◂ Noah's Ark/ Book illustration 1490 © *Superstock/* Superstock

One of the most damaging misconceptions of the Bible is that it sanctions a curse on African people because Ham was cursed. Since Ham is regarded as the father of African people, this belief implies that Ham's descendants are also cursed. Incalculable harm has resulted from this supposition. It has provided a theological justification to Caucasian Americans and others for feelings of superiority, prejudice, and actions that are oppressive to African Americans. Conversely, this assumption has created resentment and anger among African Americans and caused many to reject the Bible. The tragedy is that the belief that Ham was cursed rests on an erroneous interpretation of the Bible. The authority claimed for the curse on Ham is Genesis 9.18-29, but this passage is complex and subject to misunderstanding.

A Careful Reading of Genesis 9.18-29

This passage is made up of three distinct parts. The centerpiece is a story in vv. 20-27 about Noah's discovery of wine and how this affected relationships between him and his sons. This story is framed by a summary statement in vv. 18,19 that the sons of Noah were the ancestors of all the peoples of the biblical world, (CEV)and by the conclusion to the genealogy of Noah from Genesis 5.28,29.

According to Genesis 9.18,19, Shem, Ham, and Japheth went forth from the ark, and in obedience to God's command (9.1, 7), peopled the whole earth. These verses condense a long history but no details are given. The concern is to make clear the identity of the ancestors of the various peoples of the biblical world and to establish that it was only from "these three" that all the peoples of the world are descended. The results of the procreative activity of Shem, Ham, and Japheth are given in Genesis 10. There, some seventy different peoples are listed and all are identified as descendants of Shem, Ham, and Japheth. Thus Genesis 9.18,19 anticipate and prepare the reader for the extraordinary expansion of humankind from the three sons of Noah recorded in chapter 10.

Verses 28, 29 of chapter 9 connect back to Genesis 5, take up, and bring to a close the genealogy and the life of Noah. In keeping with the interest of Genesis 5, Genesis 9.28, 29 informs us that Noah lived 350 years after the flood, "and died at the age of nine hundred fifty." A regular feature of the genealogy of Noah's ancestors is that after their first-born, they all had "more children" (Genesis 5.4,7,10,13,16 19,22,26,30). Noticeable by its absence is any reference in 9.28,29 to Noah having other sons and daughters after the birth of Shem,

Ham, and Japheth. This relates 9.28,29 to the emphasis in 9.18,19 that it was only from "these three" sons of Noah that all humankind is descended.

The story of Noah's discovery of wine in Genesis 9.20-27 stands apart from its framing passages. Verses 18,19 of chapter 9 lead one to expect an account of the increase and dispersal of Noah's descendants following the flood. Instead, vv. 20-27 deal with the relationships of Noah's sons and their descendants in the land of Canaan or Palestine, and connect these relationships to Noah's discovery of wine. According to this story, Noah was the first to plant a vineyard and to discover wine. This new development has significant connections with the previous history of humankind.

Because of Adam's sin, the ground was cursed and Adam had to earn his livelihood by the sweat of his brow (Genesis 3.18,19). But with the birth of Noah, his father saw an omen in Noah's name and expressed the hope that "he will give us comfort, as we struggle hard to make a living on this land that the LORD has put under a curse." (Genesis 5.29). Lamech's wish was inspired by the similarity of sound between the name Noah in Hebrew, *noach*, and the Hebrew word for relief or comfort, *nicham*. Thus Noah's discovery of wine, God's gift "to cheer us up" (Psalm 104.15; Judges 9.13; Proverbs 31.6,7; Jeremiah 16.7), is regarded as the fulfillment of his father's wish and a blessing. But wine can be a mixed blessing (Proverbs 23.29-35; Hosea 4.11,18).

Ignorant of the properties of wine, Noah drank some, became drunk, uncovered himself because of the heat from the wine, and lay naked in his tent. Noah betrays no consciousness of wrongdoing in becoming drunk nor does the text condemn him, but his nakedness created problems for his sons.

From the references to nakedness in the Old Testament, it appears that the Israelites observed a modesty about their physical being comparable to that of Muslims today. Exposure of one's nakedness was a source of shame, humiliation, and degradation. To be clothed was the first need of the man and the woman after eating the forbidden fruit (Genesis 3.7). One was not to go up by steps to the altar because "you might expose yourself when you climb up" (Exodus 20.26). Prisoners were led away naked and barefoot, with buttocks uncovered (Isaiah 20). The degradation and humiliation of defeat and exile is likened to the exposure of a woman's nakedness (e. g., Hosea 2.10; Isaiah 47.3; Jeremiah 13.26; Ezekiel 16.37, 39; Nahum 3.5).

Thus Noah's nakedness posed a delicate problem for his sons, whose responsibility to respect and care for their parents is presupposed here and spelled out in Israelite tradition (Exodus 20.12; 21.15,17; Deuteronomy 27.16; Proverbs 30.17; Isaiah 51.17-19).

Ham, according to Genesis 9.22, behaved very badly. He discovered his father in his tent in his drunken condition, paused to look upon him, then went outside and told his brothers. Shem and Japheth, however, took an outer garment (*the garment* in Hebrew, probably Noah's discarded garment) which also served as a blanket (Exodus 22.26,27; Deuteronomy 24.12,13), put it "over their shoulders and walked backward [gingerly, and awkwardly, no doubt] into the tent. Without looking at their father, they placed it over his body" (Genesis 9.23). The detail and vividness of this scene emphasize the modesty, respect, and sense of duty of Shem and Japheth for their father and highlight, by contrast, the offense of Ham. Ham looked at Noah in his naked condition, made no effort to cover his father, and talked about his father's nakedness.

Some time later Noah awoke "and knew what his youngest son had done to him." Noah's son is not named in the Hebrew text of Genesis 9.24, but a few translations, as the *King James Version,* identify Noah's son in verse 24 as Ham by referring to him as the "younger son." The grammar permits either the comparative or the superlative degree, but the more natural construction because of the three sons, and the one adopted by most modern translators, is the superlative, "the youngest."

The text does not tell us how Noah came to know what had been done to him. Did Shem and Japheth tell Noah about their brother viewing and talking about their father's nakedness? Or was more involved than seeing and talking about it? In any case, Noah was highly offended and cursed his son.

In Hebrew mentality a curse has a self-fulfilling energy and power to bring about the malady prescribed in the curse. The king of Moab hired Balaam to curse Israel to prevent the Israelites from entering his land, confident that Balaam's curse was as effective as a military force (Numbers 22-24). After conquering and burning Jericho, Joshua pronounced a curse on anyone who would rebuild the city (Joshua 6.26). Centuries later in the days of Ahab, Hiel rebuilt Jericho and, because of Joshua's curse, lost his first-born and his youngest son (1 Kings 16.34). The text leads us to expect Ham to be cursed but takes us by surprise by naming Canaan as the one cursed and by identifying him as Noah's youngest son! Ham, however, is consistently referred to as Noah's middle son (Genesis 5.32; 6.10; 7.13; 9.18; 10.6). The curse is that Canaan is to be the lowest of slaves to his brothers. Canaan's brothers, whom he is to be subject to, are then named. Again the text takes us by surprise and mystifies us. The brothers Canaan is to be a slave to are Shem and Japheth! Shem and Japheth, however, are blessed and after each is blessed it is reiterated that Canaan is to be their slave, making the curse all the more binding, for repetition strengthens and intensifies (Genesis 41.32).

As a curse has a self-fulfilling energy and power, so does a blessing when rightly spoken. And the blessing, like the curse, has the power to determine destiny and to shape the future. Jacob's ascendancy over Esau (Genesis 27), Ephraim's pre-eminence over Manasseh, the first-born (Genesis 48.8-20), and the destinies of all Jacob's sons (Genesis 49.1-27) are attributed to blessing. So also the relationships of Noah's descendants in Canaan are understood in terms of curse and blessing. The motive for the blessing of Shem and Japheth is not stated, but from the context it is clearly because of their respect and care for their father.

Noah blesses Shem by way of blessing the Lord, the God of Shem. The thought here is that of Psalm 144.15, (NKJV): "Happy are the people whose God is the LORD!" To bless the Lord is to express thanksgiving and praise in acknowledgment of the Lord as God. Since among the descendants of Shem the Lord became the covenant God of Israel, Shem at this point in time represents the future Israelites. The blessing of Japheth takes the form of a wish that God may extend, *yapht* a play on Japheth, his territory and that he may dwell in the tents of Shem.

With the blessing of Japheth it becomes clear that we are not dealing with individuals alone but with groups of people and their political relationships to one another. Canaan obviously represents the Canaanites, Shem the Israelites, and Japheth, the ancestor of Greek peoples (Genesis 10.2), the Philistines, who were immigrants from the Aegean basin (Amos 9.7; Jeremiah 47.3,4). This way of referring to peoples in their relationships to one another is confirmed by Genesis 10. There, a combination of geographical, political, ethnic, racial, and linguistic relations among people are expressed in terms of genealogical relationships. When Canaan is said to be the son of Ham (Genesis 10.6), for example, this expressed the fact that Canaan is geographically adjacent to Egypt and was, from earliest times, either under the hegemony or directly ruled by Egypt. As the list of Canaan's descendants in Genesis 10.15-19 shows, the Canaanites were not properly an African people, but Semites and Indo-Europeans who all lived in Palestine.

Problems of Interpretation

One comes to the end of Genesis 9.18-29 perplexed and with a host of questions. Verse 22 implies that Ham was liable to be cursed for acting disrespectfully to his father, but it is Canaan who is cursed. One might infer that Canaan was cursed for the infraction of his father, but if this were so one would expect a reason to be given for it; but none is. In fact, Canaan is explicitly identified as the offender in verses 24, 25. "When Noah woke up and learned what his youngest son had done, he said, 'I now put a curse on Canaan!'" (CEV) Since Canaan is called Noah's son, and the brothers he is to be subjected to are identified as Shem and Japheth, how does this accord with the statement in Genesis 9.18 that the sons of Noah were Shem, Ham, and Japheth? Moreover, the descendants of Shem, Ham, and Japheth are said to populate the whole earth in 9.19, but Shem and Japheth rule, over and jointly occupy, only the land of Canaan in 9.26,27. In the flood story, Shem, Ham, and Japheth have wives (Genesis 7.7,13; 8.15,18), but Noah's sons in 9.20-27 seem to be living at home with their father and there is no mention of their wives. Why is it said in 9.18 and 9.22 that Ham was the father of Canaan, but there is no reference to Ham's other sons, Cush, Egypt, and Put? And why is there no mention of Shem and Japheth being the father of anyone? How can Ham be the father of Canaan when according to 9.24,25, Noah was the father of Canaan? When did Shem (Israel) and Japheth (the Philistines) jointly rule Canaan and did these old enemies live in peace? Finally, what is the point of the passage?

The Literary Character of Genesis

One of the established results of biblical criticism is the recognition that Genesis speaks with not one, but four voices. By paying attention to the terms used for the deity, God (Hebrew, *Elohim*) and the Lord (Hebrew, YHWH, traditionally pronounced Yahweh) together with literary style and theological point of view, scholars have distinguished two creation stories, two lists of patriarchs before the flood, two versions of the flood, two versions of the family of nations in chapter 10, etc. These different voices continue throughout Genesis and into Exodus, Leviticus, and Numbers. Scholars call the voice that consistently refers to God as the Lord, J (from the German spelling, Jahweh), and a widely accepted date is ca. 950 B.C. Another voice begins with God (*Elohim*), changes to God All-Powerful (*El Shaddai*) at Genesis 17, and to the Lord in Exodus 6. This voice has a pronounced interest in priestly matters and for this reason is called P; it is generally dated to ca. 550-450 B.C. A third voice calls the deity God (*Elohim*) until the time of Moses, then the Lord (but not consistently), but it is fragmentary and difficult to date. Because of its preference for Elohim and its place of origin in the Northern Kingdom, also called Ephraim, this voice is named E. Proposed dates range from ca. 900-750 B.C. The fourth voice of Genesis is that of the one(s) who carefully and purposefully placed J, E, and P in the order in which we now find them.

While there is a profound theological harmony between these versions of the early history of humankind, they often differ in detail. The universe in Genesis 1.1—2.4a is brought into being by eight creative acts of God's Word over a period of six days. In Genesis 2.4b-25 creation is accomplished by four creative acts by the Lord's hands and there is no reference to the time involved. In the parallel genealogies of humankind before the flood in Genesis 4.17-26 and Genesis 5, the names are sometimes spelled differently and they do not consistently follow the same order of birth. (Note also the differences in the genealogy of Jesus in Matthew and Luke.) According to one version of the flood, Noah took two of every kind of animal into the ark (Genesis 6.19,20; 7.9,15). In the other version, Noah took seven pairs of clean and one pair of unclean animals and seven pairs of birds into the ark (Genesis 7.2, 3). Nor is this phenomenon confined to the Old Testament. We have not one, but four versions of the life and ministry of Jesus, and the differences between Mark and John are as striking as anything in Genesis. But whereas the New Testament Gospels have been preserved separately, the different literary sources in Genesis have been "braided" together.

These differences in detail are the inevitable results of the oral transmission of information and traditions for generations in different geographical locales and under different historical circumstances. The Bible leaves these differences uncensored and thereby indicates that it accepts and embraces them. The combined witness of the different voices in Genesis (and elsewhere in the Bible) gives us a fuller and better understanding than any one voice alone.

Two Versions of Noah's Family

The recognition of the composite nature of Genesis provides the key to the proper understanding of 9.18-29. As there are two versions of creation, two genealogies of humankind before the flood, and two versions of the flood, so there are two versions of Noah's family. Verses 18,19 represent one tradition; verses 20-27 embody another. Verses 18,19 and also 28,29 belong with Genesis 1, 5, and 10 (the P voice) and reflect the view that the (married) sons of Noah were Shem, Ham, and Japheth and that they were the ancestors of all the peoples of the biblical world. In 9.20-27, on the other hand, the (apparently unmarried) sons of Noah are Shem, Japheth, and Canaan. In this version of Noah's sons the one cursed is Canaan and the purpose of these verses is to account for relations between Israelites, Canaanites, and Philistines in the land of Canaan. These verses speak with the voice of J, also found in Genesis 2–4; 11.1-9, and chapter 12. This tradition of Noah's sons seems also to be reflected in Genesis 10.21 where Shem is referred to as the elder brother of Japheth.

The understanding of Genesis 9.18-29 is so confused because the Hebrew text at an early stage of its transmission has been edited to harmonize the two traditions of Noah's sons. This was done by adding the note in 9.18b, "and Ham, he was the father of Canaan" (to give a literal translation of the Hebrew text), and by inserting the phrase, "Ham the father of," before Canaan in 9.22a. These editorial additions interrupt the flow of the narrative and stand out like a bandaged thumb. The concern of 9.18,19 is to establish that Shem, Ham, and Japheth, and only "these three," were the forebears of all the peoples of the biblical world. The note that explains Ham's relationship to Canaan in 9.18b introduces a new and unrelated subject. And this note is made conspicuous as an addition by the absence of similar information about Shem and Japheth.

The insertion of "Ham the father of" in 9.22 is equally intrusive and stands in conflict with 9.24. This editorial note makes Ham, the middle son of Noah, the offender, but Noah explicitly identifies the guilty party as his youngest son (9.23,24).

The editorial nature of "and Ham, he was the father of Canaan" in 9.18b is acknowledged in the translations of *The New International Version, The New American Bible*, and *Today's English Version* by placing these words in brackets or parentheses. The same should be done for "Ham the father of" in 9.22, as in the *Moffatt Translation* and the *Confraternity Version.* Notes added to the

Hebrew text by a later editor to explain changes in place names, etc. are found throughout the Bible. *The New Revised Standard Version,* the *New International Version,* and the *New King James Version* use parentheses to designate part of the following passages in Genesis as editorial additions: 14.8; 23.2,19; 35.6,19,27; 48.7. Other translations, including the *Contemporary English Version,* integrate these editorial additions into the text.

It is understandable that someone confronted by the two traditions of Noah's family in Genesis 9.18-29 would attempt to harmonize them, especially since Noah's sons are identified by name as Shem, Ham, and Japheth in the P version of the flood (Genesis 6.10; 7.13), and the P version of Noah's sons (9.18,19) stands immediately before Noah's curse and blessing (9.20-27). In the J version of the flood the sons of Noah are not named. When they are referred to, it is as Noah's "whole family" (Genesis 7.1) and "the others in the boat" (7.23). The authority for the editorial additions in 9.18 and 9.22 is Genesis 10.6, where it is stated that Ham indeed was the father of Canaan. However, the author of these editorial notes overlooks the fact that in Genesis 9.24,25 Noah is the father of Canaan.

The recognition that there are two traditions of Noah's sons in Genesis 9.18-29 opens the way to the correct interpretation of the passage. The only basis for identifying Ham as the offender is the note in 9.18, "and Ham, he was the father of Canaan," and the insertion in 9.22, "Ham the father of." When it is understood that these notes were not a part of the original narrative but later, editorial additions to the Hebrew text, the offender as well as the one cursed is Canaan. Ham was not the one cursed because in Genesis 9.1 God blessed Ham and his brothers. As Baalam could not curse Israel whom God had blessed (Numbers 22.12; 23.8), so Noah could not have cursed Ham whom God had blessed.

If the editorial notes about Ham being the father of Canaan are accepted as original, no satisfactory explanation of Genesis 9.18-29 is possible. These notes make Ham the offender but give no reason why Canaan is cursed. There is the additional awkwardness that Ham is consistently referred to as Noah's middle son, but the one cursed is identified as Noah's youngest son. Those who interpret the passage on the assumption that the notes in 9.18 and 9.22 are an integral part of the narrative are forced to resort to speculation or to declare other portions of the passage secondary. This approach has achieved no consensus of interpretation and has led to widely diverging and sometimes bizarre expositions.

The Purpose of 9.18-29

In Genesis 12.7 God promises Abraham that the land of Canaan will be given to his descendants. Preceding and following this promise (12.6; 13.7) is the notation that the Canaanites were then living in the land and therefore were the native inhabitants of Canaan. This raises an important question: What right did the Israelites have to Canaan when its native population were Canaanites? In the course of time the Israelites did occupy Canaan and subjected the native population to forced labor (Joshua 16.10; 17.12,13; Judges 1.27-35; 1 Kings 9.20,21), but they shared possession of the land with the Philistines. If God promised the land to the Israelites, why did they share it with the Philistines?

Genesis 9.20-27 provides answers to these questions. According to this passage, the Canaanites lost their right to their land because of an inherent perversity in their ancestor Canaan which was perpetuated by his descendants. The Canaanites, especially those of Sodom, were "wicked, great sinners against the Lord" (Genesis 13.13; 15.16; 18.20,21; 19; Amorites in 15.16 is a synonymous term for Canaanites). According to Leviticus 18.24, 25, it was because of the abominable sexual practices of the native population of Canaan that the land "vomited" them out (see also Deuteronomy 9.4, 5; 12.29-31; 1 Kings 14.24; 2 Kings 17.7,11). Because of the notoriety of the Canaanites for sexual misconduct, it is tempting to infer that what was "done" to Noah (Genesis 9.24) was homosexual rape and that a fuller account of what happened has been curtailed to avoid offending readers. To see the nakedness of another leads naturally to sexual relations (Leviticus 20.17). And to look upon a forbidden object opens the way to succumbing to temptation, as in the case of Eve with the forbidden fruit (Genesis 3.6) and David with Bathsheba (2 Samuel 11.2-5). In whatever way we understand what was done to Noah, Canaan did not honor his father. And as the Fifth Commandment makes clear, honoring one's parents is the basis for maintaining the tenure of one's land.

Noah's curse and blessing are in effect a theological mandate for Israel's supremacy over Canaan. A remarkable feature of this mandate is that it also includes the Philistines. The Israelites and Philistines entered Canaan about the same time and at first were rivals for control of the land. Under David, the Israelites conquered the Philistines (2 Samuel 5.17-25; 8.1,12; 2.15-22; 23.9-17), but the Philistines were allowed to retain their holding along the coastal plain of Canaan and to maintain their separate identity (see maps

3,4, and 6 in the back of the Bible). This is all the more remarkable in that the Israelites claimed the territory occupied by the Philistines. In the boundary lists of the Promised Land (Exodus 23.31; Numbers 34.3; Joshua 15.11; Ezekiel 47.20) the western boundary does not stop at Philistine territory but is placed at the Mediterranean Sea.

The wish that God may enlarge Japheth probably refers to an extension of Philistine territory in the direction of Egypt. This would not only be a blessing to Japheth but also a source of security to Israel from the threat of Egyptian incursion into Palestine.

David may have contributed to the Israelite acceptance of the Philistine presence "in the tents of Shem," for he had enduring relationships with the Philistines, especially Achish, king of Gath. David lived as a refugee with Achish for one year and four months (1 Samuel 27.7). Achish later gave David the city of Ziklag as a feudal holding (1 Samuel 27). After David became king of all Israel and conquered the Philistines, Achish continued to be king of Gath into the reign of Solomon (1 Kings 2.39). Also, there was in David's army a contingent of troops from Gath willing to follow him into exile (2 Samuel 15.18-22). And the royal bodyguard of David and Solomon was composed of Cherethites and Pelethites (2 Samuel 8.18; 23.23; 1 Kings 1.44), who were either components or relatives of the Philistines (Ezekiel 25.16; Zephaniah 2.5). In any case, it is true that personal relationships with the "enemy" and those who are different can lead to blessing and dwelling together in peace.

No Evidence of a Curse on Ham Anywhere in the Bible

Not only is there no shred of evidence in Genesis 9.18-29 of a curse on Ham; nowhere in the Bible is there any reference or even an allusion to such a curse. Genesis 10 contains a list of the descendants of Shem, Ham, and Japheth (from the P source; portions of the chapter also belong to J). If there were any negative thoughts and feelings toward Ham and his descendants, this passage, following immediately on Noah's curse and blessing, would have been the place to express them. But no disparaging remark is made about anyone. (In Deuteronomy 23.7,8 Israelites are expressly forbidden to be unkind to Egyptians because "you lived as foreigners in the country of Egypt.") Rather, all the descendants of Noah are listed as related to one another as brothers and sisters. The one person

▸ Nubians carrying offerings, among them a giraffe. Thebes, tomb of Huy, viceroy of Nubia. Photo credit: Erich Lessing/ Art Resource, New York, NY

given special attention is Nimrod, the son of Cush, and he is credited with being the first to exercise imperial political power in Mesopotamia (Genesis 10.8-12). The point of Genesis 10 is that humankind is conceived as a unity, and the diversity of peoples with "their own languages, tribes, and land" (vv. 5, 20, 31) is understood as the fulfillment of God's command to Noah and his sons to be fruitful and to multiply, and to fill the earth (Genesis 9.1, 7). As God inspected the creation in Genesis 1 and declared it to correspond exactly to the divine intention, that it is good, so Genesis 10 implies that humankind in all its ethnic and racial manifestations corresponds to God's intention and is good. Abraham had no reservation about going to Egypt, the land of Ham (Psalms 78.51; 105.23, 27; 106.22), when there was a famine in Canaan (Genesis 12.10-20). Nor did Abraham and Sarah have any qualms about using Hagar, an Egyptian, as a surrogate mother so they could have an heir (Genesis 16). In fact, Abraham would gladly have accepted Ishmael, Hagar's son, as the father of the covenant people (Genesis 17.18). The mother of the tribes of

Ephraim and Manasseh was Asenath, an Egyptian (Genesis 41.45, 50-52; 46.20), and Jacob was at pains to adopt her sons so that they could be recognized as fully Israelite (Genesis 48.5,6).

Moses was married to a Cushite (the Hebrew word for the peoples living south of Egypt whom the Greeks called Ethiopians, a word meaning literally, "burnt faces") and while Miriam and Aaron spoke out against her, the context shows that what they were really protesting was Moses' exclusive authority to speak for God (Numbers 12). If Moses' Cushite wife was Zipporah from the land of Midian where Moses found refuge (Exodus 2.11-22), then Moses accepted instruction in the administration of justice from his Cushite father-in-law, Jethro (Exodus 18.13-27). It is worthy of note that Aaron's grandson and successor as high priest (Exodus 6.25), and also one of the sons of Eli the priest (1 Samuel 1.3), given the Egyptian name, Phinehas, which means literally, "The Southerner" (in relation to Egypt), that is, the Ethiopian or the Nubian.

David had Ethiopian troops in his army (2 Samuel 18.19-32). Solomon made an alliance with Egypt and took an Egyptian wife (1 Kings 3.1). Solomon graciously received, and treated as an equal, the queen of Sheba whose kingdom embraced both Arabian and African territory (1 Kings 10.1-13).

Amos likens Israel to the Ethiopians to make the point that the distant and different Ethiopians were just as near and dear to God as the covenant people (Amos 9.7,8a). The Targum on this passage quotes God as saying: "Are you [the Ethiopians] not greatly beloved unto me."

Hezekiah made an alliance with Egypt, then ruled by the Twenty-fifth (Ethiopian) Dynasty, and with the support of his ally revolted against Assyria. Isaiah, who called for repentance and faith, objected to this alliance and makes some disparaging remarks about Egypt's help (e.g., Isaiah 30.5, 7) because the Egyptians were men and not God (31.3), but nowhere does he appeal to an ancient curse on Egypt (nor do other prophets who criticize Israel for turning to Egypt or who announce judgment on Egypt, e.g., Hosea 7.11; Jeremiah 2.18; Ezekiel 30). Hezekiah's revolt was not successful, but the Ethiopian general and later pharaoh, Tirhakah, stood by Hezekiah and fought for him (2 Kings 19.9; Isaiah 37.9).

As a result of Hezekiah's alliances with the Twenty-fifth Dynasty of Egypt, close contacts were established between the two peoples. Soon afterwards we find Ethiopians as members of Israelite society and Israelite settlers in Ethiopia. The father of the prophet Zephaniah was an Ethiopian as his name, Cushi, indicates, and Zephaniah's great-great grandfather was (King) Hezekiah of Judah (Zephaniah 1.1). Jehudi, son of Nethaniah, son of Shelemiah, son of Cushi, was a trusted member of King Jehoiakim's cabinet (Jeremiah 36.14, 21, 23). And Jeremiah's life was saved by the royal servant, Ebed-melech, "the Ethiopian" (Jeremiah 38.7-13; 39.15-18). Throughout Israel's history, Egypt and Ethiopia were places of refuge (e.g., Isaiah 11.11; Jeremiah 42–44; Matthew 2.13-15). But for Israelite refugees and converts to the religion of Israel, Zion was their spiritual home and those in foreign lands looked forward to worshipping in Zion. Isaiah 18.7 anticipates the time when gifts will be brought to the Lord by the Ethiopians. So does Zephaniah in 3.10 of his prophecy, and the Psalmist in Psalm 68.31. Psalm 87 pictures such a gathering of pilgrims in Zion, not only from Egypt and Ethiopia, but also from Babylon, Philistia, and Tyre, who all say, "I was born in Zion" (v. 4). And Isaiah 19.23b-25 (CEV) anticipates the time when "The Egyptians and the Assyrians will travel back and forth from Egypt to Assyria, and they will worship together. Israel will join with these two countries ... then the LORD All-Powerful will bless them by saying, 'The Egyptians are my people. I created the Assyrians and chose the Israelites.'" Note also the diverse peoples gathered in Jerusalem at the time of Pentecost (Acts 2.5-11), and the "large crowd ... from every race, tribe, nation, and language" gathered before the throne and the Lamb in Revelation 7.9, 10.

Simon, from the North African city of Cyrene (Matthew 27.32; Mark 15.21; Luke 23.26), was not regarded as unworthy to carry Jesus' cross. Nor did Philip feel obligated to discuss Genesis 9.18-29 with the Ethiopian minister of Queen Candace before baptizing him (Acts 8.26-40).

Origin of the Idea of a Curse on Ham

If there is no basis in the Bible for a curse on Ham, how did this idea originate? It was not until the last quarter of the nineteenth century that biblical scholars convincingly clarified the composite literary character of Genesis. To one unaware of the two traditions of Noah's family and the editorial nature of the references to Ham as the father of Canaan in Genesis 9.18, 22, the offender is obviously Ham. And if Ham is the offender, the inference naturally suggests itself that Ham was also the one cursed. A few manuscripts of the early Greek translation, the Septuagint (ca. 250-100 B.C.), name Ham as the one cursed. Ham is also named as the one cursed in the Arabic version (13th century A.D.). In early rabbinic literature and the writings of the Church Fathers, one occasionally finds references to Ham as affected by Noah's curse. But it was not until the Middle Ages that Jewish, Christian, and Moslem authorities alike began generally to identify Ham as cursed. Luther and Calvin also name Ham as cursed, as well as Canaan. Still, the interpretation of Genesis 9.18-29 during the Middle Ages for the most part was homiletical and moralistic, not intentionally racist. Ham was criticized for his immodesty or for speaking disrespectfully about his father, or for failing to care for his father, or for causing dissension in the family. Nevertheless, the focus on Ham during the Middle Ages helped establish the popular notion that Ham was cursed and made it possible for racists to seize upon this passage and to use it as theological justification for the oppression of African people.

The misunderstanding and abuse of Genesis 9.18-29 illustrate what a responsibility it is to rightly interpret Scripture. The erroneous idea that there is a curse on Ham is not the fault of the Bible. At the least, it is poor exegesis and reflects lack of knowledge of biblical scholarship. Used in a racist sense, this erroneous idea is a reminder of the ingenuity and perversity with which humans find ways to justify to themselves and to others; their sin. However one reads Genesis 9.18-29, it is absolutely clear that there is no basis for a curse on Ham in this passage. The curse is on Canaan and it is because of behavior, not race. And the passage is concerned with political relationships between Israelites,

▸ Detail, Nubians carrying offerings, among them a giraffe. Thebes, tomb of Huy, viceroy of Nubia. Photo credit: Erich Lessing/Art Resource, New York, NY

Canaanites, and Philistines in Canaan in the 10th century B.C., not with Africans or African Americans. Even if the passage is accepted as an organic literary unit speaking with a single, coherent voice, it has nothing to do with race. Read this way, its point is that the behavior of parents may bring a curse on their children. The erroneous idea of a curse on Ham stands in violent conflict with the theological heartbeat of the Bible that we are all sons and daughters of God, that we are all related to one another as members of a family, that each one of us, whatever our race, ethnicity, and nationality, is special and precious to God, and that we were created for companionship with God—and fellowship with one another.

GAMBIA NEGROES.
TO BE SOLD,
On TUESDAY, the 7th of JUNE,
On board the SHIP
MENTOR,
Captain WILLIAM LYTTLETON,
Lying at MOTTE's wharf,
A Cargoe of 156 prime healthy young Negroes, just arrived in said ship from the river Gambia, after a passage of 35 days.
The Negroes from this part of the coast of Africa, are well acquainted with the cultivation of rice, and are naturally industrious.
CONDITIONS of SALE.
To approved purchasers, bonds payable the first of January, 1786, and to those who make immediate payment in cash, rice or any other produce, a proper discount will be made thereon.
ROBERT HAZLEHURST & Co.
No. 44. Bay.

Eight

Slavery in the Ancient Near East and, Particularly, in Israel

Frank L. Gipson

In ancient Israel and the Near East, slavery had a vital role in the household. The household that was successful, having a thriving dynasty and growing wealth, also had slaves. Slaves were an economic sign of strength and political power. The patriarchs, or propertied members of society, and their households were the social paradigm for society. Although a particular deity was acknowledged as the owner of the land and its people, the king or ruler was recognized as an owner of the land and its people as well; his or her subjects and vassals were considered servants of their sovereign. Economically, the mode of production in the ancient Near East, and particularly in monarchic Israel, was tributary. This mode of production was conducive to slavery, owing to the honorific status it gave to conquerors, royalty, and ruling classes at the top of society who, by their status and power, were due tribute in exchange for protection, life, and peace.

◄ Juffureh poster at an exhibition on the slave trade. © Monica Wells PCL/Superstock

Terminology

The Hebrew term for "slave" that often translates as "a male slave" carries a range of meaning from *servant, royal subject, to minister* and even a theological title, such as *Moses, the servant of God.* The terms designating a female slave describe a female servant or a concubine in the household (Genesis 29.24, 29; 30.3; 31.33). Yet, in some references, the terms imply humility in consideration of the lowly and vulnerable status of a female slave (Ruth 3.9; 2 Samuel 14.15). The Hebrew term for *boy, lad,* or *youth* has a secondary meaning of a "young male slave, servant or retainer." This word can describe a household servant (Numbers 22.22; Judges 7.10, 11). As with all the terms the translation of the Hebrew words for "slave" depends upon the context in which they are used.

The Definition

Slavery is when one person or party has ownership over another. It is an institution when such ownership is legal and sanctioned politically as a right and privilege within a given society.

While slavery is not by definition a way of obtaining free labor, it is a means of obtaining labor at little cost, often involving mental coercion, physical force, and without any reasonable and just compensation to the person(s) producing the labor and its byproduct. In slavery, the laborers are owned and their productivity belongs to their owner(s).

In most cases slavery was a perpetual institution in the ancient Near East; e.g., a person who was born into such status would, in most cases, die in that social status. So also, the descendants of the slave remained in their station generation after generation. According to Exodus 21.2, (also Deuteronomy 15.12 and Jeremiah 34.14) however, the servitude of a Hebrew debt-slave was limited to six years.[1] Any act of manumission (release from bondage) was an official one, executed in courts or public forums. In some cases, slaves could purchase their freedom or even that of kin, but technically whatever slaves owned belonged to their masters. This would mean that owners primarily held the right of manumission. There are records of

[1] Barry Lee Eichler. "*Slavery*" *Harper Bible Dictionary*, ed. Paul J. Achtemeier. (San Francisco: Harper, 1985), 959.

owners manumitting slaves and adopting them which would entitle them to an inheritance. In Israel, there was opportunity for one to intervene and redeem a relative from debt slavery or purchase the enslaved relative out of slavery. One could become a slave through various means, such as by capture in battle, punishment for crimes committed, or debt slavery. A family member could sell a person into slavery, as was the case with Joseph, who was sold by his brothers (Genesis 37.12-36). It is well narrated in the Old Testament that the Israelites had been slaves in Egypt (Exodus 13.3, 14; Deuteronomy 5.15; 16.1; 24.18). The Egyptian officials made them slaves in order to contain and control the Israelites' population growth and their political and military potential (Exodus 1.10, 11). Foreigners were slaves in Israel as well.

The general mode of production in ancient Near Eastern societies was tributary, especially in the first and second millennia, B.C. The word "tributary" means that a ruler or country pays a conqueror for protection or peace. Slaves were used as a commodity in this arrangement. The conditions of enslavement accommodated this tributary mode of obtaining labor.

Conditions for Slavery

As a society grows in population and political and economic strength, its needs for labor availability and utilization increase. In human societies, the expansion and development of the production forces are often "due to advances and changes in at least three areas: the geopolitical arrangements; regional specialization of productive activities; and labor availability and utilization."[2] For example, a despot, overlord or nobility maximizes productivity, amasses wealth, and becomes dominant through labor availability and utilization, as well as through the use of military capability and political and class superiority. Slaves and peasants can best supply labor availability and utilization within a tributary mode of production. Slave labor or forced labor aided in producing the great monuments of the ancient Near East, such as palaces, pyramids and temples. Even King Solomon is among the rulers who used forced labor (1 Kings 9.15, 20, 21; 12.4), in part, to build the great temple, the king's palace, and the many shrines for his multitude of foreign wives.

[2] Itumeleng J. Mosala, *Bible Hermeneutics and Black Theology in South Africa.* (Grand Rapids: Wm. B. Eerdmans Publishing Co., 1989), 108.

In the ancient Near East, in places such as Egypt, Asia Minor, Mesopotamia, Achaemenid Iran and Palestine, slavery was an institution that played a major economic role. Within these societies there existed a tributary mode of production wherein the status of the societal majority ranged from peasantry to slavery. A mode of production identifies how labor is produced, how goods are exchanged, and the value given to labor and the goods that are produced. The mode of production is tributary (1) when it subsists upon tributes paid for protection, imposed by a feudal overlord who rules by intimidation, terror, oppression and/or a popular hegemonic ideology, and (2) when the tribute payments determine who is rich or poor and what status societal members hold and inherit.

Furthermore, the prophet Samuel describes this mode of production and links it with the rise of the monarchy (1 Samuel 8.11-18). It is a

▸ Slave trade in Morocco. © Bettman/ Corbis. Used by Permission

political and economic reality where one person maximizes his rule over the many which he, along with the ruling classes, reduces to servants of the state and to slavery. Also, his personage is identified with the spirit of the country he rules; consequently, what is good for him is deemed good for the country and its entire citizenry. This type of dominance over human labor and identity takes its example from the household of the patriarch or propertied member of society. Therefore, a description of the patriarchal household and explanation of slavery practiced therein follows.

Slavery in the Household[3]

Not only did kings, overlords and nobility have slaves, but slavery also existed within the households. Although scholars report that "privately owned slaves functioned more as domestic servants than as an agricultural or industrial labor force,"[4] the household in Israel was a commonwealth wherein such division of labor did not apply.

> The Family (household), in fact, was a Corporation; and he (the patriarch) was its (chief) representative or, we might almost say, its Public officer. He enjoyed rights and stood under duties, but the rights and duties were, in the contemplation of his fellow-citizens (kinsmen and others under his rule) and in the eye of the law, quite as much those of the collective body as his own.[5]

Exodus 20.17 and Deuteronomy 5.21(in the Ten Commandments or Decalogue) describe "your neighbor" or Israelite compatriots to be propertied members of society holding estates. The Ten Commandments were addressed to and for these propertied members of Israelite society. Listed among their properties, which were not to be coveted by another compatriot, are slaves, wives, livestock, and other property. Their households were not nuclear families. Here, and elsewhere, the household appears to be kinship

[3] The present writer's dissertation in progress is on the subject of local authority; from that dissertation the understanding of the patriarchal household presented here is borrowed and developed.

[4] Barry Lee Eichler, "*Slavery,*" *Harper Bible Dictionary,* 959.

[5] Henry S. Maine, "The Primitive Family and the Corporation,"*Readings in Kinship and Social Structure,* ed. Nelson Graburn. (New York: Harper & Row, Publishers, 1971), 11. Here, Maine describes a patriarch in the classical Roman household primarily, yet the description is appropriate for a patriarch within the ancient Israelite household as well.

groups organized into extended families (numbering up to fifty members or more, and may extend over four generations of living relatives), as Leviticus 18.7-16 describes.[6]

However, both the family, as the smallest segment of Israelite society, and extended families are indicated in the Hebrew term for "family." Because the household was the model social unit for all other types, this term can describe a range of social units, such as clan, tribe, and nation. The household it describes is often dynastic in leadership. The eldest son is the rightful heir of its leadership, just as the leadership was inherited in the dynasty of the Davidic monarchy, for example.

Slaves were an important part of the household and their owners did not restrict their work to "domestic" areas. The slave was not left at home while the owner of the house went to engage in agricultural or industrial labor. For example, in Judges 6.27, "Gideon took ten of his servants, and did as the LORD had told him" (*NRSV*). Genesis 32.16 calls Jacob's shepherds "slaves." This point is highly significant when one recognizes that much of Jacob's wealth was in his flocks of sheep and goats. Jacob's slaves managed his wealth. In addition, Genesis 26.15 and 19 describe Abraham's and Isaac's slaves as digging wells to sustain the households and flocks of these patriarchs. Saul's herdsman was an Edomite slave (1 Samuel 21.7). There is also record of "the use of slave labor in cultivating the land (Ruth 2.5; 2 Samuel 9.10)."[7]

The place of slaves was of immense significance in every aspect of Israelite society because, regardless of their status, they were fully functional human persons within the society. For example, in Genesis 16, Sarai gave the Egyptian slave-girl Hagar to Abraham in order to produce an heir. Of course, without an heir, the ancient Near Eastern patriarch and his household would have died out. According to the psalmist, children (sons) were a blessing from the LORD; particularly, they were a great accomplishment and source of strength (Psalm 127.3-5). Hence, Hagar's son, Ishmael, is counted among the descendants of

[6] In a series of injunctions, all sexual contact with individuals related by kin (literally "flesh") are prohibited. Mother, sister, granddaughter, half-sister, paternal aunt, maternal aunt, daughter-in-law, and sister-in-law are listed as illicit sexual partners for a man; father and paternal uncle are prohibited as sexual partners for a woman. The persons mentioned would probably be members of the household unit.

[7] Muhammah A. Dandamayev, "Slavery (OT)" *The Anchor Bible Dictionary, Volume Six, 64.*

Abraham (Genesis 25.9, 12). As recorded in Genesis 17.23, Ishmael was circumcised along with all the male slaves: "Abraham took his son Ishmael and all the slaves born in his house or bought with his money, every male among the men of Abraham's house, and he circumcised the flesh of their foreskins that very day, as God had said to him" (*NRSV*). This inclusion of Abraham's slaves as covenant members demonstrates that their importance was considerable to the patriarch. They were significant members of that household because of their irreducible contributions of vital service on its behalf. Of course, it was not possible for men like Abraham to be a patriarch or propertied member of society without owning slaves and receiving their considerable compliance and assistance.

Clearly, the owner used the slaves to provide whatever was needed or desired for the perceived good of his household. This, of course, is the message found in the story of Joseph (Genesis 39.1-6a). He was among the category of a servant or slave in Potiphar's household, which illustrates, in part, the range of possible roles and status of such a person. Upon Potiphar's purchase, he first became a slave in Potiphar's household. However, his gifts and skills led Potiphar to promote him to increasingly higher levels of status and authority, by which promotions he ultimately became the chief household steward. The status of slave, in this case, is transformed by the roles that Joseph performed. Through his role performance he transcended slavery until he met disfavor (Genesis 39.6b-20). While disfavor degraded his status, he again rebounded and became the chief minister to the Pharaoh of Egypt (Genesis 39.21— 41.57). As the story of Joseph illustrates, through the humility of a slave, Joseph's character transformed him into a savior figure. It is material that Joseph worked within the context of a household, because that is where slavery existed most acutely in the ancient Near East. However, it needs to be emphasized that the household was not a nuclear family but a commonwealth; that is, a corporation that represented a microcosm of society.

In the ancient Near East, slavery was endemic and indispensable in every society or country. If it had not been such, then allowing captives of wars to remain alive and permitting those in egregious debt to sell themselves or relatives into slavery would not have been notable social conventions or viable options. Why capture a kingdom or territory that is not strategically located and/or without the means to pay tribute? Because inexpensive sources of labor were needed, slaves were a socially sanctioned and desirable commodity; and ownership was legally enforced. Slavery was prevalent

▸ Joseph, overseer of pharoah's granaries, ancient Egypt. Courtesy of North Wind Picture Archives

because it was essential to the economic mode of production in every kingdom of the ancient Near East. Among these kingdoms Israel is included, but the difference was that the humanity of the slave was more recognized and respected in Israel.

Ideally, the master of the household was to govern in the best interest of all the members of the household, including the slaves, because they may be all that he could rely on for support, everyday survival, productivity and well being. Without this household, who would provide for him in his old age? If he were sonless, then his male slave might marry his daughter and become his heir, or he might father an heir through a female slave or concubine. Laws were in place to ensure that the highest ethical considerations were accorded slaves. Hence, there were laws that restricted the punishment and abuse that a master could mete out upon slaves (Leviticus 25.46, Deuteronomy 23.15,16, and also Job 31.13-15).

Laws Regarding Slavery

Within the Old Testament, there is a marked distinction between the status of the Israelite and foreign slaves. "Non-Israelite slaves were legally considered movable property of their masters who could dispose of them as they wished."[8]

Nonetheless, every slave was to rest on the Sabbath (Exodus 20.10; 23.12; Deuteronomy 5.14). It was a crime to premeditatedly kill the slave (Exodus 21.20), but if a slave died two days after being beaten by the owner, then the owner escaped without legal penalty. If the owner knocked out a slave's tooth or put out a slave's eye, then the slave was granted freedom to compensate for the loss (Exodus 21.26,27).

In contrast to all the laws of the ancient Near East, "Deuteronomy (23.15,16) forbade the handing over of a fugitive slave who had sought asylum from his owner."[9] In other kingdoms, abetting an escaped slave was a punishable offense; and thus it carried a heavy penalty. Under such laws, slaves remained slaves with no real protection. Slavery, regardless of its benign appearance in some texts, was very cruel and inhumane. During the period of the exile (ca. 587-539 B.C.), this point was made very clear (Isaiah 14.3,4; 47.6; Ezra 9.9). Even in Israelite society slaves were deemed inferior inasmuch as they had to honor their masters (Malachi 1.6).

Conclusion

What the Old Testament reveals about the nature of slavery and its view upon slavery is informative, but the practice of slavery is not a standard for human rights today. Full human rights and equality were not concepts or social values that dominated the Old Testament. As one reads the Old Testament through the eyes of faith, one must be guided by the Torah (law), by the prophets who point to Jesus Christ, and by Jesus Christ himself,

[8] *Ibid.*

[9] *Ibid, 65.*

for true standards of full human rights and equality. Furthermore, the Scriptures (both the Old and New Testaments) are to be interpreted through the life and teaching of Jesus and the on-going work of the Holy Spirit, who is to lead us into all truth.

According to Matthew 5.17-20, *(NRSV)* Jesus said,

> "Do not think that I have come to abolish the law or the prophets; I have come not to abolish but to fulfill. For truly I tell you, until heaven and earth pass away, not one letter, not one stroke of a letter, will pass from the law until all is accomplished. Therefore, whoever breaks one of the least of these commandments, and teaches others to do the same, will be called least in the kingdom of heaven; but whoever does them and teaches them will be called great in the kingdom of heaven. For I tell you, unless your righteousness exceeds that of the scribes and Pharisees, you will never enter the kingdom of heaven."

The remaining verses in chapter 5 (21-48) show the relationship between the Law and Jesus' teachings and reflect Jesus' standard of piety. Jesus came to fulfill the Law and the Prophets. He retells those teachings, but in light of the spirit of the Law so that there are no ethical loopholes. According to Jesus, for example, Moses allowed the bill of divorce because of the hardness of the human heart (Matthew 19.3-9); yet the Israelite custom of giving a bill of divorce was a practice never meant to be. The institution of slavery should be understood from this vantage point. This is the interpretive aim of Jesus' teaching and is the starting point for understanding the issues of slavery and human rights in the ancient Near East and, in particular, Israel. God did not intend for people to be in bondage to others; rather humankind, created in God's image, is created to "have life, and have it abundantly" (John 10.10b, *NRSV*). As children of promise, freedom in Christ "has set us free" (Galatians 5.1, *NRSV*). Slavery is a part of the pollution of sin; and to protect the disenfranchised, God created Jubilee and provided for the emancipation of those who had been in bondage (Leviticus 25.40).

Bibliography

Dandamayev, Muhammad A. "Slavery (ANE and OT)," *The Anchor Bible Dictionary, Volume Six,* ed. David Noel Freedman. New York: Doubleday, 1992.

Eichler, Barry Lee. "Slavery" *Harper Bible Dictionary,* 959, ed. Paul J. Achtemeier. San Francisco: Harper, 1985.

Mosala, Itumeleng J. *Biblical Hermeneutics and Black Theology in South Africa.* Grand Rapids: Wm. B. Eerdmans Publishing Co., 1989.

Maine, Henry S. "The Primitive Family and the Corporation," *Readings in Kinship and Social Structure,* ed. Nelson Graburn. New York: Harper & Row, Publishers, 1971.

Nine

Roman Slavery in Antiquity

Mitzi Jane Smith

Racist ideologies have been sacralized by tendentious interpretations of New Testament references to slaves and slavery. Historically, some have conveniently glossed over the most salient feature distinguishing New World slavery from slavery in antiquity (200 B.C. to 200 A.D.): New Testament slavery was not based on color prejudice. The Romans enslaved prisoners of war and foreigners, uprooting and transplanting them to foreign and hostile communities, which in praxis and in law treated them as "human property." Concessions provided to loyal, obedient slaves, i.e., manumission and "marriage," operated to encourage productive servile behavior and thus to insure the perpetuity of the institution.

◂ Slave markets of ancient Rome. Courtesy of North Wind Picture Archives.

> I had no rod wherewith to smite the stream, and thereby divide the waters. I had no Moses to go before me and lead the way from bondage to a promised land. . . . I thought of the fishes of the water, the fowls of the air, the wild beasts of the forest, all appeared to be free, to go just where they pleased, and I was an unhappy slave.
>
> —Henry Bibb, *former slave*[1]

When African Americans encounter biblical texts about slaves, it is difficult for us to dismiss mental pictures of slaves in Roman antiquity as persons of African descent who by divine decree happily and contentedly served their masters. Pro-slavery advocates have distorted history and manipulated biblical texts from the Pauline corpus (i.e., 1 Corinthians and Philemon) and from the Deutero-Pauline epistles (i.e., 1 Timothy, Colossians and Ephesians) to undergird racist ideologies that have sanctioned the enslavement of Africans in America. As a youngster, Howard Thurman read the Psalms, Isaiah and the Gospels to his grandmother, an illiterate former slave, but she forbade him to read to her from the Pauline epistles. She later explained to him the reasons for her dislike of these Pauline passages:

> During the days of slavery . . . the master's minister would occasionally hold services for the slaves. Old man McGhee was so mean that he would not let a Negro minister preach to his slaves. Always the white minister used as his text something from Paul. At least three or four times a year he used as a text: "Slaves, be obedient to them that are your masters... as unto Christ." Then he would go on to show how it was God's will that we were slaves and how, if we were good and happy slaves, God would bless us. I promised my Maker that if I ever learned to read and if freedom ever came, I would not read that part of the Bible.[2]

The significance of Roman slavery in antiquity to the American slavery debate is apparent in Josiah Priest's 1851 defense of slavery in which he justified slavery based on racist presuppositions about Roman slavery and the fallacious curse of Ham theory. (See Section Two: "The Alleged Curse on Ham," by Gene Rice.) Priest wrote:

> . . . for the *Romans*, who were also the descendants of Japheth [white race], as well as all the Grecian tribes and nations,

bought and sold negroes, even down to the time of the apostles, and for many ages after; by thousands and millions.[3]

Priest depicted Roman slavery as the enslavement of "negroes" and asserted that biblical slavery was analogous to and prescriptive for the enslavement of Africans in America. Conversely, Rev. Charles Elliott in his *The Bible and Slavery* (1851) analyzed Pauline biblical references to slaves in the historical context of Roman slavery, and concluded that "Christian slaves are bound . . . to do their utmost to be free" and that the Bible condemns slavery.[4]

African Americans, with spiritual tenacity and steadfast faith in God, have responded to racist interpretations of Scripture and one-sided accounts of history with both a hermeneutic of suspicion and a hermeneutic for liberation. The suspicions and spiritual tenacity of African Americans, and others, have stirred renewed investigations of biblical texts and historical contexts in order to uncover and recover liberating truths about God and slavery.

This article represents such an uncovering and provides a glimpse of slavery in Roman antiquity (ca. 200 B.C. to 200 A.D.).[5] Roman slavery is a necessary socio-historical context for understanding biblical texts that are traditionally used to corroborate the modern practice of slavery. As a social institution, Roman slavery uprooted and socially marginalized slaves, subjugating them to the lowest level of society. Slaves in antiquity were treated subhumanly and juridically categorized as property. Slave resistance existed alongside slaveowners' attempts to placate slaves with concessions designed to promote the servile behavior necessary to perpetuate the institution. The most salient feature that distinguished Roman slavery from American slavery was that Roman slavery was not racially motivated in the modern sense of the term. Although this is not a comparative study, the reader will recognize similarities and differences between American slavery and Roman slavery. While it is impossible to provide here a thorough overview of Roman slavery, I have attempted a provocative treatment of specific aspects of Roman slavery. I briefly cover the following topics: (1) slave ideology: Aristotle and Stoicism; (2) the acquisition and nationality of slaves; (3) the treatment of slaves; (4) slave resistance; and (5) the manumission or freedom of slaves. Finally, I provide brief comments on 1 Corinthians 7.21 and Philemon.

While African American slave narratives and testimonies relate the experience of slavery from the slave's perspective, slavery in antiquity left few, if any, biographies or autobiographies. Historians rely on epigraphs or inscriptions, the works of Greek and Roman historians and writers, Roman law, and Egyptian papyri for information about slavery in antiquity. Thus, the information available is from the slave owner's point of view. We know little of what it was like to be a slave in antiquity from the slave's perspective.

I. Roman Slavery

1. Slave Ideology

Aristotle. The Romans inherited the slave trade from the Greeks and the Phoenicians.[6] Greek ideas of slavery preceded, and to some extent influenced, Roman slave ideology. The Greek philosopher Aristotle (384-322 B.C.) propounded a classical view of "natural slavery." In his *Politica*, Aristotle asserted that nature intended for some persons to be slaves and others to be masters. Masters were born to rule and slaves were born to be in subjection. From the relationship between man and woman and master and slave, the family developed. Thus, a complete household consisted of slaves and freepersons. In the family structure, a slave existed as a "living possession," and as such he took "precedence of all other instruments." Slaves were instruments of action for maintaining life—the life of the family and the state. The slave belonged "wholly" to the master. He was a human being and a possession. (This concept is similar to the chattel nature of slavery that was practiced in the American South.) Nature normally blessed slaves with strong bodies that were suited for labor but the freedmen's bodies were fit for political life. However, sometimes nature messed up and the opposite occurred. Since slaves are inferior to their superiors, it was best for them to be under the rule of masters.[7] Natural slave theory neither originated nor ended with Aristotle, but he "was undoubtedly the high priest of natural slave theory, he elaborated it, and it was his canonical version which reverberated down the ages."[8]

Stoicism. The Stoics believed that all men shared a common logos or reason (rationality). All human beings were slaves in the sense that all persons had masters. The Roman writer Seneca (ca. 4 B.C. to 65 A.D.), a stoic, former slave, and slave owner, referred to slaves as "fellow slaves (*conservi*)," for "Fortune has equal rights over slaves and free men alike."[9] Slaves originate from the "same stock," are "smiled upon by the same skies," breathe, live, and die just as do other humans.[10] Human beings acquire character, "but accident assigns his duties."[11] The Stoics moralized slavery. The physical condition of slavery was of no consequence. A slave may possess a soul of a free person and vice versa. All persons are slaves to something — to lust, greed or ambition; all persons are slaves to fear (*timori*).[12] The Stoic theme of universality, i.e., all humans came from the same source, "sits uneasily with the notion of natural slaves and natural masters, which rests on the principle that the human race is not a unity, but includes a category of subhumans, and subrational people."[13] Stoicism, a minority position, preceded and existed contemporaneously with Christianity, but the full extent of its influence upon Christian thought is not certain.

Roman Slave Ideology: Person or Property? The Romans possessed no slave law *per se*, but laws that addressed slavery were incorporated within their *Corpus Iuris Civilis* (Body of Civil Law). One can gain only an impression of Roman slave ideology from Roman law. Generally, persons were categorized as either "free" or "slaves." Roman law defined slavery as "an institution of the law of all peoples; it makes a man the property (*dominio*) of another, *contrary to the law of nature*" (emphasis mine).[14] Contrary to Aristotle, Roman law stated that persons were not slaves by nature. The legal impression is that slaves are human property. Noted historian, M. I. Finley asserts that "[a]s a commodity, the slave is property," and the slave's human status is irrelevant, merely revealing that "he is a peculiar property."[15] Orlando Patterson offers a more vivid characterization of slavery in general: "slavery is the . . . violent domination of naturally alienated and generally dishonored persons" (emphasis Patterson's).[16] Patterson addresses the ambiguities inherent in the fact that slavery coexisted with other property relationships. The ownership of people as property extended to a number of relationships, including husband and wife.[17] Slavery must be understood as a "social institution" that tied master to slave and represented one of many asymmetrical relationships in Roman society.[18] Much like Aristotle's model, slaves as members of the *familia* or household represented the lowest property relationship to the master/father or *paterfamilias*.

2. *The Acquisition and Nationality of Roman Slaves*

According to Roman law, slaves, in Latin *servi*, are so called because it is the practice of army commanders to order captives to be sold and thus saved . . . instead of killed. Another Latin word for slaves is *mancipia,* derived from the fact that they are captured by hand from the enemy, in Latin *manu capiuntur.* They are either born slaves or enslaved afterwards. The off-spring of slave women are born slaves.[19]

Relatives or other persons could ransom captured foreigners to prevent their enslavement or murder. Thus, if not ransomed, the only alternative for the captured foreigner, short of death, was slavery. Warfare was a constant source, but *not* the only source, of slave supply throughout the central period. The Romans generally maintained the slave population by "a combination of complementary sources, warfare, trade and breeding, each of which was a constant contributor but of fluctuating relative significance . . ."[20] *Vernae* (children born to slave women) and war captives served as "mutually supportive strategies."[21] Given the demand for slaves and the effect of frequent manumissions and deaths (infant and maternal) upon the slave pool, no single source could have sufficed as a means of replenishment. Some are of the opinion that after the *Pax Romana of* 27 B.C. under Augustus, warfare ceased to be a significant source of slave supply; however, this is not the case.[22] The Jewish historian Josephus relates how the city of Japha was destroyed by the Romans under Vespasian and "the number of the slain, both now in the city and at the former fight, was fifteen thousand, and the captives were two thousand one hundred and thirty." [23] Another war under Vespasian resulted in the enslavement of 30,400 Jews, notwithstanding that "six thousand of the strongest" were sent to Nero to "dig through the Isthmus."[24] The prisoners of war or foreigners captured by the Romans included women and children, as well as men.

In addition to warfare and children born to slave women, the Romans acquired slaves by means of piracy, kidnapping (brigandage), infant exposure (the abandonment and sale of infants into slavery), and family members sold into slavery because of poverty. While the means of acquisition of slaves can be stated with certainty, the specific nationality of the slaves cannot. One would expect that slave names would be a reliable means of determining a slave's nationality, but it is difficult to ascertain a slave's nationality or race by virtue of nomenclature (naming of slaves). Slave nomenclature became Graeco-Romanized:

> The typical slave of the early empire belonged to neither east nor west: he was a product of Graeco-Roman civilisation [sic],

> an example of Rome's strange power of absorbing and assimilating aliens. His name was Greek or Roman; his speech, Latin;... He lost the great gifts of nationality, its inheritances and inspirations, its vigorous creativeness, its unique, individual quality; but he also escaped the limitations of race and tradition . . ."[25]

The following factors contribute to the difficulty of determining a slave's nationality based on nomenclature: A slave who retained her/his native name likely retained it in a Latinized or Graecized form; Greek was the language of the slave trade, and slaves could conceivably be given Greek names for ease of pronunciation; masters could arbitrarily rename slaves as they pleased; vernae (home born slaves) were likely named by their masters; early nomenclature reflected the master's identity rather than the identity of the slave; names sometimes indicated the physical and moral qualities of the "ideal slave."[26] "The nationality of the slave mattered little, so long as his physical strength sufficed for the most exacting work. (Syrians, for example, were proverbially strong)."[27] Despite the assimilation of names, it remains that the slaves were a highly heterogeneous group. The slave population consisted of many nationalities, including "Phrygians, Cappadocians, Syrians, Jews, Egyptians, Ethiopians, Numidians, Spaniards, Gauls, Germans, Thracians and Greeks."[28] With few exceptions, Romans generally were not enslaved because the slave was an "outsider" and "the earliest Roman law code explicitly provided that if a Roman were subject to enslavement as a punishment, he had to be sold abroad . . ."[29]

Although slavery in antiquity was not racially motivated in the modern sense of the term, some Romans appear to have believed that certain nationalities were more suitable for slavery than others, which is reminiscent of Aristotle's natural slave law. The Roman orator Livy (ca. 59 B.C. to 17 A.D.) wrote:

> . . . the different kinds of weapons, the many names of unheard-of peoples, Dahae and Medes and Cadusians and Elymaeans—these were all Syrians, far better fitted to be slaves, on account of their servile dispositions, than to be a race of warriors.[30]
>
> There were Macedonians and Thracians and Illyrians, all most warlike nations, here Syrians and Asiatic Greeks, the most worthless peoples among mankind and born for slavery (*servituti*).[31]

Nevertheless, Roman slave society was not racialized, that is one's nationality was not deemed superior or inferior to another because of the complexion of one's skin.

The slave's new and strange position in the family structure of Roman society required loyalty and obedience to the master's every whim and fancy. The slave's sole purpose was to please his/her master for the benefit of family and society.

3. The Treatment of Slaves

Slaves were integrated into the social structure of the Roman family hierarchy of father/master, mother, children, and slaves. According to the household codes (*Haustafeln*), the father of the family (*paterfamilias*) was entitled to complete submission by the other members of the household.[32] The slave was the lowest member of the family, and his/her purpose was to sustain and maintain the family by performing any or all tasks assigned to him/her by the master of the house.

Slaves were relegated to one of two categories according to the tasks they performed: *Rustici* referred to agricultural slaves who resided in the rural districts of the *polis* (city) and performed duties associated with the maintenance of the land. The *urbani* or domestic slaves generally lived in the households of the city districts of the *polis* and performed tasks necessary for the upkeep of the family and household. The vast majority of slaves were *rustici* who lived "in relative seclusion, at subsistence or near subsistence level" with few prospects for social mobility.[33] Whether slaves were categorized as a *rustici* or *urbani* depended solely on the type of job they performed and not where they lived. Slaves performed precise and diversified tasks. A rural slave could function as a ploughman, shepherd, herdsman, pruner, hunter, tracker, overseer (*vilicus*), maidservant, steward, potter, doorkeeper, sweeper, furniture supervisor, gardener, vilicus' wife, poultry fattener, pig breeder, agent, and provisions keeper. A domestic slave could be a water-carrier, silversmith, furniture polisher, pet child, secretary, doctor, supervisor of doctors, wetnurse, servant in charge of ceremonial dress, cook, footman, clothes mender, masseuse, servant in charge of pictures, oculist, architect, surgeon, waiter, singer, food-taster and tailor. Military service was the only occupation in Roman society off limits to slaves. Slaves could move from one job to another of greater responsibility during their lifetimes; conversely, a slaveowner could demote a slave.

Occupational hierarchy existed among domestic slaves within the urban households as well as between rural and urban slaves, the former being inferior to the latter. Diversity served to disperse and not to unite the slave population.[34]

Whether a master dealt with an urban or rural slave, his overall motives were the same. The slaveowner concerned himself with what was advantageous for the slave only if by so doing he was benefitted as well.[35] Any humane or inhumane treatment of slaves always had the ultimate physical and economic well being of the master in mind. Slaveowning served to constantly "validate and enhance the status of those who were free."[36] Seneca advised that if slaves were treated as men, rather than cruelly and inhumanely, they would readily "bare their necks for their master, to bring upon their own heads any danger that threatened him; they spoke at the feast, but kept silence during torture."[37]

▸ Pompeian ladies with their slave hairdresser, wall painting from Herculaneum, Italy, Museo Archeologico Nazionale, Naples, Italy. Photo credit: Erich Lessing/ Art Resource, New York, NY

Columella (middle late to first century A.D.), the famous agriculturalist, advised that *rustici* (rural slaves) should be cared for and clothed to enhance their "usefulness" and not their appearance. Slaves' clothing should keep them "fortified against wind, cold, and rain" so that no matter how "unbearable" the weather, they might be able to work in the field uninterrupted. The overseer (*vilicus*), himself a slave, is not to resort to cruelty but is to keep the slaves in line by "strict enforcement of labor," for slaves "when smarting under cruelty and greed . . . are more to be feared." Female slaves who are "unusually prolific" and bear a certain number of children are to be rewarded with "exemption from work and sometimes even freedom after they reared many children." If a mother had three sons, she would be exempted from work; for more than three sons she might be given her freedom. Such concessions would contribute to the profitability of the estate.[38]

Slaveowners attempted to achieve the optimum usefulness from their slaves through positive concessions or benefits (*beneficium*). The rewards for slave loyalty (*fides*) and obedience (*obsequium*) ranged from permission to enter into a *de facto* marriage to the promise of manumission.

Roman law prohibited slaves from entering into legally binding contracts. Therefore, slaves could not legally marry or make a last will and testament.[39] Nevertheless, slaveowners dangled before slaves the prospects for a semblance of married life to encourage the desired level of production and profitability. *De facto* marriages or *contubernium* often served as positive concessions for slave loyalty and obedience. *Contubernium* denoted the "dwelling together" of soldiers or animals, but referred especially to the quasi-marital and illegal union between two slaves or a slave and a free person. *Contubernium* as a "factual situation" existed only by permission of the slaveowner who reserved the "right to separate slave family members, and commonly did so."[40]

It must be noted that regardless of a slave's "marital status," slaves, male and female, were constantly subjected to sexual exploitation. Slaves were answerable "with their bodies," which meant that slaveowners had unrestricted access to slave bodies for sexual exploitation.[41] Slave dealers often catered to the sexual desires and demands of slaveowners for homosexual partners, and the practice of castrating young male slaves confirms that slaves were the "object of capricious sexual abuse."[42] Seneca, writing of the ill-treatment of slaves, relates how a slave whose task it was to serve wine had to "dress like a woman" and was forced to "remain awake throughout the night, dividing his time between his master's drunkenness and his lust; in the chamber he must be a man, at the feast a boy."[43] Not only did slaveowners exploit slaves for their own gratification (young girls and boys were purchased expressly to serve as sexual partners), but male and female slaves were forced into prostitution for as long as a master determined.[44]

Slaveowners often permitted slaves the privilege of access to *peculium.* Peculium referred to property and assets at the slave's disposal, such as cash, land, clothing, and other slaves. Peculium could be placed in the slave's possession for the purpose of conducting business transactions for the master. If a slave were offered his freedom in exchange for a sum of money (*statuliber*), the slave could use his/her peculium to pay the fee.[45] Since slaves could not own property, the peculium legally belonged to the slaveowner, but in practice it belonged to the slave.

It is of critical significance that the slaveowner's failure to "exercise all his rights over his slave-property was always a unilateral act on his part, never binding, always revocable."[46] The slaveowner could renege on any concession, including the promise of manumission.

In addition to positive concessions, slaveowners used negative reinforcement to maintain servile relations and to achieve optimum profitability from their slaves. Negative reinforcement ranged from flogging to murder. The flogging of slaves was ubiquitous and apparently required little justification.[47] Some slaveowners are said to have inflicted their slaves with 300 lashes if they were "slow in bringing the hot water."[48] Seneca admits that "we Romans are excessively haughty, cruel, and insulting" in the treatment of slaves.[49]

Cases of "extreme cruelty" by masters have been documented. One must bear in mind that it was the slaveowner who determined what constituted extreme cruelty. One recorded instance involved a friend of Emperor Augustus, Vedius Pollio, who "was allowed to punish his slaves by throwing them into his fishpond as food for his lampreys with complete impunity."[50] Slaves and criminals were regularly forced to fight against other gladiators and with wild beasts in the arena.[51]

The Romans enacted laws apparently aimed at improving the abusive nature of slavery. The Emperor Claudius declared that all sick slaves who were abandoned and survived would be freed rather than returned to their masters; if the master killed the slave instead of abandoning him/her, then he would be liable for homicide. Vespasian (emperor A.D. 69-79) passed a law that a female slave would be freed if forced into prostitution after being purchased under the condition that she would not be subjected to prostitution. Hadrian (emperor A.D. 117-138) decreed that a slaveowner could not arbitrarily kill a slave; a slave must be found deserving of death by the courts. A slave could only be sold to fight as a gladiator for good cause shown. If a slaveowner was murdered by one of his slaves, only those slaves who were "near enough to notice anything" could be questioned under torture. Antonius (emperor A.D. 138-161) declared that a master's power over his slaves must remain "unimpaired," but it is in the master's interest for slaves to be permitted relief from "cruelty" and "intolerable wrong," of course, "with just cause shown." Slaves found to have been "treated more harshly than is just" were to be sold to another owner.[52] Keith Bradley cautions that "[t]he arbitrary physical abuse of slaves cannot be said to have been dramatically alleviated by legislation of an improving kind;" lower social categories were discriminated against with regard to the application of punishment.[53] One must also bear in mind that the court officials who decided whether a slaveowner's treatment of his slave was "intolerable" were most likely slaveowners themselves and members of the higher social order, thus their decisions would not be without bias.

4. Slave Resistance

Slaves responded to the conditions of slavery in a variety of ways. Slave resistance ranged from less extreme incidents of lying, cheating, stealing, feigning sickness, working at a slow pace, petty sabotage and running away to violent acts of suicide and homocide.[54] Dio Chrysostom (ca. 40/50 A.D. to after 110 A.D.) reported that slave women (doulas) destroyed their own children before and after birth, sometimes in collusion with their husbands so as "'not [to] be involved in trouble by being compelled to raise children in addition to their enduring slavery.'"[55]

There is evidence that slaves sometimes resorted to murdering their masters. One incident involved a city prefect, Lucius Pedanius Secundus, who was murdered by one of his slaves possibly because Secundus either reneged on an agreed upon manumission price or because of rivalry in a homosexual relationship involving the slave.

In any case, Secundus' 400 slaves, women and children included, were sentenced to death because they failed to prevent the murder of their master. Gaius Cassius, a member of the senate, representing a majority opinion, declared that there was no excuse for the slaves not to have protected Secundus from death. The slaves should have suspected something or noticed "antecedent symptoms" of the crime. The slaves' failure to protect their master showed that they were not fearful for their own lives. "So long as our slaves disclose them [threats of violence and murder against masters], we may live solitary amid their numbers, secure amid their anxieties, and finally–if die we must–certain of our vengeance amid the guilty crowd." Slaves must be coerced to protect their masters by means of "terror."[56]

Slaves often resorted to running away. Escape was a direct form of resistance and a rejection of subjugation.[57] These runaways showed the inability of some slaves to endure the degradation of slavery and the uncertainty of manumission. Some slaveowners used every means to retrieve a fugitive, including the help of friends and associates, public advertisements, public officials, diviners and professional "slave catchers" (*fugitivarii*).[58] The fact that runaway slaves tried to pass as free persons serves as a reminder that "Roman slavery had no association with skin colour."[59] Fugitives could be successful in creating a new life for themselves. Their "success depended on . . . a suitable moment for departure, the ability to elude detection and to find safe refuge, . . . the capacity to cover terrain and to survive independently."[60] Fugitives were constantly exposed to the dangers of recapture no matter how great the distance achieved between master and slave and the amount of time lapsed since the escape.[61] Slave resistance served as a constant reminder that Roman slaves were by no means content with their servile status even though manumission was a legal possibility.

5. The Manumission of Slaves: Freed at Last?

There were three formal ways to manumit a slave that simultaneously conferred Roman citizenship on the freedman/freedwoman: (1) by *vindicta* (or rod) in which the owner declared his intention before the appropriate magistrate; (2) by census in which the slave was enrolled on the census list of Roman citizens by the owner's permission (taking of census was largely abandoned after 166 B.C.); and (3) by last will and testament. The *lex Fufia Caninia* (2 B.C.) required that the specific names of slaves to be manumitted must appear in the will, and it limited the number of slaves that could be manumitted at one time. A person who owned 3 to10 slaves could manumit up to one-half of his slaves; 11 to 30, one-third; 31 to 100, one-fourth; 101 to 500, one-fifth; no one could manumit more than 100 slaves at one time. An owner of less than two slaves had full freedom of manumission.[62]

The informal methods of manumission, by letter and *inter amicos* (among friends or witnesses), did not grant Roman citizenship but conferred the inferior Junian Latin status. Some slaveowners probably preferred the informal methods of manumission because it meant greater succession rights for the former master. For instance, if a freedman with full Roman citizenship died testate and at least three freeborn children survived, the patron (former master) was excluded from any access to the freedman's inheritance. But the inheritance of a freedperson with Junian Latin status would pass to the patron's heirs, since the freedman Latin's heirs were excluded from succession.[63]

The *lex Aelia Sentia* (4 A.D.) established age requirements for manumission. A slave could not be manumitted under age 30 except by *vindicta* for good cause shown before a *consilium* (council), and the master must be at least 20 years of age to manumit a slave, except by *vindicta* for good cause shown.[64] It is instructive that the life expectancy at birth of the slave was likely not more than 20 years. Thirty years was a far more advanced age than in modern times.[65] Even if a slave lived to the age of 30, this alone did not guarantee manumission—all powers of manumission rested with the master.

There existed no Roman laws that restricted manumission by virtue of race or nationality. The nationality of the slave was not a determinant for manumission and the nationality of the freedwoman/mother did not delimit the status of her freeborn child.

In theory manumission nullified the slave's former relationship with the slaveowner. Roman citizenship, which accompanied formal manumission, bestowed legal and political rights on the freedperson, and any children born to the freedwoman thereafter acquired the social status of freeborn children. However, legal obligations (*operae*) continued to bind freedpersons and women to their former masters. Under these obligations, the freedpersons were to perform certain services for a specific amount of time. Although the slave as a freedperson entered a higher social category, the master did not experience severe economic loss.[66]

The new relationship was formed with the former slave as the client of the patron (the former master). Theoretically, this new relationship was to be characterized by mutual respect. If a freedperson's patron (former owner) fell into poverty, the freedperson was expected to support the patron. Any delinquency in performing services due to the patron could result in punishment or even a return to slavery.[67] Freedpersons were expected to retain their freedom by "the same obedience (*obsequium*) which [he/she] had earned it," and "notorious offenders" "deserved to be brought back to their bondage (*servitutem*), so that fear might coerce those whom kindness had not reformed."[68] Manumission was subject to restrictions and could be revoked.

Although manumission occurred frequently, the great majority of slaves "especially those who were engaged in menial, non-domestic tasks, probably had no realistic hope of changing their status."[69] The promise of manumission was reserved as a reward for loyalty and obedience. The hope of freedom, while regularly available to all slaves, like other incentives was another means to exploit and regulate the behavior of slaves.[70] However, most of the "servile population probably never achieved freedom at all."[71]

Slavery was ubiquitous and pervasive in Roman society. Slaves, as foreigners, were forced to contribute to the social and economic well being of a society that deemed them unworthy of participation in that society. This exploitation, however, was indiscriminate in that the Romans did not enslave persons based on nationality or skin color. A slave's nationality neither delimited his/her access to the benefits proffered to obedient and loyal slaves, nor did it increase the incidence of exploitation and abuse. While slaveowners in antiquity at times treated slaves humanely, such treatment was economically motivated. Widespread and constant resistance existed in spite of the constant dangling of concessions before slaves to encourage servile behavior. Slave resistance testifies to the unbearable nature of the institution. The most coveted benefit, freedom, was restricted, uncertain and often withheld. When a slaveowner did grant manumission, a "new" servile relationship awaited the former slave, one which required loyalty and obedience to the former master, now his patron, for as long as life should continue. Although a slaveowner might celebrate the manumission of a slave, it did not always represent a personal Jubilee for the slave. Besides, the master could celebrate with the assurance that the freedperson's place had already been filled by another slave.

▸ The Forum was Rome's religious, political, and business center. Courtesy of American Bible Society Archives, New York, NY

II. Hermeneutical Considerations

A Note on 1 Corinthians 7.21

> Were you called when you were a slave? Do not let it worry you. But if you are provided with the opportunity to become a freedperson (*eleutheros*), then [certainly] make use (*mallon chrésai*) [of the opportunity to become a freedperson].

1 Corinthians 7.21 is one of the most controversial passages in the New Testament. Translations of the text in which Paul advises the slave to remain a slave have been used to provide divine sanction for the enslavement of Africans in America. Unfortunately, most readers, especially African Americans, have not had access to translations that depict Paul as advising the slaves to make use of the opportunity to become freedpersons. I will briefly address the general context of 1 Corinthians 7.21 (verses 1-16), the immediate context (verses 17-20), and the interpretation of the text itself.

The General Context of 1 Corinthians

Pauline Christian groups consisted of individuals from various social categories, including men and women, freeborn persons, freedpersons, and slaves.[72] The Corinthian group was no different in this respect. The New Testament city of Corinth was a Roman colony whose first settlers were mostly freedpersons.[73] While Paul is addressing a heterogeneous group, quite a number of them either had experienced slavery or were slaves. 1 Corinthians 7 is Paul's response to a letter he received from the Corinthian group requesting advice about specific concerns relating to male and female relationships in the world (7.1).

Paul's first advice is to husbands and wives so that they might avoid sexual immorality (7.2). Each one is to have their own husband or wife. Each party is to make sure the other receives their conjugal rights within the marriage; one partner should not withhold their affections from the other partner. Paul, however, provides an exception to this rule: Husband and wife may deprive one another of their conjugal rights but only by agreement and for the purpose of engaging in prayer (v. 5). Paul admits that everyone is not like him, presumably single and celibate, because everyone does not have the same gift (*charisma*) as God has given to him (v. 7). Paul sets down a rule and then provides an exception to the rule, and he continues this pattern in the following verses.

Next Paul advises the unmarried and the widows (vv. 8,9). The general rule is that they should "remain unmarried." The exception to the rule is: "But if" they lack self-control, then they should get married.

The third category to whom Paul offers advice is wives who are contemplating leaving their husbands (vv. 10, 11). Husbands and wives are not to separate. The exception to the rule is: "But if" the wife does leave her husband, she should not remarry and should eventually reconcile with her husband.

Finally, Paul offers his own personal advice to the "rest," those marriages in which one spouse is an unbeliever (vv. 12-16). The rule is that a believing spouse should not divorce his/her unbelieving spouse if the unbelieving spouse consents to stay in the marriage relationship. The exception is, "But if," the unbeliever leaves, so be it. The believing spouse is not bound to the marriage once the unbeliever leaves the marriage. Paul's advice is based on the fact that God has called (*kekléken*) the Corinthians to peace (v. 15). The objective is to live in the peace that God has called one.

Verses 17-20. The "golden rule" for all four situations is that each one is to live in the assignment in which God has called them (v. 17). This is the rule among the churches (*ekklésias*) (v.17). The Greek word translated "assigned" is *emerisen* (_m_risen) from the root word *merizo* meaning to divide or apportion. It is used two other times in the Pauline corpus, Romans 12.3 and 2 Corinthians 10.13. In Romans 12.3 Paul admonishes the saints not to think more highly of themselves than they ought to but to think soberly "according to the measure of faith that God has *assigned* you." The verses that follow Romans 12.3 refer to God's giving of spiritual gifts in the Church. Paul is obviously referring to a spiritual gift or grace from God, a spiritual endowment and not a social status. In defense of his apostolic ministry, Paul asserts in 2 Corinthians 10.13 that "we, however, will not boast beyond limits, but will keep within the field that God has assigned to us, to reach out even as far as you." Paul is referring to his evangelistic mission to the Gentiles as a "field that God has assigned." This assignment he received from God (Galatians 1.11).

The word translated "called" in 1 Corinthians 7.17 is *kekléken,* the perfect form of *kaleo* meaning "to call." Allan Callahan notes that when Paul speaks of those who are called he does not refer to one's social or religious position in the world.[74] Paul uses another form of *kaleo* at 1 Corinthians 1.9, the Corinthians were "called into the fellowship of his son, Jesus Christ our Lord." Nowhere in Paul's writings does he refer to marriage as a gift from God. God has called the Corinthians into fellowship with Jesus Christ and this is a free gift.

Paul now provides examples for the advice he has given. Paul admonishes one who is circumcised not to try to "remove the marks" (v. 18) and one who is not circumcised to "seek circumcision." But on the other hand, "Circumcision is nothing and uncircumcision is nothing; but obeying the commandments of God is everything" (v. 20). Paul follows the same pattern here that he has in the preceding verses by setting a rule and then introducing an exception to the rule. It seems apparent that Paul's point is that what is important is that one maintains one's relationship of obedience to God. In verse 20 when Paul says "Let each of you remain in the condition in which you were called," he is referring to a relationship of fellowship with Jesus Christ, which is freely "assigned." Whether one decides to remain celibate, marry or separate, one should remain true to the fellowship to which you were called in Jesus Christ by being obedient to his commandments. It seems that Paul's intention is to clarify the position he has taken that social status does not affect one's calling.

Paul's Admonition to Slaves: 1 Corinthians 7.21

"Were you called when you were a slave? Do not let it worry you" (v. 21a). While Paul's slave example serves the same purpose as his circumcision example, the examples are not without dissimilarities. Circumcision is normally a voluntary act which is physically irreversible. Circumcision is permanent. As we have shown above, slavery in the Graeco-Roman Empire was not necessarily a permanent, irreversible condition. When manumitted by formal means, a slave became a Roman citizen. (There also existed means by which an informally manumitted slave could achieve citizenship.) Manumission was a frequent occurrence, the promise of which was a combination of humanitarian gestures and exploitation to perpetuate servile behavior in those who remained in slavery. As evidenced by the constant widespread slave resistance, slaves, like anyone else, wanted to be free. To say otherwise would be to deny their humanity. Paul is not saying be happy in your servile status, but he is saying your slave status does not deny you access to the gifts and participation in the calling of God. Paul asserts that, "There is no longer Jew or Greek, there is no longer slave or free, there is no longer male and female; for all of you are one in Christ Jesus" (Galatians 3.28), and he maintains that "in the one Spirit we were all baptized into one body—Jews or Greeks, slaves or free—and we were all made to drink of one Spirit" (1 Corinthians 12.13). Paul is reassuring the slaves of their place and equality in the body. Vincent Wimbush asserts that Paul is saying that worldly status does not "determine status with God," and Paul provides this advice to "counter what Paul took to be the Corinthians' antiworldly understanding of Christian existence."[75]

"But if you are provided with the opportunity to become a freedperson (*eleutheros*), **then [certainly] make use (*mallon chrésai*) [of the opportunity to become a freedperson]**" (v. 21b). The second half of verse 21b presents the challenge. I have translated the subordinate clause emphatically. This represents the translation of only two Greek words, *mallon chrésai. Mallon* literally means "rather," and *chrésai* is the aorist middle imperative form of the deponent verb *chraomai* meaning "to make use of." The problem is that the Greek text does not supply a subject with which to complete the subordinate clause. So what is it that the slave is to make use of, freedom or slavery? J. Albert Harrill analyzes the text in the context of chapter 7, its social-historical context, and also provides a philological analysis (comparison with analogous literature). He asserts that *mallon* with *chraomai* carries the adversative sense with respect to the previous apodosis, "do not worry about it."[76] The slave is not to dismiss any opportunity to become freed, but to take advantage of freedom. Paul was obviously referring to the achievement of a concrete legal status, for in v. 22 he uses the proper juridical designation, "freedman" (*apeleutheros*).

Paul is consistent with his rule and exception pattern established in the previous verses. "[T]he context does not exclude the 'use freedom' interpretation . . . To the contrary, this reading naturally fits Paul's argumentative and rhetorical structure in 1 Corinthians 7 of granting particular exceptions to general principles."[77] As a rule, if you were a slave when you were called, do not worry about it. Conversely, the exception is but if you can become free, take advantage of the opportunity to become a freedperson.

A Note on Philemon

Traditional scholarship has bequeathed to us a conservative reading of Philemon as the story of the "runaway-slave—Onesimus." Onesimus is said to have found refuge with the Apostle Paul who himself is in bondage. After Onesimus has benefitted from Paul's ministry, Paul sends him back to his master Philemon. Onesimus has been so stigmatized as the "runaway-slave" of Philemon, that it is difficult for many to read the text with an untainted and open mind. However, in the text itself there is nothing that conclusively warrants labeling Onesimus as a runaway, and it is questionable as to whether he is even a slave. The major evidence used by most scholars to call Onesimus a slave is the phrase in verse 16. Philemon is to receive Onesimus "no longer as a slave but above a slave, [as] a beloved brother *(ouketi hos doulon all' hyper doulon, adelphon agapāton).*"

If we presume that Onesimus was a runaway slave, we must ask why he would flee to Paul. Paul was imprisoned under guard and would have to explain Onesimus' presence to the authorities. Thus, as a runaway slave, Onesimus would not have been safe with Paul. Paul would be guilty of harboring a runaway slave. Under Roman law, Paul was obligated to immediately notify Philemon of Onesimus' whereabouts and to send Onesimus back to his owner posthaste. Places of refuge existed for runaway slaves who ran away for just cause shown (extreme cruelty). A certain Julius Sabinus' slaves fled and sought refuge at the statue of the deified Emperor Antonius. Sabinus was found to be extremely cruel to his slaves and they were sold to another owner.[78] As a runaway slave, the wisest thing to do would be to put as many miles between oneself and one's master, and as quickly as possible.

Onesimus certainly would not seek refuge with a friend of his slaveowner. If caught, Onesimus would be severely punished for running away, and his master would likely brand him and "adorn" him with an iron collar. While Onesimus' service to Paul can be described as Christian ministry (*diakoné*), even a Christian slave was not oblivious to the Roman laws delimiting his status as a slave and the lowest member of the family and one who was under the total power (*dominium*) of the master of the house. If he was a slave, Christian or not, he knew if he were to abscond, he had better succeed or suffer severe consequences. If Onesimus were a runaway slave, it would have been almost as radical for Paul to harbor him as a runaway slave for any length of time as it would have been for Paul to encourage Philemon to manumit a runaway slave (manumission was generally withheld from runaway slaves).

I believe it is plausible to believe that Onesimus and Philemon were brothers. In his book *The Embassy of Onesimus: The Letter of Paul to Philemon*, Alan Callahan retells the story as the story of two brothers whom Paul attempts to reconcile.[79] In light of the socio-historical context of slavery, it is more likely that Onesimus was an estranged brother, possibly a younger brother under Philemon's guardianship. As *paterfamilias*, Philemon had the right to treat anyone under his roof like mere property. Even sons were sometimes treated as slaves, and conversely slaves were treated humanely at times. It is possible that Philemon had previously treated his brother as a slave, and not as a brother. Social historical considerations and the paucity of evidence favoring the depiction of Onesimus as a runaway-slave, warrant a retelling of the story.

> Once upon a time there was a man named Paul. He had a colleague named Philemon, who worked together with him in the service of their common lord, Jesus Christ. Philemon had a brother named Onesimus . . .[80]

Notes

1. Henry Bibb, *Narrative of the Life and Adventures of Henry Bibb, an American Slave, Written by Himself*, (New York, published by the author, 1850), 29-30.
2. Howard Thurman, *Jesus and the Disinherited* (Boston: Beacon Press, 1976). On rare occasions he could read the thirteenth chapter of I Corinthians, 30, 31. Howard Thurman was a theologian, preacher, and former Dean of the Howard University Rankin Chapel.
3. Josiah Priest, *Bible Defense of Slavery or the Origin, History, and Fortunes of the Negro Race, as Deduced from History, both Sacred and Profane, their Natural Relations – Moral, Mental, and Physical – to the Other Races and Mankind, Compared and Illustrated – Their Future Destiny Predicted, etc.* (Louisville, Kentucky: J. F. Bennan, 1851), 287, 309 (quotation); Priest refers to Ham as the Negro race and Japheth as the white race. For a thorough treatment of the curse of Ham theory, see Gene Rice, "The Curse That Never Was (Genesis 9.18-27)," *Journal of Religious Thought* 29 (1972).
4. Charles Elliott, *The Bible and Slavery: in which the Abrahamic and Mosaic Discipline is Considered in Connection with the Most Ancient Forms of Slavery; and the Pauline Code on Slavery as Related to Roman Slavery and the Discipline of the Apostolic Churches* (Cincinnati: L. Swormstedt & A. Poe, 1857), 298 (quotation) - 302. This was published by the Methodist Episcopal Church "to show the relation of the church to slavery, so as to point out the duties of the church in the present state of affairs," 31. While Elliott clearly found Scripture to be against slavery, he also moralized slavery.
5. Rome constitutes one of four "genuine slave societies" in the world (the other three are classical Greece (except Sparta), the Caribbean [some say Brazil], and the American South. Other societies owned slaves but are not considered to be slave societies. M. I. Finley, "The Extent of Slavery," *Slavery: A Comparative*

Perspective: Readings on Slavery from Ancient Times to the Present, ed. Robin W. Winks, (New York: New York Univ. Press, 1972), 5.

6. Mary L. Gordon, "The Nationality of Slaves Under the Early Roman Empire," *Slavery in Classical Antiquity*, ed. M. I. Finley, (Cambridge: W. Heffer & Sons, Ltd., 1964), 171.

7. Aristotle, "Politica," *The Works of Aristotle*, Vol. X (London: Oxford University Press, 1946), trans. by Benjamin Jowett, 1252a30-35, 1252b1-15 (quotation), 1253b1-5 (quotation), 253b30-35, 1254a1-25, 1254b15-40.

8. Peter Garnsey, *Ideas of Slavery from Aristotle to Augustine* (Cambridge, Great Britain: Cambridge University Press, 1996), 15.

9. Seneca, *Ad Lucilium Epistulae Morales* (Cambridge: Harvard University Press, The Loeb Classical Library, 1979), 47.1.

10. Seneca, *Epistulae Morales,* 47.10.

11. *Ibid.,* 47.15.

12. *Ibid.,* 47.17.

13. Peter Garnsey, *Ideas of Slavery from Aristotle to Augustine,* 144.

14. *Justinian's Institutes*, trans. by Peter Birks & Grand McLeod, Latin text of Paul Krueger (London: Gerald Duckworth & Co. Ltd., 1987), 1.3.2.

15 M. I. Finley, *Ancient Slavery and Modern Ideology* (New York: The Viking Press, 1980), 73.

16. Orlando Patterson, *Slavery and Social Death: A Comparative Study* (Cambridge: Harvard University Press, 1982), 13. Patterson's book is a comparative analysis of slavery. His study is based on 66 of the 186 slaveholding societies listed by George P. Murdock's sample of world societies. The 66 societies are listed in Patterson's Appendix B, 350-352.

17. Patterson, *Slavery and Social Death,* 21. While it is "impolite" to call one's spouse one's property, "[w]ith slaves politeness is unnecessary," 22.

18. Keith Bradley, *Slavery and Society,* 4.

19. *Institutes,* 1.3.3-4.

20. Keith Bradley, "On the Roman Slave Supply and Slave Breeding," *Classical Slavery,* ed. M. I. Finley, (London: Frank Cass & Co., Ltd., 1987), 58, 59 (quotation).

21. Bradley, "On the Roman Slave Supply and Slave Breeding," 50.

22. *Ibid.*, 49.

23. Josephus, *Jewish Wars,* 3.305.

24. Josephus, *Wars,* 3.540.

25. Gordon, "The Nationality of Slaves . . .," 188.

26. *Ibid.*, 178-186.

27. *Ibid.*, 181.

28. T. G. Tucker, *Life in the Roman World of Nero and St. Paul* (New York: The MacMillan Company, 1911), 68.

29. M. I. Finley, "The Extent of Slavery: M. I. Finlay [*sic*]," *Slavery: A Comparative*

Perspective, ed. Robin W. Winks, (New York: New York University Press, 1972), 5-6.

30. *Livy,* trans. by Evan T. Sage (Cambridge: Harvard Univ. Press, The Loeb Classical Library, 1965), 35.49.8.

31. *Ibid.,* 36.17.5.

32. Household codes that specifically govern the slave-master relationship are found in Ephesians 5.21–6.9, Colossians 3.18–4.1, 1 Timothy 6.1,2, Titus 2.1-10, 1 Peter 2.18–3.7. *See* Clarice J. Martin, "The Haustafeln (Household Codes) in African American Biblical Interpretation: 'Free Slaves' and 'Subordinate Women'," *Stony the Road We Trod: African American Biblical Interpretation.* (Minneapolis: Fortress Press, 1991) ed. Cain Hope Felder.

33. Bradley, *Slavery and Society at Rome,* (Cambridge: Cambridge University Press, 1994), 71.

34. Bradley, *Slavery and Society at Rome,* 58-60, 62, 63, 65, 68, 69, 70, 73.

35. Dio Chrysostom, "The Fourteenth Discourse: Slavery I," (Cambridge: Harvard University Press, The Loeb Classical Library, 1977), § 10.

36. Bradley, *Slavery and Society at Rome,* 29.

37. Seneca, *Epistulae Morales,* 47.4. Evidently some masters forbade their slaves to speak at feasts; the slaves were ordered to serve food all night "hungry and dumb." "The slightest murmur is repressed by the rod . . . " 47.3.

38. Columella, *De Re Rustica: I-IV on Agriculture,* Vol. I (Cambridge: Harvard University Press, The Loeb Classical Library, 1977) §§ I.8.9, 10 (quotation), 11, 16, 17 (quotation), 18, 19 (quotation).

39. Under Roman law marriage was legally binding only between Roman citizens, *Institutes* 1.10; Women, children or slaves did not have the capacity to make a will or serve as witnesses to a will. *Institutes* 2.10.6.; 2.12

40. M. I. Finley and K.R.Bradley, "Contubernium," *The Oxford Classical Dictionary* Third Edition, eds. Simon Hornblower and Antony Spawforth, (New York: Oxford University Press, 1996), 388. Since slaves could not enter into legal marriages, they were never guilty of adultery.

41. Finley, *Ancient Slavery and Modern Ideology,* 95, 96.

42. Keith Bradley, *Slaves and Masters in the Roman Empire: A Study in Social Control* (Bruxelles: Latomus Revue D'Etudes Latines, 1984), 115, 116 (quotation).

43. Seneca, *Epistulae Morales,* 47.7, 8.

44. Bradley, *Slaves and Masters,* 116, 117.

45. Alan Ferguson Rodger, "Peculium," *The Oxford Classical Dictionary* Third Edition, eds. Simon Hornblower and Antony Spawforth, (New York: Oxford University Press, 1996), 110.

46. Finley, *Ancient Slavery and Modern Ideology,* 74.

47. Bradley, *Slaves and Masters,* 119.

48. Ammianus Marcellinus, "Valentinianus Valens Gratianus," Vol. 3 (3 vols.: Cambridge: Harvard University Press, The Loeb Classical Library, 1972), 28.4.16.

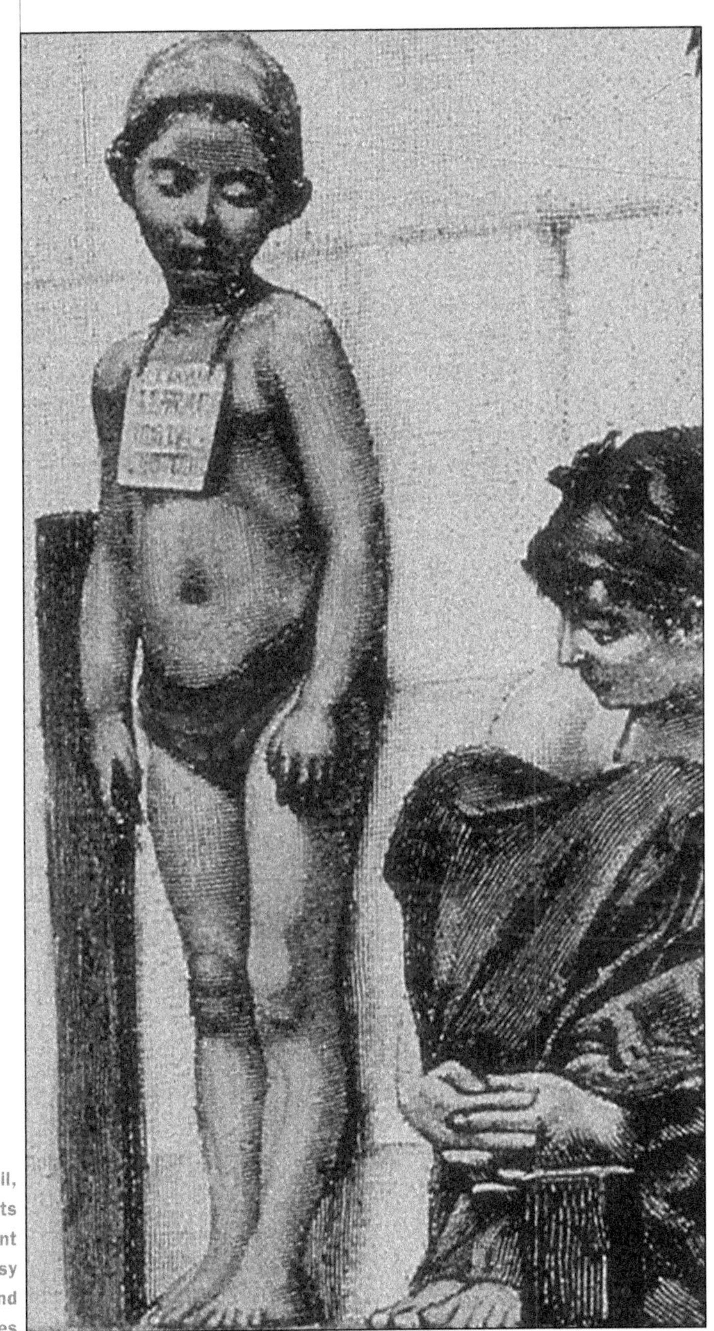

▸ Detail, Slave markets of ancient Rome. Courtesy of North Wind Picture Archives

49. Seneca, *Epistulae Morales,* 47.11.

50. Joseph Vogt, *Ancient Slavery and the Ideal of Man* (Cambridge: Harvard University Press, 1975),104.

51. Naphtali Lewis and Meyer Reinhold, eds., *Roman Civilization Sourcebook II: The Empire* (New York: Harper & Row Publishers, 1966), 229.

52. Lewis, *Roman Civilization*, 268, 69.

53. Bradley, *Slaves and Masters*, 129.

54. Bradley, *Slavery and Society at Rome,* 110, 117.

55. Dio Chrysostom, "The Fifteenth Discourse: On Slavery & Freedom II" (Cambridge: Harvard University Press, The Loeb Classical Library, 1977) § 8.

56. Tacitus, *The Annals,* Books 13-16 (Cambridge: Harvard University Press, The Loeb Classical Library, 1981), 14.42-45 , 14.44 (quotations).

57. Keith R. Bradley, *Slavery and Rebellion in the Roman World, 140 B.C.-70 B.C.* (Indianapolis: Indiana University Press, 1989), 37, 38.

58. Finley, *Ancient Slavery and Modern Ideology,* 111.

59. Bradley, *Slavery and Society at Rome,* 121.

60. Bradley, *Slavery and Rebellion*, 38.

61. *Ibid.*, 35.

62. Alan Watson, *Roman Slave Law* (Baltimore: The John Hopkins University Press, 1987), 2434. Keith Bradley notes that formal manumission was subject to taxation and this was a means by which the Roman state exploited slavery to its own pecuniary advantage. The slave might be required to pay the price of manumission as well as the extra burden of the tax. *Slaves and Masters,* 104-106.

63. Watson, *Roman Slave Law,* 35-42.

64. *Ibid.*, 29-30. The *lex Aelia Sentia* also prohibited the manumission with full citizenship or Latin status to slaves who had been chained or branded as punishment (regardless of guilt or innocence), questioned under torture for wrongdoing and found guilty, or put in the arena to fight with men or beasts, *id.*

65. Bradley, *Slaves and Masters*, 96.

66. *Ibid.*, 81, 82.

67. Lewis, *Roman Civilization*, 256.

68. Tacitus, *The Annals*, Books 13-16 (Cambridge: Harvard University Press, The Loeb Classical Library, 1981), 13.26.4, 5.

69. Watson, *Roman Slave Law*, 23.

70. Bradley, *Slaves and Masters,* 104.

71. *Ibid.*, 83.

72. Wayne A. Meeks, *The First Urban Christians: The Social World of the Apostle Paul* (New Haven: Yale Univ. Press, 1983), 79.

73. Meeks, *The First Urban Christians,* 55.

74. Allan Callahan, "A Note on 1 Corinthians 7.21," *Journal of Interdenominational Theological Center* 17 (Fall 1989 - Spring 1990), 111.

75. Vincent L. Wimbush, *Paul, The Worldly Ascetic: Response to the World and Self-Understanding according to 1 Corinthians 7* (Macon, Georgia: Mercer University Press, 1987), 16.

76. J. Albert Harrill, *The Manumission of Slaves in Early Christianity* (Tübingen: J. C. B. Mohr (Paul Siebeck), 1995), 120.

77. J. Albert Harrill, *The Manumission of Slaves in Early Christianity,*126.

78. Lewis, *Roman Civilization*, 270.

79. Dwight Allan Callahan, *Embassy of Onesimus: The Letter of Paul to Philemon.* (Valley Forge, PA: Trinity Press International, 1997), 69, 70.

80. Callahan, *Embassy of Onesimus,* 69.

Bibliography

Aristotle. "Politica," *The Works of Aristotle Translated into English,* Vol. X , Benjamin Jowett, trans. London: Oxford University Press, 1946.

Barrett, C. K. *A Commentary on the First Epistle to the Corinthians.* New York: Harper & Row, 1968.

Bartchy, S. Scott. "Slavery (Greco-Roman): New Testament," *Anchor Bible Dictionary: Si-Z* Vol. 6. David Noel Freeman, ed. New York: Doubleday, 1992.

____________. *First-Century Slavery and the Interpretation of 1 Corinthians 7.21.* Atlanta: Scholars Press/Society of Biblical Literature, 1985.

Birks, Peter and Grand McLeod, trans. *Justinian's Institutes.* London: Duckworth & Co., Ltd., 1987.

Bradley, Keith R. "Slavery (Roman)," *The Oxford Classical Dictionary,* Third Edition. Simon Hornblower and Antony Spawforth, eds. New York: Oxford University Press, 1996.

____________. *Slavery and Society at Rome.* Cambridge: Cambridge University Press, 1994.

____________. *Slavery and Rebellion in the Roman World, 140 B.C.—70 B.C.* Bloomington: Indiana University Press, 1989.

____________. "On the Roman Slave Supply and Slavebreeding," *Classical Slavery.* M. I. Finley, ed. London: Frank Cass & Co., Ltd., 1987.

____________. *Slave and Masters in the Roman Empire: A Study in Social Control.* Bruxelles: Latomus Revue D'Etudes Latines, 1984.

Callahan, Allen Dwight, *Embassy of Onesimus: The Letter of Paul to Philemon.* Valley Forge, Penn.: Trinity Press International, 1997.

____________. "A Note on 1 Corinthians 7.21," *Journal of Interdenominational Theological Center* 17 (Fall 1989—Spring 1990), 110-114.

Columella. *De Re Rustica: IV On Agriculture,* Harrison Boyd Ash, trans. The Loeb Classical Library, 1977.

Conzelmann, Hans. *1 Corinthians: A Commentary on the First Epistle to the Corinthians,* Philadelphia: Fortress Press.

Dawes, Gregory W. "But If You Can Gain Your Freedom (1 Corinthians 7.17-24)," *The Catholic Biblical Quarterly,* Vol. 52:681-97, October, 1990.

Dio Chrysostom. "Thirty-First Discourse," *Discourses 31-36,* Vol. III, The Loeb Classical Library, 1979.

______________. "The Fourteenth Discourse: On Slavery and Freedom I," *Discourses 12-30,* Vol. II, The Loeb Classical Library, 1977.

______________,."The Fifteenth Discourse: On Slavery and Freedom I," *Discourses 12-30,* Vol. II. 5 vols. Cambridge: Harvard University Press, The Loeb Classical Library, 1977.

Elliott, Charles. *The Bible and Slavery: in which the Abrahamic and Mosaic Discipline is Considered in Connection with the Most Ancient Forms of Slavery; and the Pauline Code on Slavery as Related to Roman Slavery and the Discipline of the Apostolic Churches.* Cincinnati: L. Swormstedt & A. Poe, 1857.

Feldstein, Stanley. *Once a Slave: The Slave's View of Slavery,* Narrative of the Life and Adventures of Henry Bibb, an American Slave Written by Himself, New York, 1850. New York: William Morrow & Co., Inc., 1971.

Finley, M.I. *Ancient Slavery and Modern Ideology.* New York: The Viking Press, 1980.

______________. "The Extent of Slavery," *Slavery: A Comparative Perspective: Readings on Slavery from Ancient Times to the Present,* Robin W. Winks, ed. New York: New York University Press, 1972.

Finley, M. I. and K. R.Bradley. "Contubernium," *The Oxford Classical Dictionary,* Third Edition. Simon Hornblower and Antony Spawforth, eds. New York: Oxford University Press, 1996 , 386.

Garnsey, Peter. I*deas of Slavery from Aristotle to Augustine.* Cambridge, Great Britain: Cambridge University Press, 1996.

Gordon, Mary L. "The Nationality of Slaves under the Early Roman Empire,"(originally appeared in *Journal of Roman Studies* 14 (1924), 93-11) *Slavery in classical Antiquity*. M. I. Finley, ed. Cambridge: W. Heffer & Sons, Ltd., 1964.

Harrill, J. Albert. "Paul and Slavery: The Problem of 1 Corinthians 7.21," *Biblical Research,* Vol. 39-5-28, 1994.

______________. *The Manumission of Slaves in Early Christianity.* Tübingen: J. C. B. Mohr (Paul Siebeck), 1995.

Jones, Amos. Jr. *Paul's Message of Freedom: What Does It Mean to the Black Church?* Valley Forge: Judson Press, 1984.

Kisembo, Benezeri. "The Free Man and the Freedman," *The Bible Translator,* Vol. 46, No. 2, April, 1995.

Lewis, Naphtali and Reinhold Meyer. *Roman Civilization: Sourcebook II: The Empire.* New York: Harper & Row Publishers, 1955.

Martin, Dale B. *Slavery as Salvation: A Metaphor for Slavery in Pauline Christianity.* New Haven: Yale University Press, 1990.

Martin, Clarice J. "The *Haustafeln* (Household Codes) in African American Biblical Interpretation: 'Free Slaves' and 'Subordinate Women'," *Stony the Road We Trod: African American Biblical Interpretation.* Cain Hope Felder, ed., Minneapolis: Fortress Press, 1991.

Meeks, Wayne A. *The First Urban Christians: The Social World of the Apostle Paul.* New Haven: Yale University Press, 1983.

Patterson, Orlando. *Slavery and Social Death: A Comparative Study.* Cambridge: Harvard University Press, 1982.

Priest, Josiah. *Bible Defence of Slavery; or the Origin, History, and Fortunes of the Negro Race as Deduced from History, Both Sacred and Profane. Their Natural Relations —Moral, Mental, and Physical - to the Other Races of Mankind, Compared and Illustrated - Their Future Destiny Predicted, etc.* Louisville, Kentucky: J. F. Bennan, 1851.

Rice, Gene. "The Curse That Never Was (Genesis 9.18-27)," *Journal of Religious Thought* 29 (1972).

Robertson, Archibold and Plummer Alfred. *International Critical Commentary: 1 Corinthians.* New York: Charles Scribner's Sons, 1911.

Rodger, Alan Ferguson. "Peculium," *The Oxford Classical Dictionary,* Third Edition. Simon Hornblower and Antony Spawforth, eds., New York: Oxford University Press, 1996.

Saller, Richard. "Slavery and the Roman Family," *Classical Slavery.* M. I. Finley, ed., London: Frank Cass & Co., Ltd., 1987.

Ste. Croix, G. E. M. De. *The Class Struggle in the Ancient Greek World from the Archaic Age to the Arab Conquests.* Ithaca, New York: Cornell University Press, 1981.

Seneca. *Ad Lucilium Epistulae Morales,* The Loeb Classical Library, 1979, 47.1-21.

Tacitus. *The Annals,* The Loeb Classical Library, 1981, 14.42-45.

Talbert, Charles H. *Reading Corinthians: A Literary and Theological Commentary on 1 and 2 Corinthians.* New York: Crossroad Publising Company, 1987.

Thurman, Howard. *Jesus and the Disinherited.* Boston: Beacon Press, 1976.

Tucker, T. G. *Life in the Roman World of Nero and St. Paul.* New York: The MacMillan Company, 1911.

Vogt, Joseph. *Ancient Slavery and the Ideal of Man.* Cambridge: Harvard University Press, 1975.

Watson, Alan. *Roman Slave Law.* Baltimore: John Hopkins University Press, 1987.

Wimbush, Vincent L. *Paul, the Worldly Ascetic: Response to the World and Self-Understanding according to 1 Corinthians 7.* Macon, Georgia: Mercer University Press, 1987.

Ten

A History of the Black Church

Dennis C. Dickerson

Several scholars in recent years have identified salient themes that have defined the development of the black church and the black religious experience. Charles Long, for example, indicated that the phenomena of the black church and the black religious experience are explained by the involuntary presence of blacks. Another scholar, Albert Raboteau, contended that America represented Egypt, whereas Canada, Africa, and the northern cities of America represented Israel. These symbolic destinations helped shape the sermons, speeches and songs of black Christians. Although the Anglicans started catechesis among blacks before other Christian denominations, the evangelistic successes of the Baptists and Methodists determined the religious inclinations of blacks. The rise of independent black churches and denominations provided places and personnel for the fight against slavery and its ultimate demise during the Civil War. In the first few decades during the twentieth century, the spread of pentecostalism created additional black denominations, and the black migration from the South to the North spearheaded social gospel programs within many black congregations. Support of the Civil Rights movement, and the espousal of black theology brought black clergy and black churches into the forefront of activism from the 1950s through the 1970s. When Jarena Lee started to preach in the African Methodist Episcopal Church in the 1810s and Nannie Burroughs organized the Women's Auxiliary of the National Baptist Convention in 1900, they developed precedents, during the 1980s, that brought to frontline church leadership such women as Bishop Leontine E. C. Kelly in the United Methodist Church and Bishop Barbara Harris in the Protestant Episcopal Church.

◂ A Negro camp meeting in the South, 1892. Hand-colored woodcut. Courtesy of North Wind Picture Archives

African American Christianity emerged out of the crucible of slavery. In fact "the involuntary presence of the black community in America," according to Charles Long, has been a formative and persistent factor in shaping the African American religious experience. Although Long also argues that the African background influenced African American Christianity, he and other scholars, some of whom discount the importance of the African heritage, agree that as blacks grappled with slavery, segregation, and other forms of racial oppression, they developed theological perspectives that differed significantly from those of whites.

Albert Raboteau, for example, observed that blacks interpreted "the language, symbols, and worldview" found in the Bible to explain their peculiar fate. Often African Americans turned to the story of Exodus and applied it to themselves. White Christians who fled religious persecution in the Old World also used Exodus events to explain their journey to the New World. For them Europe was the Egypt that they left behind to go to a Promised Land, an Israel that was America. Blacks found similar hermeneutical possibilities in the Exodus story. Blacks were captured and shipped from their homeland in Africa on crowded and disease-infested slave ships headed for America. Although America was an Israel for white Christians, it was a different place for blacks. America, where oppression and persecution awaited them, was like the biblical Egypt. Hence, they longed to escape Egypt in order to go to a Promised Land. Israel for southern slaves was located in the North or in Canada or in Africa. Israel was any place to which they could journey to end their bondage and become free from racial subjugation. The views of African American Christians differed from those of whites in other respects. As blacks tried to make sense of their enslaved and segregated status they developed a deeper understanding of forgiveness, reconciliation, and other fundamental tenets of Christian doctrine.

Timothy Smith, for example, observed that blacks who converted to Christianity "knew they had a lot to forgive." Those who were serious and steadfast understood better than most whites the depth of desire, discipline, and fortitude required to forgive others for their wrongful acts toward African Americans. Similarly, black Christians demonstrated their spiritual resilience when, in the face of physical persecution and abuse, they counselled reconciliation with whites rather than revenge. Moreover, they viewed God as active in history. Hence, they waited for deliverance either directly from God from divinely appointed agents on the Underground Railroad, or from Civil War soldiers in the Union Army.[1]

The founding in 1701 of the Society for the Propagation of the Gospel in Foreign Parts started the Anglican mission to evangelize African American slaves. These initiatives, mainly in the South, predated other denominational efforts to introduce Christianity to blacks. Opposition from slave owners, failure to condemn human bondage, and a tedious method of catechesis limited the number of slave converts. The Dutch Reformed Church made similar efforts in the North, principally in New York, to Christianize blacks. This pro-slavery denomination, like the Anglicans, emphasized strict "catechetical instruction," but these factors restricted its evangelical effectiveness.[2]

Most scholars have agreed that the 18th century revivals and camp meetings of the Baptists and Methodists proved more successful than the evangelical efforts of their Anglican and Dutch Reformed counterparts. Winthrop Hudson, for example, offered three explanations why most blacks became Baptists and Methodists. Aggressive and extensive evangelization, acceptance of black members on a somewhat equal basis, and opportunities to become preachers pulled African Americans into these denominations in large numbers both in the North and in the South. Their acceptance into the ministry enabled black preachers, especially in the North, when faced with racial discrimination in white churches, to form separate congregations and denominations. Between 1787 and 1822 in several northern and some southern cities, blacks withdrew to found their own Baptist, Methodist, Episcopal, Congregational, and Presbyterian churches.[3]

Will B. Gravely has contended that the rise of independent black congregations and denominations was traceable to three crucial circumstances: discriminatory behavior by whites, the desire of blacks for religious independence and autonomy, and white clergy distancing themselves from previous anti-slavery positions. As a result black Baptists started congregations in Silver Bluff, South Carolina in the 1770s, Savannah, Georgia in 1782, and Augusta, Georgia in 1793. Richard Allen, a Delaware slave converted by a Methodist circuit rider, purchased his freedom and founded the Free African Society (FAS) in Philadelphia in 1787. An ugly racial incident at St. George Methodist Episcopal Church moved Allen and his followers to become completely autonomous. Out of the FAS emerged two black congregations, St. Thomas Protestant Episcopal Church and Bethel African Methodist Episcopal Church, both dedicated in 1794. Since Allen declined to serve St. Thomas, his associate, Absalom Jones, became its priest.

Allen's Bethel congregation eventually severed all ties with Wesleyan whites and led other congregations in Pennsylvania, Maryland, and New Jersey to form the African Methodist Episcopal Church in Philadelphia in 1816.

Similar racial tensions led Peter Spencer to found another black Wesleyan denomination in Wilmington, Delaware in 1813, the Union Church of Africans. James Varick, Christopher Rush, and others established another denomination, the African Methodist Episcopal Zion Church in 1821 in New York City.[4] Although some African Americans remained within white religious structures, they, like their Baptist and African Methodist counterparts, worshiped in separate congregations. In 1807, black Presbyterians founded the First African Presbyterian Church with John Gloucester as pastor, in Philadelphia. Black Calvinist congregations spread to other cities in Pennsylvania, New Jersey, and New York. Black Congregational churches started in New Haven, Hartford, Pittsfield, Providence and other cities in New England. After the Disciples of Christ began in 1820 in Kentucky, several black congregations started in Kentucky, Ohio, North Carolina, Georgia, and Tennessee prior to 1862. Although most Roman Catholic missionaries ministered among slaves in Baltimore, Maryland; Savannah, Georgia; Mobile, Alabama; New Orleans, Louisiana; and their environs, free blacks sometimes attended mixed congregations in Pittsburgh, Washington, D.C., New York City, St. Louis, and Chicago prior to the Civil War.[5]

Black pastors and their parishioners, particularly in the North, used their churches to advance abolitionism and to support emancipation efforts during the Civil War. Samuel Cornish and Theodore S. Wright, both black Presbyterian ministers, through their own newspapers, and through cooperation with white anti-slavery groups, advocated freedom for the slaves, denounced the colonization of free blacks, and supported the establishment of black schools. J. W. C. Pennington, an escaped slave, Amos G. Beman, and Charles B. Ray, all black Congregational clergymen, joined Cornish and Wright in these endeavors. Perhaps the most prominent preacher-turned-abolitionist was Frederick Douglass who ran away from bondage in Maryland and settled in New Bedford, Massachusetts. There he became a local preacher in the African Methodist Episcopal Zion Church. Some clergy opened their churches to abolitionist meetings and offered them as stations on the Underground Railroad. Fleeing slaves often stopped at any one of several Baptist, A.M.E. and A.M.E. Zion churches in the Midwest, the Middle Atlantic and

New England states to hide from marauding slave catchers and bounty hunters anxious to recapture them and return them to bondage in the South.

A divinely inspired slave preacher, Nat Turner, in Southampton County, Virginia, believed that Old Testament justice required him to lead a slave revolt in 1831. Henry Highland Garnet, a former slave from Maryland, and a Presbyterian pastor, in 1843 called upon slaves to break the chains of their oppression using whatever means were at their disposal. During the Civil War numerous black ministers recruited soldiers to fight in the Union Army against the Confederacy. Fourteen black clergy served in the Union Army as chaplains. They performed marriages, improved morale, tended to the wounded, and taught illiterate recruits how to read and write.[6]

The Civil War destroyed slavery and freed four million persons, many of whom were without a formal church affiliation. Northern white denominations sent preachers and teachers, both white and black, into the South to evangelize among the newly emancipated. However, the Baptists and the Methodist Episcopal Church in the north outdistanced the Presbyterians, Episcopalians, and Congregationalists in their recruitment of black members. All of these denominations, however, made major educational contributions through the many secondary, collegiate, and professional

▶ The Dickerson family of Tazewell, Virginia. Courtesy of Crockett and Dickerson Families. Used by Permission

institutions that they established to train black ministers, teachers, doctors, and lawyers. Similarly, black Baptists, the African Methodist Episcopal Church, and the African Methodist Episcopal Zion Church outpaced the white denominations in their numerical success. They also founded schools and colleges for the former slaves and their children. With assistance from the American Baptist Home Mission Society, black Baptists supported Wayland Seminary in Virginia, Shaw in North Carolina, Atlanta Baptist (Morehouse) and Spelman in Georgia, and Leland in Louisiana. The A.M.E. Church established Morris Brown in Georgia, Allen in South Carolina, Kittrell in North Carolina, Edward Waters in Florida, and Paul Quinn in Texas. The A.M.E. Zion Church founded Livingstone in North Carolina as its flagship institution. Additionally, black voters in several southern states elected black ministers in significant numbers to Reconstruction legislatures and they also served as local and state officials.[7]

Southern white denominations that had slave members before the Civil War encouraged them to start separate denominations and congregations. The Methodist Episcopal, South in response to their black members agreed to establish the Colored Methodist Episcopal Church in Jackson, Tennessee, in 1870. Similarly, in 1874 in Nashville, Tennessee, the Cumberland Presbyterian Church endorsed the founding of the Colored Cumberland Presbyterian Church. Although blacks remained a part of the southern-based Presbyterian Church in the U.S., they were organized into separate synods, presbyteries, and congregations. Similar structures existed within other northern and southern white denominations. In 1889 blacks within the Evangelical Lutheran Synodical Conference of North America, for example, established the Alpha Synod of the Evangelical Lutheran Church of Freedmen in America consisting of five North Carolina congregations. Nonetheless, the vast majority of African Americans belonged to black controlled Baptist and Methodist churches.[8]

After Reconstruction, newly enfranchised blacks lost their right to vote and faced increased violence and hostility from whites. At the same time, a surge of millennial thought characterized the perspectives of leading black churchmen. They reached into their ancient past for sources of hope and assurance that the suffering that blacks endured would culminate in a golden age in which freedom for all would become a reality. Some believed their glorious African past heralded an equally promising future in which God would rebuke western society for its ill treatment of blacks.

Benjamin W. Arnett, a bishop in the African Methodist Episcopal Church and a bibliophile of black history, in an 1893 address to the World's Parliament of Religions, credited Africa with helping to spread Christianity. "In the first days of Christianity," he said, "it contributed more than its proportion of the early agents." He cited Luke of Cyrene in North Africa as the author of one of the gospels. He mentioned Simon, also of Cyrene, "who became the cross-bearer of the Son of God on his way to Calvary." Arnett's colleague, Bishop Benjamin T. Tanner published *The Color of Solomon—What?* in 1895. He argued that Solomon, through his parents, David and Bathsheba, had a Hamitic or a black origin. He also cited Solomon's "passion for women manifestly of darker hue than were the women of Israel." Tanner's point in advancing these contentions was that most translations of the Bible made "Solomon to be white when it is absolutely certain that according to the division of the human family. . . he did not belong to the White race, and all things being equal could not personally have been white, as that word is popularly understood." Arnett and Tanner believed that Christianity's ancient anchors among people of color argued for their equality in 19th century American society.[9]

The millennialism of black clergy did not obscure another influential movement among the African American community. William Seymour, a black Holiness preacher born in Louisiana, inaugurated a marathon series of revivals at the Azusa Street Mission in Los Angeles, California. Seymour preached sanctification and speaking in tongues (glossolalia). As word spread about Seymour's powerful preaching, blacks and whites flocked to Azusa Street to receive these spiritual gifts that Seymour enthusiastically espoused. The founders of numerous Pentecostal denominations drew their spiritual authority from Azusa Street to establish Holiness churches. One pilgrim to Azusa Street was Charles Harrison Mason who formally founded the Church of God in Christ in 1914. Another was G. T. Haywood, head of the interracial Pentecostal Assemblies of the World started in 1914. R. C. Lawson, a Haywood follower, founded the Church of Our Lord Jesus Christ of the Apostolic Faith in 1919. Lawson trained other clergy including Sherrod Johnson, Henry C. Brooks, J. P. Shields, Smallwood E. Williams, and Lymus Johnson who started their own Pentecostal denominations.[10]

During the era of the two World Wars the labor needs of northern industry drew millions of African Americans away from the South to major urban areas of the Northeast, Midwest, and Pacific Coast.

▸ Detail, "Baptism," Anna Belle Lee. Washington/ Superstock

Beginning in the first decades of the 1900s through the 1960s, African Americans populated plants, factories, and foundries that manufactured steel, automobiles, rubber, ships, and electrical products. As a result, African American congregations in numerous denominations experienced phenomenal growth and financial support from their blue collar parishioners. Consequently, such model congregations as Reverdy C. Ransom's Institutional A.M.E. Church and Social Settlement in Chicago, J. C. Austin's Ebenezer Baptist Church in Pittsburgh, Pilgrim Baptist Church in Chicago, and Robert Bradby's Second Baptist Church in Detroit established social gospel programs that addressed the housing, employment, and child care needs of their respective communities. Such pastors as Adam Clayton Powell, Jr. at Abyssinian Baptist Church in New York City and Archibald J. Carey, Jr. at Woodlawn A.M.E. Church and Quinn Chapel A.M.E. Church in Chicago respectively launched successful careers in national and municipal politics.[11]

African American clergy and congregations were also conspicuous in spearheading the Civil Rights Movement in the 1950s and 1960s. The landmark 1954 Supreme Court decision in *Brown vs. Board of Education* owed its origin to suits that two A.M.E. ministers, Reverend Oliver Brown of Topeka, Kansas, and Reverend Joseph A. DeLaine of Clarendon County, South Carolina, initiated. Bus boycott leaders in Baton Rouge in 1953, Montgomery in 1955, and Tallahassee in 1956 were Baptist ministers, Theodore Jemison, Martin Luther King, Jr., and C. K. Steele, respectively. Their congregations, along with several others in their respective cities, provided sites for rallies and financial support to these grassroots movements. The Southern Christian Leadership Conference, founded in Atlanta in 1957 with Martin Luther King, Jr. as president, gave material support to numerous southern communities that fought against legalized racial segregation and discrimination in the region and in the nation.[12]

Civil Rights clergy owed their activism to an earlier generation of black religious intellectuals who pressed black congregations to reinterpret Jesus and his relationship to social struggle and the place of the church in movements for social change. In the 1930s, 1940s, and 1950s the perspectives of Howard Thurman, Mordecai W. Johnson, Benjamin E. Mays, and George D. Kelsey inspired a succeeding generation of black activist clergy that included Martin Luther King, Jr. and others. Similarly, the millenialist black theology of Benjamin W. Arnett and Benjamin T. Tanner resonated in the late 1960s with James Cone, Cecil Cone, J. Deotis Roberts,

Gayraud S. Wilmore, and others who promulgated the view that African American Christianity required commitments to critique racist biblical interpretations, to oppose oppressive religious and economic institutions, and to support the black freedom struggle. Jacqueline Grant, Pauli Murray, and other black feminist writers condemned both the racism and sexism practiced by American society and black and white churches.[13]

Women also sought a place in the African American clergy. Jarena Lee whom Bishop Richard Allen initially rebuffed was licensed to preach in the A.M.E. Church in 1817. Although Bishop Henry M. Turner ordained Sarah A. Hughes as an itinerant deacon in the A.M.E. Church's North Carolina Annual Conference in 1885, his successor, Bishop Jabaz P. Campbell, rescinded this action. The denomination authorized that women could be ordained as local deacons in 1948, then as local elders in 1956, and finally as itinerant deacons and elders in 1960. The A.M.E. Zion Church authorized the full ordination of Mary Blair Smalls in 1898 in the Philadelphia-Baltimore Annual Conference. The C.M.E. Church followed the other two black Wesleyan bodies with the full ordination of women in 1966.

The election of Leontine T. C. Kelly as a United Methodist bishop in 1984, and the the elevation of Barbara Harris as suffragan bishop of the Episcopal Diocese of Massachusetts in 1989 represented significant achievements for black women in the ministry. Women also spearheaded several Pentecostal/Holiness denominations. Mary Magdalena Lewis Tate, the founder of the Church of the Living God, the Pillar and Ground of Truth, is the best example. After some Alabama revivals in 1908, Mother Tate became a Bishop and later ordained four others, including her two sons to help her supervise the growing denomination. Additionally, church mothers within Pentecostal/Holiness churches developed into important positions at the local, regional, and national levels. Their substantial influence upon clergy drew from their moral guidance and rhetorical abilities. Women assumed other leadership positions in numerous auxiliaries, especially in the historic black denominations. All the Baptist, Methodist, and Pentecostal bodies had women's missionary societies. Perhaps, Nannie H. Burrough's Women's Auxiliary of the National Baptist Convention established in 1900 is the best known.[14]

African American churches have cooperated primarily through several interdenominational groups. The Fraternal Council of Negro Churches which started in 1934, with A.M.E. Bishop Reverdy C. Ransom as president is one such group.

A.M.E. Bishop John Hurst Adams spearheaded the Congress of National Black Churches in 1978. The National Association for the Advancement of Colored People, the National Urban League, and the Southern Christian Leadership Conference were black betterment groups that have drawn consistent support from black churches throughout the 20th century.[15]

The impact of black churches also stretched elsewhere within the Americas and to Africa where major denominations established churches, schools, and hospitals. Black Baptists established the Baptist Foreign Missionary Convention of the United States of America in 1880. This body, which helped to create the National Baptist Convention in 1895, became the denomination's Foreign Mission Board. The Board founded the Providence Industrial Mission in Nyasaland in Central Africa, with Lewis G. Jordan as Corresponding Secretary between 1896 and 1921. In 1923 there were ten mission stations in Liberia and fourteen in South Africa. Bishop Henry M. Turner of the African Methodist Episcopal Church established the Sierra Leone and Liberia Annual Conferences in 1891, and he brought into this denomination the Ethiopian Church of South Africa in 1896. While he presided as the Bishop of Georgia from 1896 through 1908, Turner also launched missions in Cuba and Mexico. The A.M.E. Zion Church, the C.M.E. Church, and the Church of God in Christ inaugurated similar efforts to expand within the Americas and to Africa. Hence, black churches that have functioned as meeting places for abolitionists, as stations on the Underground Railroad, and as sites for civil rights activism also embraced a Pan African vision to include persons of color throughout the African diaspora.[16]

Three trends will likely define the future direction of black churches. First, the growing influence of mega-churches probably will continue. Such congregations as First A.M.E. Church and West Angeles Church of God in Christ in Los Angeles, California, Full Gospel A.M.E. Zion Church in Temple Hills and Clinton, Maryland, Windsor Village United Methodist Church in Houston, Texas, and Greater St. Stephen Full Gospel Baptist Church in New Orleans, Louisiana, all boast memberships in the multiple thousands and they support a broad range of social outreach, media, and housing ministries. Second, blacks in predominantly white denominations will continue to ascend to important executive positions such as Bishop Wilton D. Gregory, the Vice President of the National Conference of Catholic Bishops, and Reverend Arnold I. Thomas, the conference minister of the Vermont Conference of the United Church of Christ. Third, non-denominational churches such as Frederick K.C. Price's Crenshaw Christian Center in Los Angeles, California, Johnnie Coleman's Christ Universal Temple in Chicago, Illinois, and T.D. Jake's Potter's House in Dallas, Texas will continue to attract increasing numbers of black parishioners.

Selected Chronology

A History of the Black Church

1701 The Society for the Propagation of the Gospel in Foreign Parts started the Anglican mission to evangelize African American slaves.

1782 Several Black Baptist congregations are started in Savannah, Georgia.

1787 Richard Allen, a Delaware slave converted by a Methodist circuit rider, purchased his freedom and founded the Free African Society (FAS) in Philadelphia.

1787-1822 Blacks in several northern and southern cities founded their own Baptist, Methodist, Episcopal, Congregational, and Presbyterian churches.

1813 The Union Church of Africans was founded by Peter Spencer in Wilmington, Delaware.

1816 The African Methodist Episcopal Church was founded in Philadelphia, Pennsylvania.

1831 Nat Turner, a slave preacher in Southampton County, Virginia, leads a revolt.

1843 Henry Highland Garnet, a former slave from Maryland and a Presbyterian pastor, called upon slaves to break the chains of their oppression.

1870 The Colored Methodist Episcopal Church was established in Jackson, Tennessee.

1880 The Baptist Foreign Missionary Convention of the United States was formed by black Baptists.

1895 Bishop Benjamin T. Tanner publishes *The Color of Solomon—What?* Tanner argued that Solomon had a Hamitic or a black origin through his parents, David and Bathsheba.

1900 Nannie H. Burroughs established the Women's Auxiliary of the National Baptist Convention.

1906 William Seymour, a black Holiness preacher, organized what became known as the Azusa Street Mission.

1914 The Church of God in Christ was formally founded by Charles Harrison Mason.

1948 The African Methodist Episcopal Church began ordaining women as local deacons.

1957 The Southern Christian Leadership Conference (SCLC) was founded in Atlanta, Georgia, with the Rev. Dr. Martin Luther King, Jr. as president.

1978 The Congress of National Black Churches was spearheaded by Bishop John Hurst Adams.

Notes

1. Charles H. Long, "Perspectives for a Study of Afro-American Religion in the United States" *Significations: Signs, Symbols, and Images in the Interpretation of Religion,* Charles H. Long, ed. (Philadelphia: Fortress Press,1986), 176-179; Albert J. Raboteau, "African Americans, Exodus, and the American Israel," *A Fire in the Bones: Reflections on African American Religious History,* Albert J. Raboteau, ed. (Boston: Beacon Press, 1995), 17-36; Timothy L. Smith, "Slavery and Theology: The Emergence of Black Christian Consciousness in Nineteenth Century America," *Church History*, 41 (December 1972), 498-499.

2. Harold T. Lewis, *Yet With a Steady Beat: The African American Struggle for Recognition in the Episcopal Church* (Valley Forge, Pennsylvania: Trinity Press International, 1996), 19-23; Gerald F. DeJong, "The Dutch Reformed Church and Negro Slavery in Colonial America," *Church History,* 40, (December 1971), 430-436.

3.Winthrop S. Hudson,"The American Context as an Area for Research in Black Church Studies," *Church History*, 52, (June 1983), 157-171; Will B. Gravely,"The Rise of African Churches in America (1786-1822): Reexamining the Contexts," *African-American Religion: Interpretive Essays in History and Culture*, Timothy E. Fulop and Albert J. Raboteau, editors, (New York: Routledge, 1997), 135-151.

4. Ibid., 137-140; 144-146.

5. Andrew E. Murray, *Presbyterians and the Negro: A History.* (Philadelphia: Presbyterian Historical Society, 1966), 30-39; David E. Swift, *Black Prophets of Justice: Activist Clergy Before the Civil War,* (Baton Rouge: Louisiana State University Press, 1989), 182-185; 215; Dennis C. Dickerson, "Samuel Harrison, A Nineteenth Century Black Clergyman," *Black Apostles at Home and Abroad: The Black Christian Mission from the Revolution to Reconstruction,* David W. Wills and Richard Newman, editors, (Boston: G. K. Hall & Co., 1982), 148, 149; 151; Hap Lyda, "A History of Black Christian Churches (Disciples of Christ)

in the United States Through 1899," Ph.D. dissertation, Vanderbilt University, 1972, 23; Cyprian Davis, *The History of Black Catholics in the United States*, (New York: Crossroad Publishing Company, 1990), 67-97.

6. Swift, *Black Prophets of Freedom*, 2-4; 7-18; William L. Andrews, "Frederick Douglass, Preacher," *American Literature* 54, (December 1982), 592-597; Benjamin Quarles, *Black Abolitionists*, (New York: Oxford University Press, 1969), 83, 84; Gayraud S. Wilmore, *Black Religion and Black Radicalism*, (Maryknoll, New York: Orbis Books, 1973), 62-73; Henry Highland Garnet, "Address to the Slaves of the United States of America," (1843), *The Black Abolitionist Papers*, Volume III, The United States, 1830-1846, C. Peter Ripley, editor, (Chapel Hill, North Carolina: University of North Carolina Press, 1991), 403-411; Edwin S. Redkey, "Black Chaplains in the Union Army," *Civil War History* 33, (December 1987), 331-350.

7. William E. Montgomery, *Under Our Own Vine and Fig Tree: The African American Church in the South, 1865-1900*, (Baton Rouge: Louisiana State University Press, 1993), 38-190. On black denominational involvement in higher education see Paul R. Griffin, *Black Theology as the Foundation of Three Methodist Colleges*, (Lanham, Maryland: University Press of America, 1984) and Leroy Fitts, *A History of Black Baptists,* (Nashville: Broadman Press, 1985).

8. Othal H. Lakey, *A History of the CME Church,* (Memphis: The CME Publishing House, 1985), 131-163; Thomas D. Campbell, *One Family Under God: A Story of Cumberland Presbyterians in Black and White,* (Memphis: Frontier Press,1982), 38-40; Ernest Trice Thompson, "Black Presbyterians, Education and Evangelism After the Civil War," *Journal of Presbyterian History* 51, (Summer 1973), 174-198.

9. Timothy E. Fulop, "'The Future Golden Day of the Race': Millenialism and Black Americans in the Nadir, 1877-1901," *Harvard Theological Review* 84, (1991), 75-99; Benjamin W. Arnett, "Christianity and the Negro," *The World's Congress of Religions: Addresses and Papers Delivered Before the Parliament*, J. W. Hanson, editor, (Chicago: W. B. Conkey Company, 1894), 748-750; Benjamin T. Tanner, *The Color of Solomon—What?* (Philadelphia: A.M.E. Book Concern, 1895), 16-18; 31-38.

10. James S. Tinney, "William J. Seymour: Father of Modern Day Pentecostalism," *Black Apostles: Afro-American Clergy Confront the Twentieth Century*, Randall K. Burkett and Richard Newman, editors, (Boston: G. K. Hall & Co., 1978), 213-225; Elsie W. Mason, *The Man... Charles Harrison Mason,* (Memphis: Privately Printed, 1979); Robert C. Spellman, A Chart on Pentecostal History: Partial Development of Predominantly Black Pentecostal Organizations, U.S.A.

11. Milton Sernett, *Bound for the Promised Land: African American Religion and the Great Migration*, (Durham: Duke University Press, 1997), 87-121; 154-179; Dennis C. Dickerson, "The Black Church in Industrializing Western Pennsylvania, 1870-1950," *African Americans in Pennsylvania*, Joe William Trotter, Jr. and Eric Ledell Smith, editors, (University Park: Pennsylvania State University Press, 1997), 388-402; Reverdy C. Ransom, *The Pilgrimage of Harriet Ransom's Son*, (Nashville, A.M.E. Sunday School Union, n.d.), pp. 104-118; Randall K. Burkett, "The Baptist Church in the Years of Crisis: J.C. Austin and Pilgrim Baptist Church, 1926-1950," *African American Christianity*, Paul E. Johnson, editor, (Berkeley: University of California Press, 1994), 134-158; Cara L. Shelly, "Brad-

by's Baptists: Second Baptist Church of Detroit, 1910-1946," *Michigan Historical Review* 17, (Spring1991), 1-33; Charles V. Hamilton, *Adam Clayton Powell: The Political Biography of an American Dilemma*, (New York: Atheneum, 1991), "Archibald J. Carey, Jr.," *Encyclopedia of African Methodism,* Richard R.Wright, Jr., editor, (Philadelphia: A.M.E. Book Concern, 1947), 62, 63; Biographical Data in *Archibald J. Carey, Jr.* Papers, Chicago Historical Society, Chicago, Illinois.

12. Howard D. Gregg, *The A.M.E. Church and the Current Negro Revolt*, (Nashville: A.M.E. Sunday School Union, n.d.), 17-24; Aldon D. Morris, *The Origins of the Civil Rights Movement*, (New York: The Free Press, 1984), 40-119.

13. Thomas I. S. Mikelson, "Mays, King, and The Negro's God," *Walking Integrity: Benjamin Elijah Mays, Mentor to Martin Luther King, Jr.*, Lawrence Edward Carter, Sr., editor, (Macon: Mercer University Press, 1998), 153-184; Walter Earl Fluker and Catherine Tumber, editors, *A Strange Freedom: The Best of Howard Thurman on Religious Experience and Public Life*, (Boston: Beacon Press,1998), 6, 13, 131; Clayborne Carson, editor, *The Autobiography of Martin Luther King, Jr.,* (New York: Warner Books, 1998), 16, 23; Gayraud S. Wilmore and James H. Cone, editors, *Black Theology: A Documentary History, 1966-1979*, (Maryknoll, New York: Orbis Books, 1979), 1-11; 398-414; 418-431.

14. Dennis C. Dickerson, "'Did Not Mary First Preach the Risen Savior': Women Preachers Within Wesleyan Black Denominations," *Historical Bulletin of the World Methodist Historical Society*, Fourth Quarter 1997, 5-9; "Barbara Harris," "Leontine T. C. Kelly," *Black Women in America: An Historical Encyclopedia*, Volume I, Darlene Clark Hine, editor, (Brooklyn: Carlson Publishing Company, 1993), 537; 675; Evelyn Brooks Higginbotham, *Righteous Discontent: The Women's Movement in the Black Baptist Church, 1880-1920,* (Cambridge, Massachusetts: Harvard University Press, 1993), 150-184.

15. Mary R. Sawyer, "The Fraternal Council of Negro Churches, 1934-1964," *Church History* 59, (March 1990), 51-64; Also see the following: Mary R. Sawyer, B*lack Ecumenism: Implementing the Demands of Justice*, (Valley Forge, Pennsylvania: Trinity Press International, 1994), and Dennis C. Dickerson, "Black Ecumenicism: Efforts to Establish a United Methodist Episcopal Church, 1918-1932," *Church History* 52, (December 1983), 479-491.

16. William J. Harvey, III, *Bridges of Faith Across the Seas: The Story of the Foreign Mission Board of the National Baptist Convention, USA, Inc.*, (Warminster, Pennsylvania: Neibauer Peeress, 1989), 22; 29-33; 44, 75, 76; Stephen W. Angell, *Bishop Henry McNeal Turner and African American Religion in the South*, (Knoxville: University of Tennessee Press, 1992), 215-237; Dennis C. Dickerson, *Religion, Race, and Region: Research Notes on A.M.E. Church History* (Nashville: A.M.E. Sunday School Union/Legacy Publishing, 1995), 121-130.

Eleven

A Hidden History: African American Contributions to the Bible Cause

Robert L. Cvornyek

◂ "From Door to Door," ca. 1933. Courtesy of American Bible Society Archives, New York, NY

Despite laws forbidding them to read, African American slaves yearned to read the Bible for themselves. After the Civil War, several religious and charitable organizations supported the freed blacks in their quest for literacy. The American Bible Society was one of those organizations that not only championed the right of African Americans to an education, but also intentionally focused on providing African Americans with the Bible, "the book which must be the great educator of the Colored people of the South." In addition, the American Bible Society trained blacks as *colporteurs* or door-to-door distributors who could reach their own people with the Word of God.

▶ "1890 Graduating Class." Courtesy of American Bible Society Archives, New York, NY

The American Bible Society has worked actively to share the Word of God with the African American community since its founding in 1816, occasionally against great odds.

Before the Civil War, African American slaves in virtually every southern state were forbidden by law to read. During the Civil War, as many African Americans sought protection in Union forts and garrisons, many forts established primary schools and churches to help educate people on the path to freedom.

In the decade following the war, more than four dozen religious and benevolent organizations raised money and sent teachers to establish schools among the freed African Americans. The American Bible Society worked in conjunction with these organizations to furnish "the book which must be the great educator of the Colored people of the South." Correspondence to the Society revealed a strong desire among African Americans to learn for themselves. Individuals sometimes traveled several miles to obtain a Bible and many preferred to purchase one rather than receive it as a gift.

For the remainder of the century, though, distribution of the Bible to the African American community was spotty, due in part to the lack of structured distribution channels and in part to conflict over who was responsible for distribution.

The ABS Agency Among the Colored People of the South

In 1900, leaders of the American Bible Society responded to the new situations created by the Supreme Court's "separate but equal" decision in 1896 and the uneven distribution of the Bible in the southern states by launching the "Agency Among the Colored People of the South," a new Agency devoted solely to the distribution of the Bible among African Americans in the South.

The Rev. Dr. John Percy Wragg of Atlanta, Georgia, a pastor and presiding elder in the Savannah and Atlanta Conferences of the Methodist Episcopal Church, was chosen to lead the new Agency in June 1901. Dr. Wragg, a seminary-trained clergyman, pledged his total support and dedication to the Bible cause. Historical documents reveal Dr. Wragg's deep concern for many African American families who were without Bibles.

Dr. Wragg focused particularly on African Americans living in urban areas as a target group for ABS work. He maintained that many "drifted" into the cities, fell into bad habits, and, at last, became "lost in the great sea of city sins." Their only salvation, in Dr. Wragg's view, rested in spiritual rebirth through the Scriptures. He wanted the African American churches to take an active role in Bible work by recognizing and supporting the work of the American Bible Society.

▸ American Bible Society colporteurs reading the Bible with a southern family, ca. 1900. Courtesy of American Bible Society Archives, New York, NY

▸ Dr. and Mrs. John Percy Wragg, June, 1929. Courtesy of American Bible Society Archives, New York, NY

From 1901-1929, Dr. Wragg supervised the Agency's operation from his home at Gammon Seminary, an African American Methodist seminary in Atlanta. During that time, the Agency distributed more than 625,000 Bibles and countless portions. Public distribution was undertaken by an initial group of six colporteurs (Bible distributors) at work in six states: Georgia, Alabama, Mississippi, Tennessee, Louisiana, and South Carolina. By 1920, 16 colporteurs were at work for the Agency in 13 states.

Most of the colporteurs were seminary-trained members of the Methodist Episcopal Church. Their outreach extended to many other traditional African American denominations, including the African Methodist Episcopal Church, the African Methodist Episcopal Zion Church, the former Colored Methodist Episcopal Church (now Christian Methodist Episcopal Church), and the National Baptist Convention, U.S.A., Inc., and they reaped great rewards in distribution.

▸ Miss S. E. Harris. First female African-American colporteur, ca. 1911. Courtesy of American Bible Society Archives, New York, NY

In 1911, Dr. Wragg hired the first African American woman colporteur, Miss S. E. Harris. As a student at Atlanta University, Miss Harris had been an active volunteer for the Agency, and she became a salaried colporteur in Mississippi immediately after her graduation.

All Agency colporteurs followed the same basic Bible Society rules. They systematically visited all African American households in a neighborhood and specifically sought out families likely to be neglected. They sold Bibles at standard ABS discounted rates, giving free volumes only to the most destitute, in accordance with regular ABS policy.

Each colporteur developed his or her own style and found the approach most effective in the communities they served. They understood that the difficult work of spreading God's Word could not depend upon comfortable accommodations or good roads.

Most people received the colporteurs warmly, gathered their families together, and requested them to read selections aloud. A colporteur's arrival was a special event, which helped overcome feelings of separation and isolation for rural families.

▸ A young boy sells a New Testament in St. Petersburg, FL, ca. 1934. Courtesy of American Bible Society Archives, New York, NY

In the cities, colporteurs found established African American neighborhoods with thriving local institutions. The local African American church usually provided a focal point for introducing and carrying out the work of the Society. Bible distributors frequently entered a particular city by train, canvassed the area, and then reboarded the same line to visit other cities. The cities offered a special opportunity to visit the workplaces of many African American residents and to reach out to larger groups.

The Agency Among the Colored People of the United States

In 1919, the American Bible Society formed the National Church Advisory Council (NCAC). This inter-denominational group was formed to enhance and strengthen collaboration between the American Bible Society and Christian churches and organizations that are committed to sharing the gospel. Currently, the National Church Advisory Council provides counsel and feedback on ABS projects and programs, and helps to educate denominational staff in using and distributing ABS Scripture resources in and around their churches and communities.

In 1920, Dr. Wragg sought to extend his territory to include the whole United States. Hundreds of thousands of African Americans had fled the South since 1900 in search of economic opportunity in the North. World War I greatly accelerated this exodus as African Americans, especially those from the deep South, headed North for jobs in factories producing war materials.

Dr. Wragg's proposal was approved by the ABS, and the name of the Agency changed to reflect the new territory. Dr. Wragg moved to Bible House in New York City, establishing five regional administrative centers throughout the country.

In just ten years, the Agency distributed 1,367,828 pieces of Scripture to African Americans nationwide. More than 134,000 people received complete Bibles during that time.

A relatively new form of transportation, the automobile, became a vital element in distribution, with colporteurs relying on the vehicles not only for mobility but also to attract interest and arouse curiosity wherever they stopped.

In 1927, a major flood devastated communities along the Mississippi River. African Americans constituted a disproportionately high number of the victims who lost their homes and belongings. ABS efforts to help those affected by the flood included the production of a special edition of the Bible. During the relief period, more than 50,000 Gospels, thousands of portions and New Testaments, and more than 2,000 Bibles were distributed to African American families affected by the flooding. Agency officials contended that the prompt and generous response from the ABS strengthened the organization's appeal and legitimacy to the communities it served.

The William Ingraham Haven Memorial Agency Among the Colored People of the United States

In 1929, Dr. Wragg retired. But before leaving, he renamed the Agency for William Ingraham Haven, the ABS general secretary who had created it. Dr. Wragg and his wife, Jessie Elizabeth, also established a sizable personal endowment to continue the work of the Agency.

The reorganized Haven Agency embarked on its mission during the worst financial depression in American history. Factory shutdowns and slowdowns resulted in massive industrial unemployment, and the fall in the price of cotton and other agricultural products forced many farmers and tenants off the land. In 1931, the Agency's annual report noted "that the Negro is the last to get a job and the first to be dropped, other things being equal." African Americans suffered more acutely than any other group, with most possessing meager resources for Scripture purchase. Consequently, sales dropped precipitously during the early years of the decade and they leveled off to about 180,000 copies annually in 1941.

The Agency again sought new and creative ways to share the Word of God, turning to the business community and govern-

▸ Children distributing the Scriptures, Houston, TX, ca. 1927. Courtesy of American Bible Society Archives, New York, NY

ment programs as avenues of distribution. As unemployment and poverty escalated among African American youth, the Agency instituted special Bible study programs to increase the Bible-mindedness of the young. World War II ended the depression, but created new problems for the Bible Society. Periodic paper shortages and paper rationing restricted the production of Bibles, and transportation problems delayed shipments and limited colporteur travel within the United States.

Despite these obstacles, the Agency continued its domestic work and initiated new and expanded services to the Armed Forces. Although units were segregated in the Armed Forces, the Agency frequently donated scriptural materials to military personnel without regard to race, continuing a policy begun by Dr. Wragg during the First World War.

After the war, the program emphasized youth work, especially among the students and recent graduates of African American colleges in the South, until 1959, when ABS leaders declared the segregated work an anachronism, and an internal reorganization ended the Society's special mission among African Americans in the United States.

▸ "Conference at Orlando, FL," ca. 1933. Courtesy of American Bible Society Archives, New York, NY

The Stirrings of the Civil Rights Movement

Intensified protests against segregation and the legal movement to banish discrimination from society during the 1950s exerted a profound impact on the Bible movement. The ABS confronted its own part in the fight for human rights and chose to eliminate any aspect of its operation that bore "any semblance to segregation."

Within the context of the African American churches, the Bible played an essential role in shaping and guiding the work of civil rights leaders such as the Rev. Dr. Martin Luther King, Jr., and the Rev. Joseph Lowery of the Southern Christian Leadership Conference.

In 1968 Dr. Gilbert Darlington, a General Officer of the ABS, undertook a personal mission to distribute Dr. King's "Letter from a Birmingham Jail" in an attempt to raise public awareness of injustices to the African American community.

In the late 1960s, the ABS increased its efforts to distribute Scripture in inner-city areas, particularly to African Americans living in the cities, and it placed special emphasis on building relations with and among various African American groups.

The ABS Heritage Program

In keeping with its commitment to build a strong relationship with America's racial and ethnic heritage groups, the American Bible Society launched the Heritage Program in 1991. This inter-denominational effort invites people of all races to partner with ABS in carrying out its mission of sharing the gospel.

Participants in the Heritage Program, along with the members of the inter-racial National Church Advisory Council, help the American Bible Society to spread God's Word to every man, woman, and child – of every race and nation—so that all may come to know the saving grace of our Lord Jesus Christ.

St FRANCOIS XAVIER
SAINT PAUL

Twelve

Black Preaching in the Church

Elliott Cuff

The role of Black preaching in the spiritual and social history and lives of African Americans in America is inestimable. Additionally, the strengths of the Black church in America cannot be known without relevant and relative considerations being given to the contributions made by Black preaching in developing those strengths. Black preaching continues to be the predominant art and literary form that the Black church has derived from the Bible for the maintenance of its spiritual consciousness and moral conscience. The following article briefly summarizes the relationship the Bible and Black preaching have enjoyed in America.

◄ Stained glass in a church. Sacred Heart of Jesus Christ Church, Pondicherry, India. © V. Muthuraman/ Superstock

The publication of the Jubilee Bible by the American Bible Society presents a good opportunity to talk about the relationship of the Bible and Black preaching in America; that is, Black preaching in the church in America. This article will briefly examine that relationship historically, culturally, and theologically.

First, it needs to be understood what is meant by the term "Black preaching." In this article the term, Black preaching refers to the preaching done by those persons of African descent who have, for the most part, done most of their preaching in what is commonly understood as the Protestant Black church in America (Lincoln and Mamiya, 1990). In other instances, the term "Black preaching" has been called African American preaching. The Black church, however, is not a monolithic religious institution. The Black church is made up of many Protestant denominations as well as a few non-Protestant denominations. They vary in their sociological descriptions, class, and cultural definitions. Black preaching is also a significant part of Roman Catholic worship experiences and liturgy. Therefore, Black preaching in the church is not a monolithic proclamation driven solely by cultural, racial, or class interests. Black preaching is simply the spiritual, artistic, and linguistic expression used by the preacher to help those persons in the Black church and in the church in general to hear the Word of God (Romans 10.14, 17).

It also needs to be understood that while Black preaching is mostly done by Black preachers in the Black church, there have been preachers of other nationalities and racial backgrounds who have done what can be called "Black preaching." This "non-Black" Black preaching is marked primarily by its acceptance among Black preachers and congregations and not by any definable literary or artistic form (Brueggemann, 1978; Buttrick, 1994). Also, many Black preachers have done Black preaching in other churches not commonly understood as being Black nor interracial. Moreover, due to the historical and the relevant societal concerns of people of African descent in America, the pulpit for Black preaching has been set up in the political and social forums beyond the conventional and traditional trappings of the church (Abernathy, 1970). Black preaching has become known by its cultural theater, its biblical and theological emphasis, and its spiritual acceptance among those persons in the church who have come to recognize what is and what is not Black preaching (Mitchell, 1979). This generalization can be borne out more succinctly by reviewing Black preaching in the church historically.

In many ways, the role of Black preaching in the church historically parallels the major doctrinal and historical themes set forth in the Bible. Themes such as creation, redemption, restoration, liberation, nation building, exile, new creation, and community building mark the emphasis of the earliest Black preaching done in the church. While there are no exact records about when or where the first Black preaching was done, it is commonly believed that the earliest Black preaching emerged and evolved during slavery in America (Franklin, 1967; Woodson, 1921).

Slaves who had heard the preaching of white preachers, white missionaries, and white abolitionists soon grew in knowledge, although limited, of the Bible and began to preach to other slaves about God. Imbued with the power of the Holy Spirit, the earliest Black preaching was directed at sustaining the hopes of a people for a new day of freedom and liberation from slavery in heaven (Franklin, 1967). It was this "otherworldliness" of Black preaching that initially characterized and shaped the literary forms of Black preaching. It is indeed remarkable how Black preachers were able to shape and hone an idiom and language for preaching, given the near universal bar, both by legal and societal consensus, against slaves learning to read and write. Moreover, there was a general fear among white slave owners and the free masses that any forms of free association and public speaking by slaves, be it for religious purposes or otherwise, were dangerous to law and order. Into such a societal context, Black preaching was created. To echo and embellish a preaching dictum attributed to a famous European preacher in the preceding century, "...with the Bible in one hand and [the power of God] in the other hand," Black preachers helped to create fluid and elastic spheres of faith among a people whose hopes were anchored in the God of their oppressors. While much of what Black preachers initially preached was a mimic of what they heard white preachers say about God, it was not long before an identifiable context of biblical content became the distinguishing characteristic of Black preaching.

There appeared to be, and understandably so, more spiritual fervor and emotional passion derived in Black preaching when the content of the preaching focused on biblical stories of creation, redemption, restoration, liberation, and the like that mirrored the plight of the slaves. So, Black preachers preached about Daniel being delivered by God while in the lions den (Daniel 6), the three Hebrew boys escaping the fiery furnace (Daniel 3), the children of Israel being led by Moses from Egypt to the Promised Land (Exodus 3–24), and other biblical stories and themes that emphasized hope

▸ George Liele, 1750–1820. Illustration by Nancy Lane.

in God. In nearly every instance, Black preachers paralleled the context of the situations faced by their hearers. In most cases, due to the lack of access to the language of the King James Bible and to the language of their oppressors, Black preachers were forced to compensate rational linguistic forms with their own imagination, language creativity, and retained African cultural art forms that would eventually set Black preaching apart from all other forms of the white evangelistic and missionary preaching that the slaves first heard (Franklin, 1967). This is not to say that early Black preaching was not eloquent nor heard more widely. The very opposite is true.

Recent scholarship has reported that there were "so-called slave preachers" whose preaching had become so effective and so eloquent that the general masses longed to hear them. There are now verifiable stories and folklore about such Black preachers as Harry Hoosier or "Black Harry" (1750-1810) who became such a great orator of the Bible that many of the famed leaders of that generation marveled at the incomparable speaking skills that he possessed. Then there was George Liele. Liele was a slave converted to Christianity around 1772. Liele would later be recognized for his worship skills and would be ordained as a preacher and granted the privilege to preach to slaves on a plantation near Silver Bluff, Georgia. The influence of Liele's preaching is attributed to the establishing of the first Baptist church in America (Woodson, 1921).

Henry Highland Garnet was one of the most famous Negro orators in the period before the Civil War. He was born a slave in New Market, Maryland, about 1815, and escaped with his family to New York City in 1824. Two years later he entered New York African Free School where his schoolmates included S.R. Ward (who was Garnet's second cousin) and Alexander Crummell, both of whom were to become active in the anti-slavery movement. From 1828 to 1830, Garnet worked as a cabin boy on a ship to Cuba and as a bound-out servant. In 1831 he entered the high school for Negro youth in New York City and also attended the Sunday school of the First Colored Presbyterian Church where he came under the influence of the Rev. Theodore S. Wright. Garnet attended the academy in Canaan, New Hampshire, but this school was destroyed by an anti-Negro riot and students were forced to flee. From 1838 to 1840, he studied at the Oneida Institute, which was under the direction of Beriah Green, a noted anti-slavery leader. While editing an abolitionist paper, *The Clarion*, at Troy, New York, Garnet turned to the study of theology. After several years of study under Dr. Berman, he was licensed by the Presbytery of Troy in 1842. From 1842 to 1848 he served as pastor of the Liberty Street Presbyterian Church of Troy while continuing his anti-slavery activities.

▸ Richard Allen, 1760–1831. Richard Allen was the first bishop of the African Methodist Episcopal Church and the first recognized national leader of the black community. Illustration by Nancy Lane.

The African American Episcopal (A.M.E.) Church, among other things, largely owes its origins to the preaching of Richard Allen (1760-1831). Allen, who first gained acceptance as a preacher among whites, was involved in one of the most triumphant socio-religious movements in American religious history at the St. George's Methodist Church in Philadelphia, Pennsylvania. It was out of this movement at St. George's that the A.M.E. Church was born and for which Allen was revered for his powerful preaching and his dynamic leadership. There were other Black preachers, many of them slave preachers, who were respected both for their preaching abilities as well as their leadership abilities. Again, mirroring their historical African roots and paralleling the preachers and prophets of the Bible, especially the Old Testament, the development of Black preaching, historically in the church in America, would give the Black preacher the prime responsibility as the leader of his community. As the Israelites looked to Moses and others (Exodus 3–24), the Black church and the Black community would recognize the Black preacher in a similar way. This historical current in Black preaching is still very prevalent today in many churches. However, there may be indications that the traditional cultural aspects of Black preaching are on the decline.

Culturally speaking, Black preaching has always been at home in what is commonly understood as the Black spiritual cultural context. This is a context that is derived largely from the traditional African religious expression (Herskovits, 1958). It is a spiritual context shaped by what is understood about God through the verbal declaration, the physical demonstration, and the imaginative storytelling. First, the context was socially innate in the slaves, slavery notwithstanding, and then maintained and sustained by the Black church throughout its history (Franklin, 1967; Lincoln 1974). So, then, the earliest cultural expressions in the religious experience of Black people were focused around prayer, song, and dance. While some have mistakenly marked the cultural accentuation of this experience as "illiterate, slavish, or backward," these expressions have shaped and formed the foundations for Black preaching in the church (Johnston, 1974; Woodson, 1921).

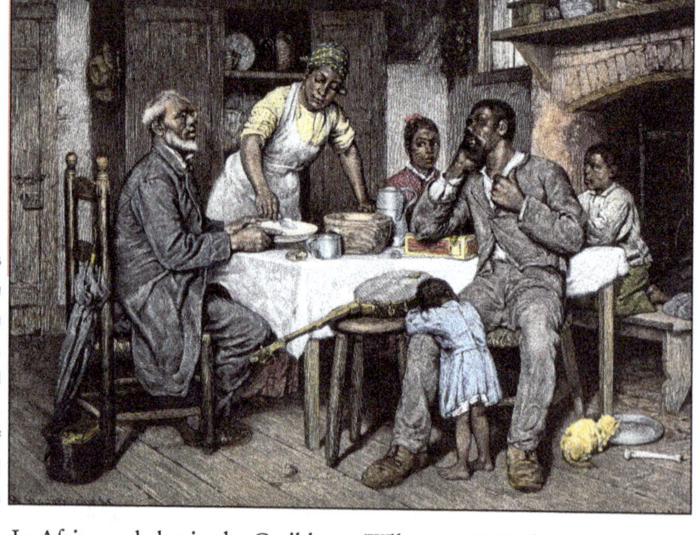

▸ The pastor's visit to an African-American family. 1800s, hand-colored woodcut. Courtesy of North Wind Picture Archives

In Africa and also in the Caribbean (Wilmore, 1983) the contexts of the celebrations were feasts, songs, fellowship, and adoration (praise) to the Supreme Being or God. As the slaves were converted to Christianity, they continued this tradition in their expressions of Christian faith. Black preaching connected to this experience by incorporating, in many instances, the song-style, the physical dramatic expression, the fellowship, and the praise of the recognizable cultural context in telling stories or preaching about God. The fellowship of Black preaching is understood as the interaction between the preacher and the hearers as both interact in the Spirit. This interaction in Black preaching was and is still audibly recognized by the antiphonal or "call and response" attribute associated with Black church worship.

In this regard, the fellowship aspect of Black preaching is very critical in how preaching is viewed and defined culturally by both preachers and congregations. Although many Black congregations and preachers have not recognized this aspect of Black preaching, they seem to favor a cultural aspect that is accompanied by song, prayer, and praise. It is also shaped by distinct religious interests based upon class and social status preferences. On the other hand, the most recognized traditional and cultural aspect of Black preaching is sometimes referred to as "tuning up," "pulling it," "gravy," or "whooping."

"Tuning up" usually happens near the conclusion of the sermon, although in any given church context it might occur at any point in the sermon. Sometimes, the "tuning up" aspect of Black preaching today is accompanied by musical intonations, usually from the Hammond organ or a piano in the church. Before Black churches could afford to have musical instruments, "tuning up" was accompanied by the vocal musical tonal inflections of the members of the church. These vocal musical tonal inflections were similar to the chants associated with West African and Caribbean religions (Wilmore, 1983). In many churches today this aspect of the fellowship in Black preaching still exists and is formally recognized by many, preachers and congregations alike, as the measure of the ability to preach. In fact, there are some denominations in the Black church experience who have developed recognizable subcultures for this type of preaching (commonly referred to as the Late Night Services) where the whole subculture is contrived on "tuning up." Others, usually more interested in the more substantive aspects of Christian Education, have called this continued preaching practice of "tuning up" as only being done in response to the itching ears of the culture rather than as preaching being done to the glory of God (1 Timothy 4.1-3). Again, with the new preaching being done in the Black religious context, there is a clear break from the traditional and conventional forms of Black preaching as it is historically understood. This might be further underscored by briefly looking at the theological aspects of Black preaching.

Theologically, the heart and mind of Black preaching are, and always have been, Jesus, Calvary, and "the third day." While it is true that, historically, the great character and theme stories of the Old Testament in the Bible have a large place in the canon of the Black preaching experience, there is more identification theologically with Jesus, Calvary, and "early Sunday morning" as understood from the perspective of the New Testament. Regardless of the style or type of

Black preaching that was and is being done, and no matter where the Black preacher takes a preaching text in the Bible, at some point in the preaching, usually at the end, the preaching must go by Jesus at Calvary. In Black preaching, Jesus must die, be buried, and then be resurrected. This resurrected Jesus is the most practical theology of hope understood universally in the Black Church experience. The whole of the Black experience can be understood in preaching, biblically and theologically, by identifying with what happened to Jesus.

Jesus suffered needlessly, and Black people suffer needlessly. Jesus received injustice, and Black people receive injustice. Jesus was marginalized by the majority, and Black people, too, are marginalized by the majority in America. Jesus identified more readily with the oppressed, the downcast, the poor, the imprisoned, and the powerless minorities in societies (Luke 4.18,19; 15); and Black people hold their theological identity more closely being associated with what happened to Jesus.

Jesus would eventually be triumphant over every form of sin, sickness, and evil; and Black people believe that with Jesus they, too, can be as triumphant. This is at the heart and mind, theologically, of the Black preaching experience. Jesus was crucified, buried, and has risen triumphantly; and Jesus has all power over the kingdoms of this world and the next (1 Corinthians 15). This is the holistic aspect of the Black preaching experience where every aspect of broken humanity in Black life is hermeneutically, that is, biblically interpreted, through the contexts of what Jesus went through. Therefore, the struggles, setbacks, hurts, and hopes of a people, historically denied and yet still denied, have been addressed in the proclamation of a triumphant Jesus as set forth in the Bible. It was this type of theological understanding that underscored the Black preaching done in one of the most telling periods in our nation's history, the Civil Rights Movement.

▸ Martin Luther King, Jr. speaking in Montgomery © Bettman/Corbis Used by Permission

Martin Luther King, Jr., as well as others who believed in the movement, helped to shape a Black preaching ethic based on the liberation and freedom grounded in a theology primarily shaped by what happened to Jesus. Although not roundly received with great popularity during that time, nonetheless it was the liberation and redemptive preaching done by a host of others that moved an entire nation toward its true biblical identity with God (Proverbs 14.34; 29.18).

As we celebrate the publication of the Jubilee Edition of the Bible, the relevance of preaching a triumphant Jesus is still existent in our world today. There are hard questions Black preaching must face in and for the next millennium. For instance, how will the rapid increases in the continued impersonalization of ministry through the electronic media affect how conventional preaching forms are used? Will the reliance upon a type of preaching that pays almost

▸ Tenth Memorial Baptist Church, Philadelphia, PA. Photographs and Prints Division, Schomburg Center for Research in Black Culture, The New York Public Library, Astor, Lenox and Tilden Foundations, ca. 1940's

no attention to any of the classical preachers or the historical scholarship of Black preaching create a new understanding of Romans 10.14-17? With the continuing social formation of the "mega-churches" around the nation, where the boundaries of race, nationality, class (in some instances), and denominational preferences are becoming less distinguishable, will it mean that Black preaching, as it is known, will soon meet its mainstream demise? What, if any, effect will the availability and proliferation of Christian information among the masses have on the demand for biblically relevant expository preaching in the church?

Even before the dawn of a new millennium, more and more Black female preachers have been making their voices heard. Modern society, as a result of civil and equal rights laws and policies, is increasingly elevating the status and role of women in virtually all areas of professional secular life. A similar, albeit protracted and hesitant, parallel of such elevation of women in the proclamation ministries can also be seen in the Black church. Thus, the gospel of Jesus Christ is now increasingly being proclaimed in the pulpits of churches and seminaries by female voices which had previously been silent or suppressed. While society and the Black church (as well as the church in general) have yet a long way to go in this regard, Black preaching is already reaping the benefits. Further, an increasing number of articles and books championing the contributions of Black female preachers are now available. This new vista can only strengthen the future of Black preaching, theologically, biblically, and culturally.

For the most part, Black preaching has had a glorious past, enjoys a good, but unpredictable and amorphous present, yet still has hope for a bright future in God! As long as Black preaching in the church can have the Bible in the church and keep the Bible in its preaching, God shall be victorious in all of humanity!

Bibliography

Abernathy, Ralph. "Our Lives Were Filled With Action," in *Martin Luther King, Jr.* C. Eric Lincoln, ed. New York: Hill & Wang, 1970.

Brueggemann, Walter. *The Prophetic Imagination.* Minneapolis: Fortress Press, 1978.

Buttrick, David. *A Captive Voice: The Liberation of Preaching.* Louisville: John Know/Westminster Press, 1994.

_________. *Preaching Jesus Christ.* Philadelphia: Fortress, 1988.

Franklin, John Hope. *From Slavery to Freedman.* New York: Alfred A. Knopf, 1967.

Herskovits, Melville. *The Myth of the Negro Past.* Boston: Beacon Press, 1958.

Johnston, Rubye F. *The Development of Negro Religion.* Garden City, NY: Anchor/Doubleday, 1974.

_________ and Lawrence H. Mamiya. *The Black Church in the African American Experience.* Durham: North Carolina University Press, 1990.

Mitchell, Henry. *Black Preaching.* New York: Harper & Row, 1979.

_________. *Celebration and Experience in Preaching.* Nashville: Abingdon Press, 1990.

Wilmore, Gayraud S. *Black Religion and Black Radicalism.* 2nd Ed. Maryknoll, NY: Orbis, 1983.

Woodson, Carter G. *The History of the Negro Church.* Washington, DC: Associated Publishers, 1921.

Voices of Black Women Who Have Proclaimed the Gospel

Amanda Berry Smith (1837-1915)

▸ Amanda Berry Smith. Illustration by Nancy Lane.

Amanda Smith was first a preacher in the African Methodist Church. Later, she became a missionary evangelist who preached in the United States, as well as in England, Scotland, Africa, and India. Against the most adverse circumstances, beginning her life as a slave, she not only preached God's Word, but she lived it. She also encouraged Christians to achieve "spiritual perfection." Amanda dedicated her life to helping women and children. She was referred to as "God's image carved in ebony."

Lulu (Louise Cecilia) Fleming (1862-1899)

Lulu Fleming was born during slavery, but became a career missionary in the Women's American Baptist Foreign Mission Society of the West. During her short life, she served God in Africa. Miss Fleming was the valedictorian of her class at Shaw University. She also received a medical degree from the Pennsylvania Women's Medical College, in preparation for a position as a medical missionary in the Congo.

▶ Lulu Fleming. Illustration by Nancy Lane.

Jarena Lee (1783-1857)

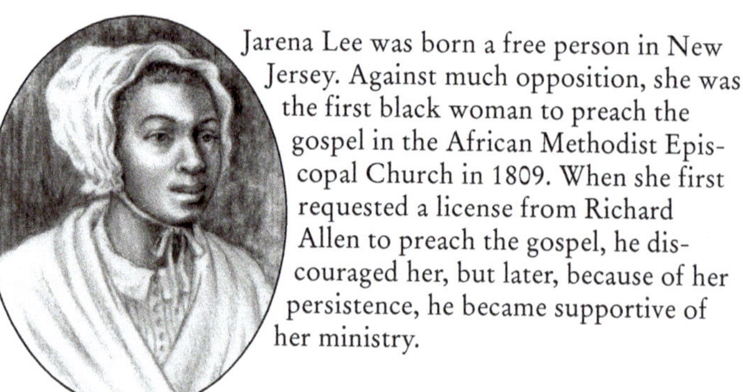

Jarena Lee was born a free person in New Jersey. Against much opposition, she was the first black woman to preach the gospel in the African Methodist Episcopal Church in 1809. When she first requested a license from Richard Allen to preach the gospel, he discouraged her, but later, because of her persistence, he became supportive of her ministry.

▶ Jarena Lee. Illustration by Nancy Lane.

Zilpha Elaw (c. 1790)

Zilpha Elaw was converted at a camp meeting in 1817. At the same time, she received a call to the ministry. Zilpha Elaw ministered in the south to congregations of slaves even though she was a free black woman from the north. There was a danger of her being captured and sold as a slave, but this did not deter her. Eventually, she joined with Jarena Lee to form a preaching team.

▶ Zilpha Elaw. Illustration by Nancy Lane.

Julia A. Foote (1823-1900)

Julia A. Foote. Illustration by Nancy Lane.

Julia A. Foote was the first black woman to be ordained a deacon in the African Methodist Episcopal Zion Church. She was the second black woman to be ordained an elder in 1900. She had a very special conversion experience and received a call to a preaching ministry. Julia overcame much resistance to answer the Lord's call to service.

Nannie Helen Burroughs (1883 - 1961)

Nannie Helen Burroughs Illustration by Nancy Lane.

Nannie Helen Burroughs devoted her life to working on behalf of and for black women in their struggle for visibility and recognition of their gifts and talents in the Black Church. She was instrumental in forming the Women's Convention of the National Baptist Convention; and her great achievement was her role as the founder of Women's Day in the Black Church.

Sources Cited

Deen, Edith. *Great Women of the Christian Faith.* New Jersey: Barbour & Co., 1959.

Ruether, Rosemary R. and Skinner, Rosemary K. *In Our Own Voices: Four Centuries of American Women's Religious Writing.* San Francisco: Harper Collins, 1996.

__________. *Women and Religion in America.* Vol. 3: 1900-1968. San Francisco: Harper & Row, 1986.

Riggs, Marcia Y. *Can I Get A Witness? Prophetic Religious Voices of African American Women: An Anthology.* Maryknoll, NY: Orbis Books, 1997.

"*The Gallery: Thumbnail Sketches of Significant Leaders, Evangelists, Thinkers, and Movers in Baptist History.*" Christian History Magazine. Vol. IV, No. 2, Issue #6.

Black Women Educators

Mary Jane Patterson (? -1894)

▸ Mary Jane Paterson. Illustration by Nancy Lane.

Mary Jane Patterson was the first black woman in America to receive a bachelor's degree in 1862. She attended Oberlin College in Ohio. Oberlin was well known for its abolitionist policies. Charles Finney, the great revivalist of the nineteenth century was also president of Oberlin at that time, and advocated coed classes. Oberlin College was a "station on the Underground Railroad" and helped many slaves achieve freedom. Mary Jane Patterson, from a family of slaves, graduated and pursued a teaching career in the north.

Mary McCleod Bethune (1875 - 1955)

▸ Mary McLeod Bethune. Illustration by Nancy Lane.

Mary McCleod Bethune was an outstanding educator and humanitarian, as well as an eloquent lecturer. She was an advisor to Franklin D. Roosevelt and she was the Founder-President of Bethune-Cookman College in Florida. She availed herself of every opportunity to crusade on behalf of decent public schools and civil rights.

Phillis Wheatley (1753 - 1784)

The title page of Phillis Wheatley's book "Poems on Various Subjects, Religious and Moral," printed in London in 1773. Wheatley was kidnapped from Senegal at the age of nine and taken as a slave to Boston, where she began to write poetry in English five years later. She was quickly recognized as a prodigy, and her writings became particulaly popular in England.

▸ Portrait of Phillis Wheatley. © Corbis

Virginia W. Broughton (c. 1850)

Virginia W. Broughton, the first black woman to receive a college degree in the south (Fisk University), dedicated her life to home missions and forming Bible study groups for women. She was very active in Sunday School work, and what was called the "Bible Band." Virginia W. Broughton was a fine example of a person who combined her faith with her teaching.

▸ Viirginia W. Broughton. Illustration by Nancy Lane.

Sources Cited

"God's College and Radical Change." Christian History Magazine. Vol. VII, No. 4, Issue #20.

Ruether, Rosemary R. and Skinner, Rosemary K. *In Our Own Voices: Four Centuries of American Women's Religious Writing.* San Francisco: HarperCollins, 1996.

__________. *Women and Religion in America.* Vol. 3: 1900-1968. San Francisco, Harper & Row, 1986.

Riggs, Marcia Y. *Can I Get A Witness? Prophetic Voices of African American Women: An Anthology.* Maryknoll, NY: Orbis Books, 1997.

Thirteen

Music in the Black Church

William H. Collins, Jr.

All great music finds its roots in the church, and in the Black experience, it is no different. The music of Black people—rhythm and blues, soul, jazz, and folk—finds its origin in the Black church. Music in the forms of spirituals, hymns, anthems, traditional gospel, contemporary gospel, and praise and worship is the root and inspiration of the sound of music in the Black community. The melodies, rhythms, and harmonies are born out of a desire to give God the glory due him and to lift up the name of Jesus, our Lord and Savior.

◄ "The Jubilee Singers," by Edward Havel, (British, 1835-1908). Oil on canvas, Fisk University Franklin Library Special Collections. Used by Permission

Music has always been an integral part in the lives of black people. It carries over from everyday life into the church and has been very important in helping to keep the emotional balance necessary for the joy, peace, and spirituality of the individual. Its purpose is, therefore, that God may be glorified and people edified. "I will sing unto the LORD as long as I live: I will sing praise to my God while I have my being" (Psalm 104.33, *KJV*).

In 1619, a Dutch vessel landed twenty Africans at Jamestown, Virginia. They were bought by colonial settlers. This was the beginning of the African slave trade in the American colonies. Slaves came from various localities in Africa. In this country they were cut off from the moorings of their culture, having to adjust to a completely alien way of life, having to learn a strange language, and having to endure a barbaric system of slavery. Yet, it was within this cruel milieu, and from these oppressed people, that beautiful melodious spirituals originated. The music and words of the black spirituals are noble and their sentiments are exalted.

Many of the spirituals used in worship in the black church grew out of the everyday struggles for existence and survival. Songs were sung to ease the adverse circumstances—uncertainties of the future, harsh and painful treatment, and the wounding of the psyche. These circumstances characterized the lives of the slaves; yet, they were able to communicate with their Maker through the spirituals.

Some of the spirituals were also sung to transport messages to one another in their endeavors to escape from slavery by way of the Underground Railroad. Songs such as "Go Down Moses," "Deep River," "Stan, Still Jordan," "Walk Together Children," and "Swing Low, Sweet Chariot."

The slaves came to America endowed with musical talent to begin with; and the spirituals possess many of the fundamental characteristics of African music. African-American spirituals are built upon this foundation, but they contain a higher melodic quality and an added harmonic development.

All great music finds its roots in the church, and in the black experience, it is no different. The music of black people—folk, rhythm and blues, soul, and jazz—finds its origin in the black church. The black church has always been a breeding ground for the talent, gifts, and creativity of its community. Its music, found in the forms of spirituals, hymns, gospel, contemporary gospel, and praise and worship songs are very prominent in the church—"Speaking to yourselves in psalms and hymns and spiritual songs, singing and making melody in your heart to the Lord" (Ephesians 5.19, *KJV*). The melodies, rhythms, and harmonies are born out of a desire to give God the glory due him and to lift up the name of Jesus, our Lord and Savior.

The only difference between the root of gospel and its offspring is the lyrical content and the focus of the music. In the best of gospel, the lyrical content is Word-based, right out of the Scriptures. The focus of the music is the Lord, Jesus Christ, "the only wise God our Saviour" (Jude 24, *KJV*), to the glory of God the Father.

During the 1730s, the Great Awakening brought with it a demand for the use of livelier music (rather than anthems and canticles) in the worship services. These "livelier"songs were called hymns. The new style of texts by Dr. Isaac Watts (1674-1748) and Charles Wesley (1707-1788) appealed to blacks because of the vitality of the words, wider use of intervals than in psalm tunes, and their rhythmic freedom. The book, *Hymns and Spiritual Songs*, was published by Dr. Watts in 1707, and *A Collection of Psalms and Hymns* (1742) was published by John Wesley (1703-1791) together with his brother, Charles. These hymnbooks became the most widely used; and the latter book ultimately became the forerunner of the official *Methodist Hymnal.*

Toward the end of the eighteenth century, blacks began to break away from white congregations to establish their own places of worship. They brought to their own worship services some semblance of the white church worship format; however, the music gained another dimension by the addition of the African-Americans' indigenous experiences. The creation of new musical forms began—black hymns and spirituals.

The most prolific writer of the black hymn was Dr. Charles Albert Tindley (1856-1933). For many years, he pastored the Tindley Temple United Methodist Church in Philadelphia, PA. His period as a composer was from 1901-1906. However, his hymns did not become well known in the black churches until after World War I. Some of the hymns written by Dr. Tindley are: "Some Day" (Beams of Heaven), "Nothing Between," "Leave It There," "I'll Overcome Someday," "Stand by Me," "We'll Understand It Better By and By," among others.

Black gospel music came into existence during the latter part of the nineteenth century. This music was generally classified as "gospel" songs because they were inspired by the four gospels of the New Testament. They dealt with the teachings of Jesus and the life of the believer. Some black ministers, at first, did not permit gospel singing in their churches because of the rhythmic beat and its close relationship to the blues. Eventually, however, gospel began seeping into the churches.

Eileen Southern states in her book, *The Music of Black Americans*, "When the black people began pouring into the nation's cities during the second decade of the twentieth century, they took their joyful spirituals with them, but found the rural born music to be unsatisfactory in urban settings and unresponsive to their needs." Consequently, the church singers created a more expressive music to which they applied the term, gospel, but which displayed little resemblance to the traditional gospel song of the whites. Composer Thomas A. Dorsey developed and made popular the "gospel blues." His "Precious Lord, Take My Hand" became a musical staple of the black churches across the U.S. Black gospel music, then, became essentially the sacred counterpart of the city blues, sung in the same improvisatory tradition with piano, guitar, or instrumental accompaniment.

The music of the black church is also born out of its experience and relationship with the Lord, Jesus Christ. Our thanksgiving, praise, and worship is heartfelt and soulful because God has shown himself to be a great and good God unto us as a people. The love, care, and compassion of God toward us causes us to sing the way we do. We have experienced God as Savior, Liberator, Deliverer, Redeemer, Creator, Great Emancipator, Protector, Master, King, Judge, Supplier, etc., and the music in the black church reflects it. Black music addresses God for his keeping power through our formidable and toilsome past and our current struggles in today's burdensome society. The strength of African Americans can be viewed in light of the music that has been generated from their history.

God has graced the black church musician with creativity, ingenuity, and a wonderful ability of improvisation. Black worshipers join in, and celebrate with them in, the joyous renditions to magnify and glorify the Lord, for the Lord is the great source of music. All of the diversity within the musical realm emanates from God, who possesses multi-faceted and manifold wisdom in and through his creation, and music is just one of the examples.

▸ "Rise, shine for thy light has come!" by Aaron Douglas, ca. 1930. Gouache on paper. The Howard University Gallery of Art, permanent collection, Washington, DC

God uses the experiences of the gospel psalmists in the church. The black church, although joined universally with those in Christ, does not have the same heritage, culture, experiences, or history as others, so its music is unique and diverse in its forms.

One of the primary reasons for the black church service is for the people of God to come together to worship God for who he is and all that he has done. Therefore, the music, lyrics, and presentation must reflect the purpose of worship and be conducive to setting such an atmosphere in the house of the Lord. One must know what worship, praise, thanksgiving, and supplication are before being able to offer them worthily to the Lord. The music in the black church, through its lyrics, melodies, rhythms, and harmonies, enables and inspires these expressions in the service of the Lord.

Music must have the ability to open the hearts of the worshipers so they may yield and be available to God, to express praises and thanksgiving for his glory. Music, in many instances, enables the repentant to confess sorrow about sin. Music can be utilized to entreat God's presence among the people, and ushers the people into the presence of God. The music itself must be fitting and of a spiritual quality that welcomes the presence of a holy God. It must anticipate the anointing of the Holy Spirit to empower, deliver, and prosper the people of God, and whoever may be in the midst. Music should prepare our hearts and minds to hear from God so that we "might have life, and. . . have it more abundantly" (John 10.10b, *KJV*).

Music in the black church aids us in expressing ourselves in a way that is uniquely our own. As we sing, leap, dance, and shout praises, give thanks, and worship, the Lord God enthrones himself in our midst. It is reminiscent of Moses as he sang a song of victory (Exodus 15.1, 19), Miriam and the women who sang, danced, and played the timbrels (Exodus 15.20, 21), and David who danced before the Lord because the Ark had been carried safely into Jerusalem (2 Samuel 6.12-16). The liberty and freedom that we, as a people, have found in God's presence has long kept us sane and alive in the midst of the worst social injustices and oppression against humanity. Our music has been most instrumental in bringing us near to the great God our Savior, Jesus the Lord.

As a background accompaniment, music aids the preacher in proclaiming the Word of God in the worship service, especially near the climax of the message or sermon. When the Holy Spirit begins to move upon the preacher to speak the Word of God, there is a flow in the way the message is being spoken. Hence, the phrase, "the flow of conversation." In the moving of the Holy Spirit, there is sensitivity and timing; and hearts are open and receptive to the Word of God. Music inspired by the Holy Spirit assists the preaching moment by fostering sensitivity to God, as well as providing the timing necessary through its Word-based lyrics, melodies, rhythms, and harmonies. Music helps the anointing mount higher and higher as God uses his preaching instrument to sound his message to the people. The preacher can focus, tune in, tune up, and hear accurately from God. Music has prepared the atmosphere with the spiritual ambiance necessary for worship. Can the preacher preach by the Spirit of God without music? Yes, but it is very sweet with musical accompaniment. Consecrated music stills the soul of the preacher so that he or she may hear from God and proclaim the Word.

> "Then the priests left the Holy Place. All the priests who were present had purified themselves, whether or not they were on duty that day. And the Levites who were musicians—Asaph, Heman, Jeduthun, and all their sons and brothers—were dressed in fine linen robes and stood at the east side of the altar playing cymbals, harps, and lyres. They were joined by 120 priests who were playing trumpets. The trumpeters and singers performed together in unison to praise and give thanks to the LORD. Accompanied by trumpets, cymbals, and other instruments, they raised their voices and praised the LORD with these words:
>
> 'He is so good!
> His faithful love endures forever!'
>
> At that moment a cloud filled the Temple of the LORD. The priests could not continue their work because the glorious presence of the LORD filled the Temple of God."
> (2 Chronicles 5.11-14, *New Living Translation*)

Dr. William B. McClain states, "the Spirit has descended often when slaves and ex-slaves have gathered in worship and sung the Negro spirituals. These spirituals reveal the rich culture and the ineffable beauty and creativity of the black soul and intimate the uniqueness of the black religious tradition."

The slaves—having found themselves far from their native land, despised by those among whom they lived, experiencing the hurt of their separation from loved ones on the auction block, knowing the hard task master, feeling the lash—seized Christianity, the religion of compensations in the life to come, to help them endure the hurts suffered in their current existence. For the black slaves, Christianity gave them the hope that in the heavenly world there would be a complete reversal of conditions.

▸ Yoruba Drum for Ifa Ijebu Area. From A Ijebu-Igbo, England, London. © Christie's Image Primitive Art. Christie's Images Ltd./ Superstock

Having experienced the heartaches and struggles of everyday life, black people enter their churches with much hope and trust in the God who sends the sunshine and the rain, the God who is very much alive and active, and who has not forsaken those who are poor, oppressed, and out of work. Fear is turned to hope as they burst into songs of praise and celebration in sanctuaries large and small, and in storefronts. They did not need the services of psychologists, psychiatrists, or analysts because all of their inner frustrations were released to Almighty God in their outbursts of singing, shouting, dancing, and praises.

The importance of music in the black church can be seen through its ability to unify people. Group singing is done in practically every black church. It is a way of sharing joy, grief, and love. Congregations that sing together are brought closer through this experience. God has placed emphasis on music in his Word because it has a tremendous power to unify his people. "Thy watchmen shall lift up the voice; with the voice together shall they sing: for they shall see eye to eye, when the LORD shall bring again Zion. Break forth into joy, sing together, ye waste places of Jerusalem: for the LORD hath comforted his people, he hath redeemed Jerusalem" (Isaiah 52.8, 9, *KJV*).

The song of the Christian ought to include meaningful praise and thanksgiving to the LORD if the scriptural examples of music in worship and life are to be followed; e.g., Romans 15.9; Colossians 3.16; Hebrews 2.12.

"TO GOD BE THE GLORY"

Bibliography

Cleveland, J. Jefferson. *Songs of Zion*. Nashville: Abingdon/Parthenon Press, 1981.

DuBois, W.E.B. *Suppression of the African Slave-Trade*. New York: Longmans, 1896.

Garlock, Frank and Woetzel, Kurt. *Music in the Balance.* Greenville: Majesty Music, 1992.

Heilbut, Tony. *The Gospel Sound: Good News and Bad Times*. New York: Simon and Schuster, 1971.

Johnson, James Weldon and Johnson, J. Rosamond. *The Book of American Negro Spirituals*. New York: Da Capo Press, 1954.

Katz, Bernard. *The Social Implications of Early Negro Music in the United States.* New York: Arno/The New York Times, 1969.

National Baptist Publishing Board. *The New National Baptist Hymnal.* Nashville: National Baptist Publishing Board, 1977.

Southern, Eileen. *The Music of Black Americans*. New York: W. W. Norton, 1971.

Sometimes I feel like a Motherless Child

Negro Spiritual
Arranged by
H. T. BURLEIGH

*) The original form of this measure was written [music notation] In order to facilitate vocalization I have taken the liberty of altering it as above. *H. T. B.*

116496 – 4

Sometimes I feel like a Motherless Child
(continued)

N. Y. 1433

Sometimes I feel like a Motherless Child
(continued)

N. Y. 1433

Going to Shout all over God's Heav'n.

Joyfully, but not too fast.
1. I've got a robe, you've got a robe, All of God's children got a robe;
2. I've got a crown, you've got a crown, All of God's children got a crown;
3. I've got a shoes, you've got a shoes, All of God's children got a shoes;
4. I've got a harp, you've got a harp, All of God's children got a harp;
5. I've got a song, you've got a song, All of God's children got a song;
When I get to Heav-en, goin' to put on my robe, Goin' to
When I get to Heav-en, goin' to put on my crown, Goin' to
When I get to Heav-en, goin' to put on my shoes, Goin' to
When I get to Heav-en, goin' to play on my harp, Goin' to
When I get to Heav-en, goin' to sing a new song, Goin' to
shout all o - ver God's Heav'n.
shout all o - ver God's Heav'n.
walk all o - ver God's Heav'n.
play all o - ver God's Heav'n.
sing all o - ver God's Heav'n.
Refrain.
Heav'n*, Heav'n, Ev-'ry-bod-y talking 'bout
heav'n ain't going there, Heav'n, Heav'n, Goin' to shout all o - ver God's
* Let the last syllable of heav'n be a hum.

Rise and Shine.
CHORUS.
Oh, rise an' shine, an' give God de glo - ry, glo - ry, Rise an'
shine, an' give God de glo - ry, glo - ry, Rise an' shine, an'
give God de glo - ry, glo - ry for de year of Ju - ber - lee.
Je - sus car - ry de young lambs in his bo - som, bo - som,
Je - sus lead de ole sheep by still wa - ters, wa - ters,
Car - ry de young lambs in his bo - som, bo - som, Car - ry de
Lead de ole sheep by still wa - ters, wa - ters, Lead de

Rise and Shine.—Concluded.

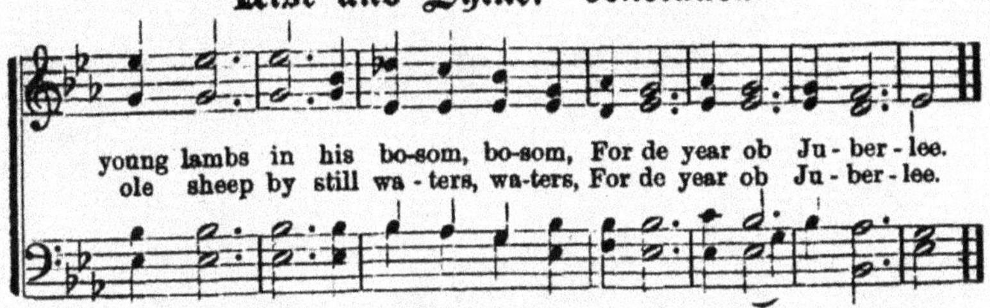
young lambs in his bo-som, bo-som, For de year ob Ju - ber - lee.
ole sheep by still wa - ters, wa-ters, For de year ob Ju - ber - lee.

2 Oh, come on, mourners, get you ready, ready,
Come on, mourners, get you ready, ready, (*bis*),
For de year ob jubilee;
You may keep your lamps trimmed an' burning, burning,
Keep your lamps trimmed an' burning, burning, (*bis*),
For de year ob jubilee.
Cho.—Oh, rise an' shine, &c.

3 Oh, come on, children, don't be weary, weary,
Come on, children, don't be weary, weary, (*bis*),
For de year ob jubilee;
Oh, don't you hear dem bells a-ringin', ringin',
Don't you hear dem bells a-ringin', ringin', (*bis*),
For de year ob jubilee.
Cho.—Oh, rise an' shine, &c.

Fourteen

The Bible in African American Spirituality

Michael I. N. Dash

The Bible has always had a place in the religious experience of African Americans. It was through the Bible that many of their slave ancestors learned to read. Indeed, the Bible became the primary source book for their devotion to the Christian faith and their life journey. The Bible is equally foundational in sustaining them amidst challenges today. African Americans' spirituality is woven into the texture of everyday living. Their knowledge and use of the Bible is a significant resource that helped their ancestors make meaning out of dehumanizing conditions in the slave society. That meaning is enriched through their identification with biblical characters and the story of the drama of the divine-human encounter.

◄ "Family Reunion," John Holyfield. Courtesy of John Holyfield, Holyfield Studios

There is a persistent impression which has imprinted itself into my consciousness—a pencil drawing that hung on an office wall. It was the picture of an old black woman. She must have been in her late eighties, perhaps even nineties. She is seated in a chair, bent over with a distinct curvature of her back at the shoulders, a hump, as if stricken with osteoporosis. She has woolly white hair. One of her fingers is placed, perhaps marking the spot in the book she is reading. It is the Bible.

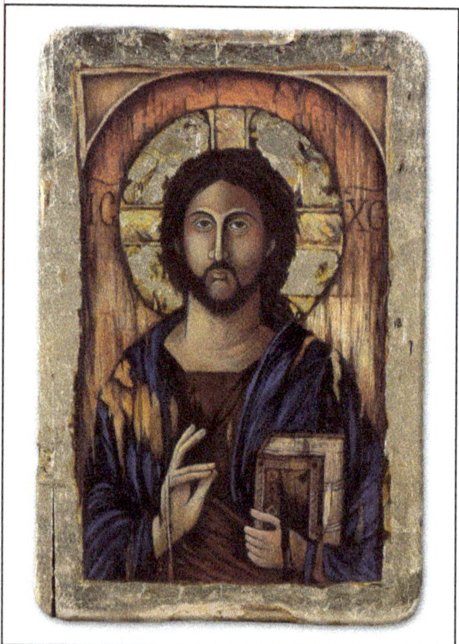

▸ "Word of Life," by Dianne Minnaar. Mixed media on board. © 2009 Dianne Minnaar

Looking at this old woman studied in her attention, I imagined how the Word must have been her succor over the long years of her life's journey. And now as I recall the picture of this woman in her evening years, I wonder how many of her friends and companions along the way are dead. Is she experiencing aloneness? Could it be that she is finding the words of the psalmist an assurance and affirmation of God's goodness? "O God, from my youth you have taught me, and I still proclaim your wondrous deeds. So even to old age and gray hairs, O God, do not forsake me, until I proclaim your might to all the generations to come. Your power and your righteousness, O God, reach the high heavens. You who have done great things, O God, who is like you?" (Psalm 71.17, 19, *NRSV*).

Then my mind turned to imagine a similar scene in the period of the slave society. Our ancestors too, like that woman in my picture, were acquainted with the Book, both through an oral tradition and later through the text itself. It was in the Bible that our ancestors found the promise of deliverance from the bondage to slavery and sin. It was in the Bible that they found inspiration, solace, and a word of hope. Albert Raboteau reminds us that, "the biblical orientation of slave religion was one of its central characteristics" (Raboteau, 1978, 239).

In this brief article, I will examine the use of the Bible by African Americans and how that use helped to inform and shape their spirituality, indeed their lives. For Africans, as well as African Americans, life is life in the Spirit. Life, as understood by our ancestors, and experienced by us, their children, is always in the totality of our beings—body, mind, and spirit. How then did, and does, the Bible impact and influence the totality of our lives and the tales that we tell? This is the question that is being explored in this article.

The Bible for Us

As Christians, we would claim that the Bible is the source book of our faith. It is the story of humankind's response to God's actions. That response has sometimes been rejection and rebellion, sometimes acceptance and obedience. Jesus Christ is God's act of acts. The acts of God are narrated in the Old Testament (Hebrew Bible) and lead us to Jesus Christ. In the New Testament, the acts of God recorded there flow from him, so that Jesus himself is revealed in his full meaning, or as we see him, in the total context of the biblical witness.

We affirm that the Bible is both a word in a particular historical situation, as well as word for us today. Our challenge in using the Bible is to rediscover the faith of the Bible. This rediscovery will lead us to meet the God of the Bible who reveals who God is in the Word. So as we engage the Bible, we pray:

> Break Thou the bread of life, dear Lord, to me,
> As Thou didst break the loaves beside the sea;
> Beyond the sacred page, I seek Thee, Lord,
> My spirit pants for Thee, O living Word.
>
> Mary Artemisia Lathbury, *The Bread of Life*

"You search the scriptures," said Jesus, "because you think that in them you have eternal life; and it is they that testify on my behalf. Yet you refuse to come to me to have life" (John 5.39, 40, *NRSV*). It is the witness of the Scriptures that is the determining factor. They point beyond themselves. Eternal life is not in them but in him to whom they point. When we have finished using all the critical tools available to us for a study of the Bible, we still have to wrestle with the witness of the passage that we are studying. The genius of African American spirituality, and its inheritance from our slave ancestors, is that there is this openness to discover God as revealed in the Word. It is a witness to a concern for every single aspect and area of our daily human existence.

Biblical Christianity enabled our slave ancestors not only to deal with the contradictions of their life, but also to make affirmations about God. This spirituality that enabled their survival was no escapism from their everyday existence. Rather it expressed in those conditions a transcendence that affirmed the presence of the divine-human encounter and relationship.

The Bible has always occupied a significant place in the lives of African Americans. It was from the Bible that many of the slave ancestors learned to read. This ability to read was both dangerous and liberating. Those slaves who could read kept this knowledge secret for fear of bodily harm. Indeed, many had been known, to lose parts of their bodies because they could read. Still others, recognizing the values of learning, were prepared to take that and other risks. They stole out at nights for meetings in deep gullies, to study there by torchlight and have a little time "wid Jesus."

This knowledge gained through reading the text for themselves enabled them to reject the interpretations that contradicted their own sense of humanity and justice. They sought to embrace those interpretations that helped them to make sense and meaning of their harsh daily realities. A sense of community, of belonging to one another is also evident in the slave period. Stories are told of how they learned from one another and shared this learning with others.

On the other hand, there were masters who were anxious for their slaves to learn to read. Slaveholders hoped that if slaves were taught the Bible that they would become docile and obedient slaves. The admonition from Ephesians 6.5 is often offered to support this viewpoint: "Slaves, obey your masters." It is ironic that, observing how the masters used the Bible, some slaves made clear distinctions between their own experiences of the Christian faith through the Bible and the "Bible Christianity" of their masters. The slaves' response was a freedom-oriented faith.

"It was in the spirituals, above all, that the characters, themes, and lessons of the Bible became dramatically real and took on special meaning for the slaves" (Raboteau, 1978, 243). Those "sorrow" songs forged out of the crucible of pain and suffering, were affirmations of God out of the experience of brutality. Through those spirituals slaves sang of a hope that "trouble don't last always." For them, the present harshness they were experiencing could be endured, and become meaningful, in light of a different and better future to which they looked forward.

Throughout the history of African Americans in this society, the Bible has continued to be influential and affective in their lives. A supercilious visitor once said to a young uneducated black woman in one of the southern small towns, "I see you are reading the Bible." "No, sir," she replied, "the Bible is reading me." She was expressing a profound understanding, that the Word has that capacity to lay bare our souls. "Indeed, the word of God is living and active, sharper than any two-edged sword, piercing until it divides soul from spirit, joints from marrow; it is able to judge the thoughts and intentions of the heart. And before him no creature is hidden, but all are naked and laid bare to the eyes of the one to whom we must render an account" (Hebrews 4.12,13, *NRSV*). It is this awareness of who God is and who we are in God that makes the Christian life possible, because it is a life lived before, in and with God. God is always working on us. The assertion is always being made that "God isn't finished with us yet." These perspectives of life that inform the spirituality of African Americans find their source in the Bible.

Spirituality

Explorations into Meaning

Within the last decade there has been a heightened interest in spirituality. It is often characterized by a deep hunger for meaning in empty lives. Henri Nouwen, one of the spiritual guides of our age, has written,

"One way to express the spiritual crisis of our time is to say that most of us have an address but cannot be found there" (Durback, 1997, 60). There is an ongoing frenetic search for that meaning in many places except where it could ultimately be found, that is, in the center of one's being. "Too many of us seem to be searching for something 'out there' to make our lives complete. We feel alienated, lonely, and empty. No matter what we do or have, we never feel fulfilled. This feeling of emptiness or intense loneliness is our clue that we are off course, and that we need to correct our direction.

Often we think the correction lies in a new mate, house, car, job or whatever. Not so. I believe that what all of us are really searching for is this divine essence within ourselves" (bell hooks, 1995, 342).

Many people's lives are like huge warehouses filled with a variety of things that refuse to suggest why they are there and what is their purpose. Yet we continue to warehouse our addictions, obsessions, violence, failures, fantasies, narcissism, disillusionment about marriage, family, relationships. Such lives are no homes. Very often the hidden cause of the emptiness we sense is a result of a painful and essential alienation from our spiritual selves, the integrating center of our beings. The manifestation of this reality is a truly spiritual experience, a movement of the Spirit in our lives. The Spirit needs a home with large spaces, a home where it is free to move, to grow, to expand. This quest for spirituality is only properly realized as we empty our lives of all the bitterness that we possess, cherish, cling to; and open them to become living spaces for the Spirit. God fills every empty space. Jesus offered the following counsel to someone who was obsessed with filling life with an abundance of things: "one's life does not consist in the abundance of possessions" (Luke 12.15b, *NRSV*).

As we discover the need and the way to let go of the "stuff" of everyday living, then the real meaning in our lives is found. "The spiritual life is like making prints from negatives. Often it is the dark forest that makes us speak about the open field. Frequently prison makes us think about freedom, hunger helps us to appreciate food, and war gives us words for peace...often someone's careful and honest articulation of ambiguities, uncertainties and painful conditions of life gives us new hope. The paradox is indeed that new life is born out of the pains of the old" (Durback, 1997, 53).

The spiritual life is simply a life in which all that we do comes from the center of that life in God. It is a life in which we acknowledge God's reality and claim, and yield ourselves to God's will. Spirituality is living life in the Spirit and discovering there the presence of God as love, who challenges us to find and manifest that love through our relationship with others and in God's world. Indeed it is the ordering of our lives so that the Holy Spirit has a chance. It is a way of being open to God in Jesus Christ through the Spirit.

Self-awareness, discovery, discernment, meaning making, attention, journey, relationship, integration, love, justice, community, wholeness, are words that may be used when exploring spirituality. All these words reflect how effective the Bible has been in shaping our life and our behavior. One does not have to labor at making the point that the strong sense of family and community and belonging to one another, being fellow travelers on the journey through life, are evidences of the way in which life is ordered for Africans and African Americans.

This sense of discovering God in the center of one's being and living out of that center is at the core of African and African American spirituality. It is holistic and encompasses the totality of being for African Americans—who we are, what we know, what we feel, and what we do. The conventions of African American spirituality embrace and encompass the totality of our beings. They are unconfined to any exclusively religious expression. One important reason for this is that the distinction between sacred and secular disappears in the African and African American experiences. We are affirming that the encounter with God and the expression of the meaning of that encounter is a total human experience. It calls forth every part of our being—body, mind, and spirit—for expression. This is equally true of the biblical admonition: to love God "with all your heart, and with all your soul, and with all your strength, and with all your mind; and your neighbor as yourself" (Luke 10.27b, *NRSV*).

A fundamental understanding of spirituality both for Africans and African Americans is that it is woven into the texture of everyday life and living. Spirituality is not experienced, discussed, nor relegated exclusively to the religious or sacred realm. Howard Thurman, who continues to be influential in any discussion on spirituality, writes about using "the raw materials of everyday life" as sources for reflection on the meaning of life's experiences. For Africans, the dichotomy between "sacred" and "profane" was never present. Indeed, one might claim that in every aspect of the slave's life in community, fusion and linkage occurred such that the ordinary was pervaded by the sacred.

It is impossible to discuss spirituality without referencing how it impacts the totality of one's life. "For the African, life is one integral whole. There is an interrelationship among the several aspects of life. Social life, politics, economics, morality, spirituality all constitute the "stuff" of life. Human life and existence are guided by religion as a motive principle" (Dash et. al., 1997, 24).

This is equally so for African Americans. There is an inherent unity of personality that illustrates integration created by self-awareness which is inclusive of who they are, what they do, what they know, and what they feel. This configuration also reflects a totality of being and informs any spirituality that may be described. "It is no accident that our ancestors' songs were called 'spirituals'; that others describe us as a 'spiritual' people, 'spirited' people, or 'soulful' people when the context, they assume, is secular rather than spiritual..."(Wade-Gayles,1995, 4).

When Jesus declared that "the kingdom of God is among you" (Luke 17.21b, *NRSV*), he was suggesting that this search for one's identity and integrity finds its fulfillment in the discovery of God within the center of one's being. The actual Greek for "among you" is *entos umon*. One interpretation of the Greek here is that the kingdom is fundamentally a spiritual experience. Its discovery is recognition of God within. The movement of the Spirit in one's life, especially at those points of difficulty and trouble, are opportunities for the discovery of God within and with us through the power of the Spirit to sustain and give hope. George Cummings observes: "The Spirit's sustaining power/presence was nurtured in the secret meetings where black slaves disobeyed their masters' orders and served God, sustained their sense of personal identity and well being, and provided mutual support for each other by giving meaning and hope to their tragic existence" (Cummings, 1991, 49).

The ancestors of African Americans were herded together with others, with their fellow tribespeople from the motherland, with whom they came to share a common condition of servitude. To be sure there was some degree of cultural overlap. These enslaved Africans were compelled to create a new language, a new religion, and a precarious new lifestyle. This lifestyle was to exert a formidable influence on American religious culture. It emerged as a significant force in the shaping of a people and their lives, and consequently, their spirituality.

Spirituality and the Bible

The African American Experience

Slave religion was a continuity of African ancestral religion. In contact with European Christianity on American soil, African American religion became an inventiveness within a tradition. The discussion about cultural continuities reflects not only expressions but content as well. In North America, African culture traits are

▸ For the People 2, 2004 Marsha Hatcher (b. 20th C. American), Acrylic. © Marsha Hatcher/ Superstock

evident in transformations more than in survivals. African American spirituality, birthed under conditions of travail and suffering, provided, and continues to provide, a means of survival and hope for a people who claim wholeness for their lives. This claim is grounded in the belief in a God whom they encounter in the totality of their daily existence, at work, at play, and in worship.

The Bible gave them a language to articulate their thoughts, ideas, and feelings about their life and their lives in God, who was for them very present in their daily journey. On the plantation, in their labors in the fields, from sunup to sundown, the slave ancestors were on the journey to freedom. It began when the first shackles were placed on their hands and feet, and our slave ancestors sought to break loose or cast themselves overboard during the Middle Passage. As Theophus Smith contends, "the black story… [is] the pilgrimage of a people toward freedom." (Smith, 1991, 373.) The words of one of the old songs remind us that the slave ancestors "woke up this mornin' wid my mind stayed on freedom." Emancipation, when it came for the slaves, was celebrated with great jubilation. Indeed, that day of deliverance was spoken of as the "day of Jubilee."

Biblical concepts of freedom are significant in themes, in the preaching, in the songs. "Before I'd be a slave, I'll be buried in my grave, an' go home to my Lord and be free." We may assert and indeed suggest that African American spirituality is a liberating spirituality. "In slave religion the figural vision of the emancipation as a type of biblical exodus provides the paradigm for subsequent strategies and acts of political imagination. The exodus figure has informed Afro-American political projects from the post-Reconstruction period to the recent civil rights…" (Smith, 1991, 391).

In the New Testament Jesus teaches about the Holy Spirit in a farewell discourse to his disciples. He promises them that the Spirit will be for them what he was to them. Caleb Oladipo offers some interesting insights into this passage. "There are two words for 'another' in Greek. One is *allos*, and the other is *heteros*. In John 14.16, Jesus promised 'another' paraclete to stay with believers forever. His word 'another' here was *allos* (not *heteros*). Thus, Jesus Christ was describing the Holy Spirit as distinct or separate, but not different or strange from him." Oladipo concludes that "the function of the Holy Spirit...[is] to help the believers attain both the subjective and the objective Christian experience" (Oladipo, October 1989, 39).

African American spirituality is expressed through many conventions. They all illustrate the inclusiveness and totality of life experience for African Americans as it is for Africans. A common core of its expression is the black religious experience, which manifests itself, among other ways, in full sensory engaging worship, triumphant singing, religious education, and prophetic imaginative preaching. We must be reminded that the religious experience profoundly affects the whole of life for African Americans.

Perhaps it is the worship experience that is a most readily observable expression of African American spirituality. This sense of experiencing God during worship through the Spirit is in our heritage. "The spirit realm is conceived as one of freedom. Slaves who were shackled could experience a bit of absolute freedom by abandoning themselves to God's spirit. Through the careful coordination of visual, audio, olfactory, and tactile stimuli, good worship becomes a form of spiritual therapy in which human wholeness is actualized through communion with God" (Franklin, 1997, 31).

Much has been written about the "spirituals." But no exploration of spirituality can avoid some commentary about them and their enduring significance for African American life and culture. Indeed, their contribution is equally an important part of the larger American cultural heritage. They reflect both individual and communal religious experiences and hopes. The spirituals helped to affirm an identity with God for the slave ancestors. Central to that identity was their several understandings of the relationship they had with Jesus. "It is out of this sense of being a child of God that the genius of the religious folk songs is born. There were three major sources from which the raw materials of the Negro spirituals were derived: the Old and New Testaments, the world of nature, and the personal experiences of religion that were the common lot of the people, emerging from their inner life. Echoes from each source are present in practically all the songs" (Thurman, 1975, 18). The spirituals were also creatively adapted and used as freedom songs during the civil rights period (Spencer, 1990, 83-105).

Summary

African ancestors, transported as slaves to labor on American plantations, brought their beliefs, practices, and culture to their life on this continent. These beliefs in God had always informed their daily existence. Indeed, there was no division of life into sacred and secular. For them all life was sacred, filled with the presence of the divine. The individual discovered identity in community and this became a means of survival. It is these aspects of a worldview that were to shape and influence their response to the brutal and dehumanizing experiences during the slave period and a heritage that they bequeathed to their descendants. There was an interconnecting unity in the rhythm of life for our slave ancestors. It was manifest in the totality of human experience—work, play, and worship.

Toward the end of the eighteenth and in the early decades of the nineteenth century, vigorous efforts were pursued to spread

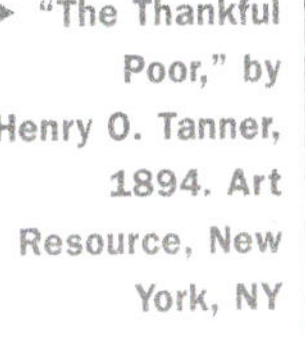

▸ "The Thankful Poor," by Henry O. Tanner, 1894. Art Resource, New York, NY

Christianity among those early African Americans, both slave and free. For them, the Bible became a significant source of spirituality. This spirituality was evident in all of their lives and found expression in their appropriation of the Bible story—the divine-human encounter and the characters through whom that drama was played. The major character in that drama was Jesus, with whom they identified in many ways. Jesus became not only a personal friend and brother, Jesus was also the subject of sermons and songs, which became known as "spirituals." Jesus became the symbol of suffering, survival, salvation, and hope.

A Concluding Reflection and an Invitation

Carolyn C. Denard tells the story of her grandmother who was dying with Alzheimer's. Communication between them had become impossible. She attempted to address this challenge by, as she puts it, talking "around her so that she could hear the conversation." In the middle of such an engagement, Denard and her sister began to recall old songs that they used to sing, one of which was "A Charge To Keep I Have." When neither of them could recall the second line, Denard "leaned over to Grandmother in a half-hearted gesture to include her in the conversation and asked, 'What were those other words, Grandmother?' 'A charge to keep I have...charge to keep I have...' I repeated searchingly, not expecting a response. And then a miracle happened: as clear as a bell with no stuttering or moaning, and from a woman who had not spoken even her name clearly in almost a year, she answered, 'A God to Glorify'" (Denard, 1995, 131f). The spirit within a body and mind deteriorating spoke loudly of who she was and affirmed an understanding of who God was for her and the commitment she had made to that God. The anticipation of coming face to face with Jesus is heard in that plaintive cry, "Oh, when I come to die, Give me Jesus."

Spirituality is inclusive of the whole of life for African Americans. It reflects interrelationships between body, mind, and spirit; work, worship, and play. An important characteristic is the discovery of self in relation to God and inevitably to others. It is the kind of life of which the Bible speaks and a demand that God makes on our lives. We are free to make that choice in response.

Sources Cited

Cone, James H. *The Spirituals and the Blues: An Interpretation*. New York: Seabury, 1972.

Cummings, George. "The Slave Narratives as a Source of Black Theological Discourse: The Spirit and Eschatology," *Cut Loose Your Stammering Tongue: Black Theology in the Slave Narratives*, Dwight N. Hopkins and George Cummings, eds. Maryknoll, New York: Orbis Books, 1991.

Dash, Michael I. N., Jonathan Jackson and Stephen C. Rasor. *Hidden Wholeness: An African American Spirituality for Individuals and Communities*. Cleveland, Ohio: The United Church Press, 1997.

Denard, Carolyn C. "Defying Alzheimer's: Saving Her Spirit in Song," *My Soul Is A Witness: African American Women's Spirituality*, Gloria Wade-Gayles, ed. Boston: Beacon Press, 1995, 131f.

Durback, Robert, ed. *Seeds of Hope: A Henri Nouwen Reader.* New York: Bantam Books, 1989.

Franklin, Robert M. *Another Day's Journey: Black Churches Confronting the American Crisis*. Minneapolis: Fortress Press, 1997.

hooks, bell. "Walking in the Spirit," *My Soul Is A Witness: African American Women's Spirituality*, Gloria Wade-Gayles, ed. Boston: Beacon Press, 1995, 342.

Oladipo, Caleb Remi. "The Holy Spirit: Distinct but not different from Jesus" *International Christian Digest* (October 1989), 39.

Raboteau, Albert J. *Slave Religion: "The Invisible Institution in the Antebellum South."* New York: Oxford University Press, 1978.

Smith, Theophus H. "The Spirituality of Afro-American Traditions," *Christian Spirituality: Post Reformation and Modern*, Louis Dupre and Don E. Saliers, eds. New York: The Crossroad Publishing Company, 1991, 373, 396.

Spencer, Jon Michael. *Protest and Praise: Sacred Music of Black Religion*. Minneapolis: Fortress Press, 1990.

Thurman, Howard. *Deep River and The Negro Spiritual Speaks of Life and Death*. Richmond, Indiana: Friends United Press, 1975.

Wade-Gayles, Gloria, ed. *My Soul Is A Witness: African American Women' s Spirituality.* Boston: Beacon Press, 1995.

Fifteen

Homegoing

Diane M. Ritzie

◄ "Funeral Procession," by Ellis Wilson, 1940. Aaron Douglas Collection. The Amistad Research Center, Tulane University, New Orleans, LA

During America's darkest hour, slavery, with its devastating physical afflictions upon enslaved Africans, was probably the leading cause of death. Escapes, attempted escapes, challenging the slave owners, or standing up for one's rights, could result in death. Learning to read, needing or wanting the neccesities of life—things that were taken for granted by others—also could lead to death.

This article attempts to discuss how death is viewed in the Bible, in the ancient world, and how Africans enslaved in America perceived death in light of their horrific circumstances. The stages of death, based on Kubler-Ross' classic work, are illustrated with biblical examples. A few Negro spirituals that deal with death as a release from bondage are also cited. For the slaves, as well as for African Americans today, homegoing marks the entrance to a blessed, peaceful eternity with the Lord.

Introduction

When I was a child, my grandmother told me all about my mother. My mother had a terminal illness when she gave birth to me and my twin sister. She lived for two more years and then died at the age of nineteen. My mother had received medical care, but to no avail. She refused drastic medical means to prolong her life, and she would not go south to change her environment. My grandmother explained that my mother said she was satisfied with the life she had. It was very difficult for me to understand as a young child, and even now sometimes, how my mother could have been satisfied with her life at such a young age. I wanted to know what was the substance of her life—what she had experienced with God in her life that allowed her to accept death at an early age. As I grew up and learned about the Lord that my mother loved, I began to experience the rich satisfaction of the presence of the Lord in my life. My grandmother told me that my mother prayed for me and for my sister very much before she died. So, her prayers in life, and her acceptance of God's will in death, have given me spiritual strength for experiences with dying and death in my life and in my ministry.

From the moment that a newborn baby takes the first breath, that child is on the road to deterioration and, finally, death. One's life is headed in that direction in spite of whatever achievements may have been accomplished during that lifetime. The human condition, as we know it, mandates the continuation of life and also demands its cessation. One looks optimistically at the processes of growth, maturation and self-actualization; yet these stages of life eventually lead to death.

The Yearning for Death: Release from Bondage

During the period of bondage in the United States, slaves were not permitted to read; nor were they even allowed to learn to read. As they heard the stories from the Old Testament that bore witness to release from bondage by a God who delivers, and as they heard of a Savior called Jesus who promised release from their torturous way of life into an eternal life of peace and joy, the emotions and musical abilities of the slaves ignited the sparks for their beautiful spirituals that emanated from their existence. In this way, slaves became familiar with stories from the Bible which they re-interpreted through song in light of their experience of enslavement.

Many of the Negro spirituals gave affirmation to the fact that slaves were overwhelmed in their plight of bondage. They were without earthly hope and, through song, they expressed a desire for death as a means of release from their oppressive conditions. Howard Thurman, in *Deep River and the Negro Spiritual Speaks of Life and Death,* states "the other-worldly hope looms large, and this of course is not strange; the other-worldly hope is always available when groups of people find themselves completely frustrated in the present. When all hope for release in this world seems unrealistic and groundless, the heart turns to a way of escape beyond the present order. The options are very few for those who are thus circumstanced. Their belief in God leads quite definitely to a position that fixes their hope on deliverance beyond the grave... There is desolation, fear, loneliness, but hope, at once desperate and profound!" Thus death and the afterlife are prominent themes in Negro spirituals. "Soon—a Will Be Done a—with the troubles of the world," a mournful Negro spiritual, communicates the weariness of life for a slave who had no earthly hope. He or she would sing, as this spiritual goes on, "I want t' meet my Jesus, I'm goin' to live with God." Death was viewed as a release from this life and an entrance to a blessed, peaceful eternity with the Lord.

These spirituals—intense with desires, expressions, and yearnings to journey to the afterlife—were also a form of criticism that gave the slaves voice to rail against the intolerable conditions of slavery in everyday life. Yet the spirituals overwhelmingly speak to the blessed hope that is centered in Christ Jesus—a "hope of sharing the glory of God" (Romans 5.2b, *NRSV*). This is a hope that emanates from suffering, endurance and character (Romans 5.3-5), and the slaves drew their strength from Jesus who suffered, endured shame, and conquered death. The hope of the slaves was grounded in their trust in the Lord and the assurance that they had "redemption through his blood" and would inherit spiritual blessings (Ephesians 1.3-14).

The Ancient World

In the ancient world, biblical people, including those in the surrounding cultures, lived with the reality of death (Psalm 49.10-12). Most cultures were preoccupied with the "hereafter" — a destiny that they could not control. Quite frequently they were involved with appeasing the gods and caring for the burial places of their deceased loved ones.

Death was accepted in the Ancient Near East as the end of life—be it full or wanting. Although death was unavoidable, people still looked forward to long lives. It is characteristic of humans everywhere to make all attempts to postpone the inevitable; the survival instinct is innate in our humanity.

If one escaped the dangers associated with childbirth (mother and/or child), experienced success against the rigors of life, and eluded deadly illnesses, one generally lived to a "good old age," a term which renders a sense of maturity and completeness. In the Old Testament, there are accounts of people living to a "good old age"—ages which are never reached in our lifetimes. Chapter five of the Book of Genesis records the lifetimes of Adam and his descendants: Adam lived for 930 years, Seth lived for 912 years, Enos for 905 years, Cainan for 910 years, and Enoch lived for 365 years (which was not very long at that time). According to the Bible, the oldest person who ever lived was Methuselah -969 years. These were all remarkable life spans.

Well after the period of the flood and soon after the patriarchal period, the human life span was shortened. Psalm 90, a prayer attributed to Moses, records these words in verse 10 *(NRSV)*: "The days of our life are seventy years, or perhaps eighty, if we are strong; even then their span is only toil and trouble; they are soon gone, and we fly away." This is approximately what the normal life expectancy is today, and life spans of seventy, eighty, or even ninety years of age are not uncommon.

The biblical record also makes mention of persons whose significant contributions to Bible history, in terms of their callings, did not occur until late adulthood: Abraham was seventy-five years of age when the LORD called him out of his father's house; he was one hundred years old when Isaac was born, and he died at one hundred and seventy-five years of age (Genesis 12.4; 21.5; 25.7). Sarah was ninety years old when she gave birth to Isaac, and she died at one hundred and twenty-seven years of age (Genesis 17.17; 23.1). Moses and Aaron were eighty years old and eighty-three years old respectively when they spoke to Pharaoh about freeing the people of Israel from the bondage of slavery (Exodus 7.7). Moses died at one hundred and twenty years of age in his full strength (Deuteronomy 34.7).

Daily life was difficult in the Ancient Near East. Many times this caused people to cry out to God in their times of distress when they desired the end of life. The ancients believed that the locus of death was the nether world. The "direction" of the grave was downward, leading to the nether world. The grave, referred to as *Sheol* in Hebrew, was considered the abode of the dead. It was not considered just a place for the wicked in the Hebrew mindset, but it was a refuge for respite from a weary, troubled, and undignified life.

Jacob said in his great sadness, when he believed that Joseph was dead, "I will go down into the grave unto my son mourning" (Genesis 37.35b, *KJV*). When Jacob did not want Benjamin to return to Egypt with his brothers for fear of losing him, he told them, "ye shall bring down my gray hairs with sorrow to the grave" (Genesis 44.29b, *KJV*). Job asked the unanswerable question, "Why is light given to one in misery, and life to the bitter in soul, who long for death, but it does not come, and dig for it more than for hidden treasures; who rejoice exceedingly, and are glad when they find the grave?" (Job 3.20-22, *NRSV*).

In the Old Testament there is no consistent view of death. There are divergent views which are expressed, for the Bible also contains accounts of persons who cry out to God for deliverance from death. The psalmist cried out to God to spare his life, saying, "Return, O LORD, deliver my soul: oh save me for thy mercies' sake. For in death there is no remembrance of thee: in the grave who shall give thee thanks?" (Psalm 6.4, 5, *KJV*). Psalm 88 is a prayer psalm, a strong cry for deliverance from death. The psalmist implores the Lord to spare his life because: (a) Sheol is a place where he would be separated from God who could save his life (verses 1-3); (b) he did not want to be just another number (verse 4); and (c) he would not be remembered anymore (verse 5).

King Hezekiah was told by the prophet Isaiah that the Lord had set the time of his death. So he prayed diligently to the Lord, saying "Remember now, O LORD, I implore you, how I have walked before you in faithfulness with a whole heart, and have done what is good in your sight" (2 Kings 20.3, *NRSV*). The Lord heard Hezekiah's prayer and added fifteen extra years to his life (2 Kings 20.1-7). As these accounts illustrate, whether the people were seeking death or trying to avoid it, they acknowledged that life and death were in the hands of God. Yet humans, in their sometimes desperate attempts to prolong life and prevent death, protest against the discretion of the Lord who has control over human destiny.

Resurrection in the Old Testament

The Old Testament teaching of the resurrection can be found in a few Scriptures. The writers did not have a complete understanding of what the resurrection was or how it would occur. They had some knowledge, which included the anticipation of eternal life. "O that thou wouldest hide me in the grave, that thou wouldest keep me secret, until thy wrath be past, that thou wouldest appoint me a set time, and remember me!" (Job 14.13, *KJV*). Job had a hope of the resurrection, that God would not leave him in the grave forever. Job looked forward to life after death when he said, "For I know that my Redeemer liveth, and that he shall stand at the latter day upon the earth: and though after my skin worms destroy this body, yet in my flesh shall I see God: whom I shall see for myself, and mine eyes shall behold, and not another; though my reins be consumed within me." (Job 19.25-27, *KJV*).

The Book of Daniel has the major teaching of the resurrection in the Old Testament. The angel told Daniel, "And many of them that sleep in the dust of the earth shall awake, some to everlasting life, and some to shame and everlasting contempt" (Daniel 12.2, *KJV*). The meaning was not revealed to Daniel "for the words are closed up and sealed till the time of the end" (Daniel 12.9b, *KJV*).

The Old Testament records several resurrection events. The widow of Zarephath had a son who was raised by Elijah (1Kings 17.17-22); a Shunammite woman had a son who was restored to life by Elisha (2 Kings 4.18-37); and an unnamed man, who was cast into Elisha's sepulchre, was raised to life when his body touched Elisha's bones (2 Kings 13.20,21). The ancient Hebrews trusted in God and knew that the grave did not have the power to hold them forever.

The Hebrews' views and attitudes toward death constitute a theological issue with which to wrestle—the tension between the desire to die and the hope to live. One can examine these perspectives and consider how they may relate to our thinking about dying and death in today's world.

Resurrection in the New Testament

At God's appointed time, Jesus Christ entered humanity's history to announce the Kingdom of God and to confront the works of Satan's kingdom. Salvation is totally God's work in which a right

▸ "Building More Stately Mansions" by Aaron Douglas. Fisk University Galleries, Nashville, TN

relationship is effected between God and humankind through the sacrifice of Jesus Christ. Through Christ's death and resurrection, believers receive salvation and the assurance of eternal life (1 Corinthians 15.12-19). During his ministry, Jesus raised people from the dead. These miracles accompanied his preaching of the gospel in order to demonstrate the power of God through Christ Jesus.

Jesus had compassion on the widow of Nain and restored to life her only son (Luke 7.11-17). The most detailed account of a resurrection is that of Jesus' calling Lazarus out of a tomb (John 11.1-44). Lazarus had been dead four days, and his body had already begun to decompose (verse 39). Yet, Jesus resurrected Lazarus, thus demonstrating that he had power over Satan who had the power of death. This was when Jesus declared, "I am the resurrection and the life" (verse 25a *NRSV*).

Our resurrection is based on Jesus Christ's resurrection from the dead. His resurrection seals the believers' resurrection. "But in fact, Christ has been raised from the dead, the first fruits of those who have died. For since death came through a human being, the resurrection of the dead has also come through a human being; for as all die in Adam, so all will be made alive in Christ. But each in his own order: Christ the first fruits, then at his coming, those who belong to Christ." (1 Corinthians 15.20-23, *NRSV*). This is the hope for the believer—the only hope. Christ's resurrection was accomplished because it was not possible that death's power should be able to hold the Son of God (Acts 2.24). The Holy Spirit raised up Jesus Christ and the Spirit will also give life to believers (Romans 8.11).

Humanity's dilemma over death has been conquered by Jesus Christ. We have a great hope and anticipation before us. ". . . through death he might destroy the one who has the power of death, that is, the devil, and free those who all their lives were held in slavery by the fear of death" (Hebrews 2.14b, 15, *NRSV*). The wonderful achievement is that one no longer has to be in bondage to the fear of death (Hebrews 2.15). Fear forces people to do things that they may not desire to do. So, this freedom in Christ enables the believer to live holy before God and, as life ends, to go to God in great anticipation of the blessed hope of the resurrection (Romans 6.5-11).

The Different Stages of Dying and Death

As we read the Bible, we meet persons who express various views concerning death at different stages of their dying process. Each one speaks according to his or her situation. For example, Rachel dies giving birth to her second son. In her last words, she names him *Ben-oni*, meaning "son of my sorrow" (Genesis 35.18 *NRSV*). This must have been heartbreaking for her—she is dying while giving birth and will not be able to participate in her son's upbringing, nor experience the joys of his childhood. The psalmist who cries out in Psalm 88 must have been suffering for a long time. For he says to God, "why do you cast me off? Why do you hide your face from me?" (Psalm 88.14, *NRSV*). So people are at different places along the road to the end.

Dr. Elizabeth Kubler-Ross, in her classic treatise on death and dying, established five stages of the dying process. The first stage is **denial and isolation** in which a person refuses to accept the prognosis of a terminal illness. Kubler-Ross states that this is a psychological defense mechanism which allows the person to gradually get used to the idea of dying. The **isolation** aspect of this stage is that family members and close friends begin to stay away from a dying person because they do not want to face the reality that their loved one is in the final stage of life. This is especially difficult for the dying person who feels rejected because of his or her impending death. Jesus himself experienced such rejection at the time of his betrayal and arrest (Matthew 26.56).

A dying person may also isolate him/herself from family and friends. Jephthah's daughter, who had to be sacrificed to the LORD because of her father's careless vow in return for a military victory (Judges 11.30,31), went away from her father to be alone with her friends for two months to mourn the life that she would never have (Judges 11.37-40). The essence of her life would have been the rearing of children, for this was a vital responsibility for the female in the ancient world, and also a sense of accomplishment and achievement. What Jephthah's daughter mourned was the loss of a fulfilled life. It was not just her impending death itself for which she and her friends grieved, but life's essence or potential that death brings to a halt.

The second stage is **anger** in which a dying person resents him/herself, family, friends, the doctors, and even God. The anger may be suppressed or expressed in strong words and/or actions. A number of psalms express such anger. For example, the psalmist writes: "How long, O LORD? Will you forget me forever? How long will you hide your face from me? How long must I bear pain in my soul, and have sorrow in my heart all day long? How long shall my enemy be exalted over me? Consider and answer me, O LORD my God! Give light to my eyes, or I will sleep the sleep of death." (Psalm 13.1-3, *NRSV*)

The third stage is the **bargaining process** in which the person begins to realize that it does no good to be angry with God. So promises are made to God if God will let the person live. Many times people promise to change their lives for the better if God will heal them. But many times these promises are short-lived. When requests for physical healing are not granted, it does not mean that God is uncaring, even though some may interpret it as such. There are many questions for which there are no sufficient answers. Then there is the point in each and every life when it will be "the end."

In the biblical text, Hezekiah denies the termination of his life and prays to the Lord for an extension of time. He bargains with God by explaining how faithful he has been, and God chooses to extend his life (2 Kings 20.1-7). When God told Moses that he would not be permitted to enter the Promised Land and that he would die, Moses sought to bargain with God. But God told Moses to stop asking for what he wanted; rather Moses was instructed to encourage and strengthen Joshua because God had chosen Joshua to lead the people across the Jordan, and had decreed that Moses would die on the mountain overlooking Canaan (Deuteronomy 3.23-29; 32.48-52; 34.4-8).

The examples of Hezekiah and Moses illustrate how people bargained with God and how God dealt with each one individually according to God's own purpose. In the case of Moses, whose request was denied, we learn from the New Testament that Moses appeared at Jesus' transfiguration. Luke's account tells us that Moses and Elijah spoke with Jesus concerning Jesus' impending suffering, death, and resurrection (Luke 9.28-31).

The fourth stage is **depression** in which a dying person becomes physically exhausted and emotionally depleted. There are two types of depression—one in which the person has lost self-esteem, a job, etc., and also the type of depression in which loss and separation is anticipated. King Saul experienced both types of depression after being told of his impending death. He was very weak and refused to eat (1 Samuel 28.20-25).

The fifth and final stage is **acceptance**, in which a person accepts death. When Jacob was near death, he outlined the plans for his burial (Genesis 47.30; 48.29-33) and blessed his family (Genesis 48, 49).

In the New Testament it is recorded that, when Jesus was about to go to the cross, he prayed diligently in the Garden of Gethsemane. He prayed, "My Father, if it is possible, let this cup pass from me; yet not what I want but what you want" (Matthew 26.39b, *NRSV*). The cup could not pass from Jesus. In him was humanity's only hope. The thief on the cross asked Jesus to remember him when Jesus came into his kingdom (Luke 23.42). This thief had accepted his fate and his hope was centered in Christ.

We are not sure whether or not the people of the Bible cited above went through all five stages outlined by Kubler-Ross. These are but a few examples from the Bible that depict how some people reacted to impending death. From these witnesses of the faith, we learn that their experiences were not unlike those of people today.

Conclusion

Even with the modern scientific competence to examine the dying and analyze the different stages of death, its process cannot be understood completely. The fetus in the womb can be examined before birth, and an autopsy can be performed on a body after death, but the complete knowledge of dying and death still rests with God.

People today are no different from ancient men and women. The same perplexities about dying and death also plague us. As believers, the difference is our belief in Christ with the hope of the resurrection and the promises of God that are revealed in the Bible. We will receive glorified bodies (Romans 8.23; 1 Corinthians 15.35-57; Philippians 3.21); new heavens and a new earth (Isaiah 65.17-25; 2 Peter 3.13); and the physical and emotional healing promised in Isaiah 25.6-10a and in Revelation 21 and 22.

Mother and Son

As a prison chaplain, I receive requests for different types of assistance from family members of inmates. One day I received a request to help a dying mother who desperately wanted to see her son for the last time. The son was in prison many miles away, and it was very difficult to arrange for a compassionate visit. Although the authorities were working on arranging it, the mother was deteriorating rapidly. Yet she was holding on with everything she had to be granted her last request. Due to some intractable circumstances, I was told that the visit could not be arranged. I was asked to go to the hospital to break this dismal, heart-wrenching news to the mother. I felt helpless and weak—I did not have the strength to do it. I fell to my knees and prayed for strength and wisdom to carry out this request. My prayer to God was for this mother not to die in disappointment and sadness. As I was about to leave for the hospital, the phone rang, and I was told to delay giving her the news because the authorities were going to make one more attempt. I felt encouraged and went on to the hospital to minister to the mother.

When I arrived at the hospital, the mother and I were introduced to each other. She was extremely weak, and I knew that she was using all her strength to hold on. She asked me if any progress had been made regarding the visit. I told her that we were still trying. She told me she was trying to accept whatever the outcome would be. I asked her if she knew the Lord Jesus Christ. She said "no" and then asked me if I thought it was now time. I said "yes" and she said she wanted to know the Lord. So I read some Scriptures and then we prayed. She received Jesus Christ as her Lord and Savior. She told me she experienced a sense of release and relief and was at peace.

The mother's sister called me the next morning to tell me that the mother had the first night of a complete peaceful sleep. She was praising God on her deathbed. Within a few days, the mother died. She never had the opportunity to see her son, but she did meet the Son, the Son of Righteousness, Jesus Christ our Lord and Savior. She experienced "homegoing" and the joy of being welcomed by Jesus into his loving arms.

The song, "Goin' Home" by William Arms Fisher (1861-1948) and sung to Anton Dvorak's "Largo" from his "New World Symphony," captures the hope shared by those who believe and trust in God's everlasting love.

"Goin' Home"

Goin' home, goin' home, I'm a-goin' home;
Quiet like, some still day, I'm jes' goin' home.

It's not far, jes' close by, Through an open door;
Work all done, care laid by, Gwine to fear no more.

Mother's there 'spectin' me, Father's waitin' too;
Lots o' folks gathered there, All the friends I knew.
All the friends I knew.

(Home, home, I'm goin' home!)

Nothin' lost, all's gain, No more fret nor pain.
No more stumblin' on the way,
No more longin' for the day,
Gwine to roam no more!

Mornin' star lights the way, Res'less dream all done;
Shadows gone, break o' day, Real life jes' begun.

Dere's no break, ain't no end, Jes' a-liv-in' on,
Wide awake, with a smile, Goin' on and on.

Goin' home, goin' home, I'm jes' goin' home;
It's not far, jes' close by, Through an open door.
I'm jes' goin' home.
Goin' home.

Jesus said, "I am the door: by me if any man enter in, he shall be saved..." (John 10.9, *KJV*). Jesus is the open door for our "homegoing." The apostle Paul counsels that we are not to grieve "as others which have no hope. For if we believe that Jesus died and rose again, even so them also which sleep in Jesus will God bring with him. ... Wherefore comfort one another with these words." (1 Thessalonians 4.13,14,18, *KJV*). Our hope is indeed grounded in "goin' home" to the Lord.

Works Consulted

Cooper, John W. *Body, Soul, & Life Everlasting.* Grand Rapids: Eerdmans, 1989.

Kubler-Ross, Elizabeth. *On Death and Dying.* New York: Macmillan, 1969.

Miller, Patrick D. *They Cried to the Lord: The Form and Theology of Biblical Prayer.* Minneapolis: Fortress Press, 1994.

Thurman, Howard. *Deep River and the Negro Spiritual Speaks of Life and Death.* Richmond: Friends United Press, 1990.

Sixteen

The Blessing: Restoring Hope for African American Youth

Maxine M. Walker

According to *Harper's Bible Dictionary* hope is "the expectation of a favorable future under God's direction." The four components of hope mentioned in the article, Promise, Purpose, Perseverance, and Prosperity, are pregnant with the activity of God and are waiting to be delivered toward the fulfillment of purpose in the lives of our youth. It is the intent of this article to encourage our youth to see themselves partnered with God to work toward the fulfillment of purpose in their lives. The Blessing is the extension of the lifeline of hope to present and future generations and encourages them to seek their place in salvation history.

◄ "Family," by Charles H. Alston, 1955. Courtesy of Whitney Museum of American Art, New York, NY

Historically, African Americans have found comfort and direction from the generational sharing of ancestral stories. In addition to chronicling vivid and moving accounts of slave journeys, these stories have also been sources of strength and lessons in motivation, pride, determination, and perseverance to many generations. The value of the stories is enhanced by their poignant rehearsal of motivation, pride, determination and perseverance which enabled our ancestors not only to survive, but also to bequeath a legacy of uncompromising faith, an unsurpassed love for God, and a blessing of promise. This legacy is ours. Our ancestral parents lived their existence in hope. This is the blessing they handed down to us, and to our youth.

Living in an era of mixed media and mixed messages, our young people often find it difficult to embrace the legacy of their ancestral history and yet be fully in tune with today's society. Because of peer pressure and other outside influences, there is an ambivalence on the part of our youth to link the rich history of their heritage with the social norms of the prevailing culture.

As we witness many of our neighborhoods being torn apart by domestic and societal violence and inadequate community services, it is imperative that we teach our youth that hope is alive. Hope makes room for creative resources in reconciling brokenness and conflictual messages. Hope is a gift from God and part of the legacy bequeathed to us from our ancestral parents. Yes, there is still hope. Despite the enemy's desire to rob our youth of this knowledge, the Bible reminds us that without vision (or hope) our people will perish (Proverbs 29.18). In hope, God created order out of chaos. The message to our youth, then, should be that God is still creating order.

Our young people who have grasped a glimmer of this hope are doing marvelous things! We watch proudly as our youth excel in city or statewide exams; we beam at those who at year's end throw their mortar boards high in the air—graduates of some fine institution of learning; we stand in the wings as we see our young people become lawyers, sanitation workers, entrepreneurs, carpenters, teachers, secretaries, nurses, construction workers, army personnel, loving home-makers, professional athletes, historians. Like the village elders, we pat our chests because we know it takes a village to raise a child. We know how important the stories are; we know just how important the blessing of hope is.

As a benefactor of this blessing, I remember the indelible impact that my great-grandmother made on me at the tender age of five.

When I was five years old my great-grandmother was an awesome figure for me. I would spend hours on end listening to her fascinating and rich stories. Her hopes, her faith, and her love for God was paramount in shaping my reality. At five years of age I was inserted into the age-old story that is lineal. My great-grandmother's stories were strong and full of traditional and cultural truth. Her truth, which later became my own, had its foundation in pride and hope. This is indeed the blessing of an old, illiterate African American woman who was very articulate and powerfully eloquent in expressing her faith and hope.

Our historical theological concept is rich in hope, born out of our grief, pain and suffering, and our belief in the eternal hope of God. It is a transformative hope, which takes its historical context from our desire for change. This context was no louder heard than from the traditional black church with its consciousness relating to dynamic social change and cultural transformation.

Not all our youth have fully understood the blessing. Parents, as well as the church, have an awesome responsibility in keeping the message of hope alive. We need to challenge those young people who have not claimed their blessing to believe in a God who is bigger than any system. Our God can provide them with a future and give them a reason to prepare themselves for one. As we hand down the wisdom we were taught, and expect more from our youth, they will, in turn expect more of themselves, and hope will become visible.

In order to secure the survival of generations to follow, African American youth must be steered toward renewed spiritual values. The answer is not in a *new* way of worship, but rather a worship that would incorporate cultural identity, reestablish strong and nurturing faith communities, grounded in hope. Moreover, they can be proud of a culture and heritage that instill good work ethics, strong moral character, and a steadfast faith nurtured in hope. This is the blessing of our ancestral parents. This is the gift we continue to offer our youth. If the story grows weak, and the faces of our ancestral parents grow dim, then the stain of their blood fades into oblivion, and we lose our purpose and direction.

Purpose or direction is vital for survival. Our youth are inheritors of the blessing handed down to them from ancestors who believed that their offspring would continue to spread the good news of love and forgiveness; that each generation would find its purpose and persevere; that they not be tainted by the ignorance of the hatred they experience because of the color of their skin; that they would fight for justice and a chance to move forward toward a prosperous future. The fight must continue; but without hope, it is impossible. We, as adults, must continue to echo the message from the past by telling them to "press on." African American youth must be encouraged to receive the blessing and not be deceived by the enemy.

▸ Anchor and rope on stained glass. Minneapolis, MN. © Fotosearch/ Superstock

Hebrews 6.19 says that hope is the anchor of the soul. The hope that Hebrews speaks of, and our ancestral parents left us, is Christ. This hope extends the scope of forgiveness of sins, love, liberation, justice, peace, and eternal life. In other words, it is a hope of inner and outer transformation that anchors our faith in Jesus Christ. If this hope is not solidly anchored, our youth will wander without direction. As adults, we must not neglect our responsibility to serve as prophetic voices for our youth.

The message of the gospel is good news and it is available for everyone. Our youth are entitled to hear all of the good news. Surely, the most important is salvation and eternal life, but Christ promises more. In hope, young people can find the liberation of spirit, mind, body, talent, and the ability to succeed in life. They are entitled to hear, and choose to claim as their own, the message, because the message of hope will keep them grounded, focused, and confident toward the fulfillment of their purpose. It affords them the opportunity to live in expectation of things to come: "I wait for the LORD, my soul doth wait, and in his word do I hope" (Psalm 130.5, *KJV*).

Hence, African American youth should be encouraged to embrace moral living, to have ambition, to dream dreams and to keep the faith. Hope liberates and frees one's spirit to breathe life into one's aspirations. It can grow out of the doubt that one experiences in failure. Hopelessness and a sense of powerlessness find no home where hope abides. So, then, hope grows out of faith and is sustained by faith which undergirds its birth. "Thus in the Christian life faith has the priority, but hope becomes a utopia and remains hanging in the air. But without hope, faith falls to pieces, becomes fainthearted and ultimately a dead faith." (*Moltmann, Theology of Hope,* p. 20)

African American youth have been dealt a devastating blow. They have been left without direction but are expected to move ahead. They are told how they shouldn't be, but they have no clear understanding of how they should be. They feel betrayed by a God who promises to protect and by Christians who don't practice what they preach. They have been robbed of their blessing, the message of hope, and they should have it back; and it is our responsibility to see to it that they do. I would encourage our youth to become more accountable, seek God's grace, and experience hope in the act of love on the cross; and for us as adults to be accountable to our responsibility for their care and nurture, to support and to encourage them toward restored wholeness.

The church has the awesome responsibility of keeping the message of hope alive in the lives of young people despite the many distractions they face. It is challenged to nurture them in the faith, instill in them a pride that makes them cognizant of who they are in Christ, and remind them of the history of their race.

First, our youth must discover the **promise in hope.** The transforming power, grounded in the promise, encourages one to strive toward where one desires to be. Where can youth discover this except in seeing themselves as part of that promise and a part of the same story, which began many years ago? It was in Israel's hope-giving promise that Israel found its truth. As African Americans we need to know that the promise speaks to us from the cross as we participate in salvation history. This promise we bring to our youth—a promise that is sustained in the tests of present perils. Our youth must be able to see the transcendence of God through Jesus Christ and Christ transcendent through African American adult Christians. The transforming promise that Christ offers is liberation, inclusivity, and a social order that opposes the injustices of society. To live in the promise of hope is to live positively in the present. The promise serves as a healing salve for the pain and betrayal that has been inflicted on our youth. It becomes imperative that youth are receptive and forgiving.

Secondly, our youth must be able to discover the **purpose in hope.** Why should we hope? Purpose gives reason to continue in one's efforts toward attaining one's goals. Purpose deters doubt and keeps one focused in spite of obstacles. Hope gives one a base from which to work, and purpose gives one a target for which to aim.

▸ "The Banjo Lesson," by Henry O. Tanner. Oil on canvas. Collection of Hampton University Museum, Hampton, VA

The restlessness, hopelessness, and the belief that nothing will change for the better makes a powerful impact on how one perceives him/herself and the future. Purpose teaches one how to build and not destroy, to hope rather than to despair, to work for peace rather than warring against each other, to love rather than to hate. This is the purpose in hope. It builds strong and lasting stories to be handed down proudly to one's children's children. It sustains life. There are times when the purpose in hope teaches us to wait, and there are other times when it teaches us to seek. This is part of the blessing our forebears handed down through generations.

When to wait and when to seek was thematic in the mentality of our slave mothers and fathers. The purpose in hope became their focus for survival. They believed in the eschatological teaching of Christ who promised to liberate them from the cruelty of slavery. The slaves believed in a God who loved them, accepted them, and identified with their suffering. This gave them purpose toward survival, that purpose in part, being reason enough to work toward securing our race and our rightful place in salvation history. Their purpose was to secure the blessing for generations to come.

Hope does not accept things as they are, but Moltmann surmises that it is alive and progressing with reason to believe that change can take place. Our youth today can be proud of such a rich history, a story not told often enough. They should be encouraged to see the importance of having such a legacy on which to build and to live out their purpose. There is a need to hear the prophetic voices from the past as they speak from the riverbanks of old. Our youth have a right and a responsibility to continue the blessing. They must be **taught** that they are the continuance of salvation history. They must **believe** that with every generation, God will bring forth leaders who will carry on the traditions of the African American race, and who will have a positive impact on every race, color, and creed. As they are endowed with the blessing, these voices of young, strong, visionary African Americans will speak with fervor, wisdom of revelation, renewed strength and restored hope.

Thirdly, our youth are encouraged to seek assurance and conviction which wills them to **persevere,** all the time recognizing God's grace to enable them in their struggles. They must stay focused, remain steady, and tune out negative influences. To help them, we must build a strong bridge of positive, open communication in which they feel free to share their aspirations as well as their fears.

It is imperative for the survival of our youth that they experience God's redeeming love and the nurture of a caring community.

I recall my great-grandmother's teaching and nurturing, her confidence in me, and her belief in a loving God to protect me. Because of the hope she instilled in me at an early age, I have persevered. She blessed me with the good news and continued to assure me of God's love, and I always needed to hear it. We can never remind our youth too much that the same is true for them. Too many of our youth do not have the same reference as I and many others of my generation had, but we, as adults, should see each child as an extension of ourselves and instill in him/her the tools for success. Further, each child should be encouraged to live and to persevere towards his/her purpose in life. For example, the emerging of a butterfly from a cocoon signifies life and celebration. The message of hope is new life. The cross and the resurrection stand as reminders that all can be recipients of new life. For this reason our youth should be directed to look to the cross and the resurrection, to embrace them both in order to become empowered to persevere so that they may grow in God's grace and fulfill their purpose and gain eternal life.

I also encourage our youth to explore the certainty of **prosperity in hope.** Prosperity assures them of a favorable future with God. They can invest in that future under God's direction to build a trust fund that reaches maturity at the consummation of the last day. As long as they are fully confident of its payoff, hope will never fail them (Romans 5.5).

Long after my great-grandmother died, hope continued to find its way through stories told within my faith community. This community helped me build a dream so vivid I was compelled to make it my reality. We must help young people build dreams, teach them how to succeed, allow them the freedom to explore and to exercise hope for themselves.

Young people are included in God's plan for the world. For God so loved the world that God gave God's best to the world—the gift of life, now and eternal. Youth have within themselves all the potential to be the best they can be. It is important that young people's lives be so impacted by the message to persevere that they will experience the fulfillment of hope.

The author of Hebrews tells us what hope is and what hope does. Jurgen Moltmann brings hope from the eschatological to the present.

▸ Multicultural group of children around a globe. © Belinda Images/ Superstock

In order to move forward and to remain a part of salvation history, young people must continue the blessing of their ancestral parents, seek after justice, live in hope, and share the good news of the gospel. In other words, they must be willing agents and catalysts for a transforming change for all humankind.

As African Americans, we learned this sitting at the feet of our ancestors. In their own way, they were articulate and eloquent in living out their belief system. As an emotional people (no apology) we have always been able to achieve spiritual health and wholeness through our cultural practices, which included stories, dance, and exerting other kinds of motion or physical energy. We have been affirmed by these stories handed down through generations, and we have been empowered through Jesus Christ. This has always made sense in our culture. This was and should always be the premise by which we "live and move and have our being" (Acts 17.28b, *NRSV*). This is the blessing we hand down to our young people. It is in the hope of this premise that they find coherence, balance, and fortitude.

Hope keeps us connected to Jesus Christ. Our ancestral parents knew this, no matter where they were: in the fields, in the big house, or under the slavemaster's whip; somehow, they were able to feel the nearness of God. The anchor of hope liberates us and transforms us to meet the ultimate challenge of experiencing the fulfillment of God's promise of eternal life while keeping us in the presence of today. Soren Kierkegaard called hope the passion for what is possible. It complements our faith.

Our young people are our most precious resource. We must continue to instill in them that faith undergirds hope, and hope is the ***promise*** that allows us to live in expectation of eternal life and all the blessings of God; ***purpose*** allows us to remain focused toward eternal life and all the blessings of God, ***perseverance*** teaches us to remain constant so that we can experience eternal life and all the blessings of God, and ***prosperity*** is the reaping of the harvest. This is the blessing.

▸ Africa, West Africa, Guinea-Bissau, Bijagos Archipelago, Canhabaque Island (or Roxa Island). © Photononstop/ Superstock

The Scriptures (Proverbs 14.26,27) tell us that the blessings of prosperity involve the fear of the Lord and that this fear or "aweness" not only secures a place for the parents, but the children are also promised a fortress and a refuge. The children will reap the rewards of the faith of the parents, and the children are encouraged to embrace the promise that God will be their protector and will cover them in honor of the parents' faith, trust and hope.

Young people, this is your legacy. This is your blessing. Be wise enough to accept it graciously, and in return, hand it down for generations to come. You have been endowed with the richest inheritance which cannot be compared to any other. Guard it carefully. Proverbs says it best, "He who fears the LORD has a secure fortress, and for his children it will be a refuge" (Proverbs 14.26, *NIV*).

Sources Cited

Evans, C. Stephen. *Soren Kierkegaard's Christian Psychology*. Bellingham, WA: Regent College, 1995.

Moltmann, Jurgen. *Theology of Hope*, New York: Harper & Row, Publishers, 1976.

www.ingramcontent.com/pod-product-compliance
Lightning Source LLC
Chambersburg PA
CBHW060005100426
42740CB00010B/1401
9781585161287